### online and in-print Internet directories in medicine

# Bioterrorism
# and
# Public Health

## An Internet Resource Guide™

**Consulting Editors**

John G. Bartlett, M.D., *Chief, Division of Infectious Diseases,*
*The Johns Hopkins University School of Medicine*

Tara O' Toole, M.D., M.P.H., *Director*
Thomas V. Inglesby, M.D., *Deputy Director*
Michael Mair, *Senior Research Assistant*

*The Johns Hopkins Center for Civilian Biodefense Strategies*

---

**Visit Bioterrorism and Public Health**
**at www.eMedguides.com**

**Access code: 5439**

---

**THOMSON**
**PDR**

D0962686

Copyright © 2002 and published
by Thomson PDR
at Montvale, NJ 07645-1742.
All rights reserved.

For electronic browsing of this book, see
http://www.eMedguides.com/bioterrorism

The publisher offers discounts on the PDR eMedguides
series of books. For more information, contact:

Bill Gaffney, Trade Sales
Thomson PDR
5 Paragon Drive
Montvale, NJ 07645-1742
*tel*      201-358-7930
*fax*     201-722-3878
*e-mail*  Bill.Gaffney@medec.com

This book is set in Avenir, BaseNine, Gill Sans, and
Sabon typefaces and was printed and bound in the
United States of America.

10 9 8 7 6 5 4 3 2 1

ISBN 1-56363-427-9

# eMedguides™.com

## Bioterrorism and Public Health
### An Internet Resource Guide

**Consulting Editors:**

John G. Bartlett, M.D., *Chief,*
*Division of Infectious Diseases, The Johns*
*Hopkins University School of Medicine*

Tara O' Toole, M.D., M.P.H., *Director,*
*The Johns Hopkins Center for*
*Civilian Biodefense Strategies*

Thomas V. Inglesby, M.D., *Deputy Director,*
*The Johns Hopkins Center for*
*Civilian Biodefense Strategies*

Michael Mair, *Senior Research Assistant,*
*The Johns Hopkins Center for*
*Civilian Biodefense Strategies*

**Editorial Staff:**

Daniel R. Goldenson, Publisher

Gregory Colon, Associate Editor

**Corporate Contacts:**

Paul Walsh, Executive Vice President

Mukesh Mehta, R.Ph., V.P., Strategic Initiatives &
Clinical Communications

Dik Barsamian, V.P., Sales & Marketing

Valerie Berger, Director, Product Management

Jeff Dubin, Senior Product Manager

Mike Bennett, Senior Director,
Publishing Sales & Marketing

Bill Gaffney, Director, Trade Sales

**THOMSON**
**PDR**

## 2002–2003
## Annual Editions

Allergy & Immunology

Anesthesiology & Pain Management

Arthritis & Rheumatology

**Bioterrorism
and Public Health**

Cardiology

Dental Medicine

Dermatology

Diet & Nutrition

Emergency Medicine

Endocrinology & Metabolism

Family Medicine

Gastroenterology

General Surgery

Infectious Diseases & Immunology

Internal Medicine

Neurology & Neuroscience

Nurse Practitioners

Obstetrics & Gynecology

Oncology & Hematology

Ophthalmology

Orthopedics & Sports Medicine

Osteopathic Medicine

Otolaryngology

Pathology & Laboratory Medicine

Pediatrics & Neonatology

Physical Medicine & Rehabilitation

Psychiatry

Radiology

Respiratory & Pulmonary Medicine

Urology & Nephrology

Veterinary Medicine

# Disclaimer

eMedguides.com, Inc. and its parent company, Thomson Healthcare Inc., hereinafter referred to as the "Publisher," has developed this book for informational purposes only, and not as a source of medical advice. The Publisher does not guarantee the accuracy, adequacy, timeliness, or completeness of any information in this book and is not responsible for any errors or omissions or any consequences arising from the use of the information contained in this book. The material provided is general in nature and is in summary form. The content of this book is not intended in any way to be a substitute for professional medical advice. One should always seek the advice of a physician or other qualified healthcare provider. Further, one should never disregard medical advice or delay in seeking it because of information found through an Internet Web site included in this book. The use of the eMedguides.com, Inc. book is at the reader's own risk.

All information contained in this book is subject to change. Mention of a specific product, company, organization, Web site URL address, treatment, therapy, or any other topic does not imply a recommendation or endorsement by the Publisher.

## Non-liability

The Publisher does not assume any liability for the contents of this book or the contents of any material provided at the Internet sites, companies, and organizations reviewed in this book. Moreover, the Publisher assumes no liability or responsibility for damage or injury to persons or property arising from the publication and use of this book; the use of those products, services, information, ideas, or instructions contained in the material provided at the third-party Internet Web sites, companies, and organizations listed in this book; or any loss of profit or commercial damage including but not limited to special, incidental, consequential, or any other damages in connection with or arising out of the publication and use of this book. Use of third-party Web sites is subject to the Terms and Conditions of use for such sites.

## Copyright Protection

Information available over the Internet and other online locations may be subject to copyright and other rights owned by third parties. Online availability of text and images does not imply that they may be reused without the permission of rights holders. Care should be taken to ensure that all necessary rights are cleared prior to reusing material distributed over the Internet and other online locations.

## Trademark Protection

The words in this book for which we have reason to believe trademark, service mark, or other proprietary rights may exist have been designated as such by use of initial capitalization. However, no attempt has been made to designate as trademarks or service marks all personal computer words or terms in which proprietary rights might exist. The inclusion, exclusion, or definition of a word or term is not intended to affect, or to express any judgment on, the validity or legal status of any proprietary right that may be claimed in that word or term.

# About the Editors

## John G. Bartlett, M.D.

Since 1980, Dr. John G. Bartlett has been Professor of Medicine and Chief of the Division of Infectious Diseases at The Johns Hopkins University School of Medicine. He has also held an additional appointment in the Department of Epidemiology in the School of Hygiene and Public Health, also since 1980.

With major research interests in HIV/AIDS, diarrhea, community-acquired pneumonia, and anaerobic infections, Dr. Bartlett has been the author of more than 300 peer-reviewed articles, 256 book chapters, reviews and letters, and a dozen books. He is a member or fellow of ten professional societies, including past president of the Infectious Diseases Society of America. Dr. Bartlett serves on the editorial boards of numerous publications, and currently he is the editor of *Infectious Diseases in Clinical Practice* and *The Hopkins HIV Report*.

A graduate of the Upstate Medical Center School of Medicine in Syracuse, Dr. Bartlett held residencies at Peter Bent Brigham Hospital in Boston as well as at the University of Alabama, followed by a fellowship at the UCLA School of Medicine and Wadsworth Veterans Administration Hospital in Los Angeles.

Dr. Bartlett was a co-founder, with Dr. Donald A. Henderson, of the Johns Hopkins Center for Civilian Biodefense Strategies.

## Tara O'Toole, M.D., M.P.H.

Dr. O'Toole is currently the Director of the Johns Hopkins Center for Civilian Biodefense Strategies and a member of the faculty of the School of Hygiene and Public Health. The Center, sponsored by the Hopkins Schools of Public Health and Medicine, is dedicated to informing policy decisions and promoting practices that would help prevent the use of biological weapons. She is a member of the Defense Science Board summer panel on biodefense technologies and the Maryland Department of Health and Mental Hygiene steering group on public health response to WMD events, among other advisory and consultative positions related to bioterrorism preparedness.

In 1993 Dr. O'Toole was nominated by President Clinton to be Assistant Secretary of Energy for Environment, Safety and Health and served in this position until 1997. As Assistant Secretary, Dr. O'Toole managed a staff of 400 professionals and an annual budget of approximately $200 million. She served as principal advisor to the Secretary of Energy on matters pertaining to protecting the environment and worker and public health from DOE operations. During her tenure, Dr. O'Toole conducted four major "Vulnerability Studies" that identified major safety and environmental hazards at the nation's nuclear weapons complex and focused resources on the most serious threats; established the department's first nuclear safety rules and professional enforcement office; and led a multi-agency, multi-million dollar task force that oversaw the government's investigations into human radiation experiments conducted during the Cold War.

From 1989-1993, Dr. O'Toole was a Senior Analyst at the Congressional Office of Technology Assessment (OTA) where she directed and participated in studies of health impacts on workers and the public due to environmental pollution resulting from nuclear weapons production, among other projects. She has served as a consultant to industry and government in matters related to occupational and environmental health, worker participation in workplace safety protection, and organizational change. Dr. O'Toole is a Board-certified internist and occupational medicine physician with clinical experience in academic settings and community health centers and has participated in many advisory committees dealing with bioterrorism, including the National Academy of Sciences Biological Weapons Working Group and the Defense Science Board.

She received her bachelor's degree from Vassar College, her M.D. from the George Washington University, and a Master of Public Health degree from Johns Hopkins University. She completed a residency in internal medicine at Yale and a fellowship in occupational and environmental medicine at Johns Hopkins University.

### Thomas V. Inglesby, M.D.

The Deputy Director of the Johns Hopkins Center for Civilian Biodefense Strategies, Dr. Thomas V. Inglesby is Assistant Professor in the Division of Infectious Diseases and on the medical staff of the Johns Hopkins Hospital.

Dr. Inglesby has served in a number of advisory and consultative capacities to federal and state agencies on issues relating to bioterrorism preparedness. He was a principal designer, author, and controller of the "Dark Winter Exercise" of June 2001, and was first author of the articles entitled "Anthrax as a Biological Weapon: Medical and Public Health Management" and "Plague as a Biological Weapon: Medical and Public Health Consequence," both published in the *Journal of the American Medical Association*. He was also principal author of "Smallpox Management," which appeared in *JAMA*.

In addition to co-authoring clinical disease management guidelines in bioterrorism, Dr. Inglesby is the author/co-author of papers, articles, and case studies in his field, and is a frequent speaker on the subject of bioterrorism preparedness.

### Michael Mair

Michael Mair is a Senior Research Assistant in the Johns Hopkins Center for Civilian Biodefense Strategies in Baltimore, Maryland. He is currently engaged in compiling a major database of Web-based resources in the field of bioterrorism.

In June of 2001, Mr. Mair was involved with the "Dark Winter Exercise" hosted by the Center for Strategic and International Studies in Washington, D.C., the Johns Hopkins Center for Civilian Biodefense Strategies, the ANSER Institute for Homeland Security, and the Oklahoma National Memorial Institute for the Prevention of Terrorism. This senior-level war game examined the national security, intergovernmental, and information challenges of a biological attack on the American homeland.

# TABLE OF CONTENTS

---

## RATINGS AND SITE SELECTION

### Site Selection Criteria

Our research staff has carefully chosen the sites for this guide. We perform extensive searches for all of the topics listed in our table of contents and then select only the sites that meet established criteria. The pertinence and depth of content, presentation, and usefulness are taken into account.

The sites in this guide contain detailed reference material, news, clinical data, and current research articles of interest to professionals and to consumer audiences. The large majority of our Web sites are provided by government, university, medical association, and research organizations. Sites operated by private individuals or corporations are only included if they are content-rich and useful to the reader. In these cases, we clearly identify the operator in the title or description of the site.

### Ratings Guide

Those sites that are selected based on these criteria are subsequently rated on a scale of one apple (🍎) to three apples (🍎🍎🍎). This rating only applies to the pool of sites that are in this guide; many sites are not included in this volume. A one-apple site, therefore, is considered worthy of inclusion but may not be outstanding. A three-apple site tends to have greater depth and more extensive information, or particularly hard-to-find resources.

# INTRODUCTION

The sudden appearance of cases of both cutaneous and inhalational anthrax following the terrorist attacks on the World Trade Center and the Pentagon on September 11, 2001 raised for the first time the very real and frightening specter of bioterrorism on U.S. soil. Although investigators have not found any connection between the September 11 terrorists and the anthrax-laced letters, there is no question that certain individuals, whether domestic or foreign, intentionally sought to spread the deadly anthrax bacteria through the mail.

Agencies of the federal government, including the FBI and the Centers for Disease Control and Prevention, immediately moved into high gear to identify the source and potential impact of anthrax on the population at large. Little historic and epidemiologic experience existed regarding anthrax as a biological weapon, other than simulated studies and laboratory research at secret military installations in the U.S., Russia, and certain other countries, both friendly and hostile.

Biological and chemical weapons of mass destruction have been on the drawing boards for many years, even in the U.S., while international commissions have sought to outlaw their existence. What the public has not been prepared for is the actual deployment of these weapons in the U.S., and the corresponding public health, social, and psychological impact of these weapons.

The purpose of this book is to bring together the extensive resources that now exist, both organizational and informational, in the bioterrorism and public health arenas. The unique focus of this book is its directory section of more than 500 Web sites covering government agencies, organizations, research centers, and clinical and public health information sources. Enhancing this content is material from the new federal Office of Public Health Preparedness, the Centers for Disease Control and Prevention, and the Johns Hopkins Center for Civilian Biodefense Strategies.

We hope our readers will find this compilation useful from several points of view. General information is available on bioterrorism, including biological, chemical, agricultural, and waterborne biowarfare. Readers will also find Web sites posting the latest news and developments, along with online newsletters from federal and public health agencies related to bioterrorism and homeland security. Policymakers will find resources on public policy guidelines, conventions, analysis, and legislation, while emergency response professionals will find sections on public preparedness and response, hazardous materials, and decontamination.

Information on specific infectious diseases associated with bioterrorism will be of interest to clinicians and epidemiologists, accompanied by disease management guidelines and consensus statements. A section specific to mental health is also included. Consumer-oriented information includes guidelines for personal health and safety and disaster readiness, as well as listings of hotlines, mailing lists, and alerting services.

Finally, public health professionals will find a variety of resources covering educational opportunities, implementation of public health response plans, and conferences and symposia. Overall, we believe that this guidebook will be a useful resource for many different audiences, and that it will serve as an educational guide for the American public as we face these new challenges as a nation.

Daniel R. Goldenson
Publisher

# GETTING ONLINE

The Internet is growing at a rapid pace, but many individuals are not yet online. What is preventing people from jumping on the "information highway"? There are many factors, but the most common issue is a general confusion about what the Internet is, how it works, and how to access it.

The following few pages are designed to clear up any confusion for readers who have not yet accessed the Internet. We will look at the process of getting onto and using the Internet, step by step.

It is also helpful to consult other resources, such as the technical support department of the manufacturer or store where you bought your computer. Although assistance varies widely, most organizations provide startup assistance for new users and are experienced with guiding individuals onto the Internet. Books can also be of great assistance, as they provide a simple and clear view of how computers and the Internet work, and can be studied at your own pace.

**What is the Internet?**
The Internet is a large network of computers that are all connected to one another. A good analogy is to envision a neighborhood, with houses and storefronts, all connected to one another by streets and highways. Often the Internet is referred to as the "information superhighway" because of the vastness of this neighborhood.

The Internet was initially developed to allow people to share computers, that is, share part of their "house" with others. The ability to connect to so many other computers quickly and easily made this feasible. As computers proliferated and increased in computational power, people started using the Internet for sending information quickly from one computer to another.

For example, the most popular feature of the Internet is electronic mail (e-mail). Each computer has a mailbox, and an electronic letter can be sent instantly. People also use the Internet to post bulletins, or other information, for others to see. The process of sending e-mail or viewing this information is simple. A computer and a connection to the Internet are all you need to begin.

## How is an Internet connection provided?

The Internet is accessed either through a "direct" connection, which is found in businesses and educational institutions, or through a phone line. Phone line connections are the most common access method for users at home, although direct connections are becoming available for home use. There are many complex options in this area; for the new user it is simplest to use an existing phone line to experience the Internet for the first time. A dual telephone jack can be purchased at many retail stores. Connect the computer to the phone jack, and then use the provided software to connect to the Internet. Your computer will dial the number of an Internet provider and ask you for a user name and password. Keep in mind that while you are using the Internet, your phone line is tied up and callers will hear a busy signal. Also, call waiting can sometimes interrupt an Internet connection and disconnect you from the Internet.

## Who provides an Internet connection?

There are many providers at both the local and national levels. One of the easiest ways to get online is with America Online (AOL). They provide software and a user-friendly environment through which to access the Internet. Because AOL manages both this environment and the actual connection, they can be of great assistance when you are starting out. America Online takes you to a menu of choices when you log in, and while using their software you can read and send e-mail, view Web pages, and chat with others.

Many other similar services exist, and most of them also provide an environment using Microsoft or Netscape products. These companies, such as the Microsoft Network (MSN) and Earthlink, also provide simple, easy-to-use access to the Internet. Their environment is more standard and not limited to the choices America Online provides.

Internet connections generally run from $10-$30 per month (depending on the length of commitment) in addition to telephone costs. Most national providers have local phone numbers all over the country that should eliminate any telephone charges. The monthly provider fee is the only direct charge for accessing the Internet.

## How do I get on the Internet?

Once you've signed up with an Internet provider and installed their software (often only a matter of answering basic questions), your computer will be set up to access the Internet. By double-clicking on an icon, your computer will dial the phone number, log you in, and present you with a Web page (a "home" page).

**What are some of the Internet's features?**
From the initial Web page there are almost limitless possibilities of where you can go. The address at the top of the screen (identified by an "http://" in front) tells you where you are. You can also type the address of where you would like to go next. When typing a new address, you do not need to add the "http://". The computer adds this prefix automatically after you type in an address and press return. Once you press return, the Web site will appear in the browser window.

You can also navigate the Web by "surfing" from one site to another using links on a page. A Web page might say, "Click here for weather." If you move the mouse pointer to this underlined phrase and click the mouse button, you will be taken to a different address, where weather information is provided.

The Internet has several other useful features. E-mail is an extremely popular and important service. It is free and messages are delivered instantly. Although you can access e-mail through a Web browser (AOL has this feature), many Internet services provide a separate e-mail program for reading, writing, and organizing your correspondence. These programs send and retrieve messages from the Internet.

Another area of the Internet offers chat rooms where users can hold roundtable discussions. In a chat room you can type messages and see the replies of other users around the world. There are chat rooms on virtually every topic, although the dialog certainly varies in this free-for-all forum. There are also newsgroups on the Internet, some of which we list in this book. A newsgroup is similar to a chat room but each message is a separate item and can be viewed in sequence at any time. For example, a user might post a question about Lyme disease. In the newsgroup you can read the question and then read the answers that others have provided. You can also post your own comments. This forum is usually not managed or edited, particularly in the medical field. Do not take the advice of a chat room or newsgroup source without first consulting your physician.

**How can I find things on the Internet?**
Surfing the Internet, from site to site, is a popular activity. But if you have a focused mission, you will want to use a search engine. A search engine can scan lists of Web sites to look for a particular site. We provide a long list of medical search engines in this book.

Because the Internet is so large and unregulated, sites are often hard to find. In the physical world it is difficult to find good services, but you can turn to the yellow pages or other resources to get a comprehensive list. Physical proximity is also a major factor. On the Internet, the whole world is at your doorstep. Finding a reliable site takes time and patience, and can require sifting through hundreds of similar, yet irrelevant, sites.

The most common way to find information on the Internet is to use a search engine. When you go to the Web page of a search engine, you will be presented with two distinct methods of searching: using links to topics, or using a keyword search. The links often represent the Web site staff's best effort to find quality sites. This method of searching is the core of the Yahoo! search engine (http://www.yahoo.com). By clicking on Healthcare, then Disorders, then Lung Cancer, you are provided with a list of sites the staff has found on the topic.

The keyword approach is definitely more daring. By typing in search terms, the engine looks through its list of Web sites for a match and returns the results. These engines typically only cover 15 percent of the Internet, so it is not a comprehensive process. They also usually return far too many choices. Typing lung cancer into a search engine box will return thousands of sites, including one entry for every site where someone used the words lung cancer on a personal Web page.

## Where do eMedguides come in?

eMedguides are organized listings of Web sites in each major medical specialty. Our team of editors continually scours the Net, searching for quality Web sites that relate to specific specialties, disorders, and research topics. More importantly, of the sites we find, we only include those that provide professional and useful content. eMedguides fill a critical gap in the Internet research process. Each guide provides more than 1,000 Web sites that focus on every aspect of a single medical discipline.

Other Internet search engines rely on teams of "surfers" who can only cover a subject on its surface because they survey the entire Internet. Search engines, even medical search engines, return far too many choices, requiring hours of time and patience to sift through. eMedguides, on the other hand, focus on medical and physician sites in a specialty. With an eMedguide in hand, you can quickly identify the sites worth visiting on the Internet and jump right to them. At our site, http://www.eMed guides.com, you can access the same listings as in this book and can simply click on a site to go straight to it. In addition, we provide continual updates to the book through the site and annually in print. Our editors do the surfing for you and do it professionally, making your Internet experience efficient and fulfilling.

Our new e-Link identification code is the fastest way to surf the Internet. Simply append the code number to the eMedguides address (http://www.eMedguides.com/b-0101) to be taken directly to the site you are reading about in the book.

**Taking medical action must involve a physician**
As interesting as the Internet is, the information that you will find is both objective and subjective. Our goal is to expose our readers to Web sites on hundreds of topics for informational purposes only. If you are not a physician and become interested in the ideas, guidelines, recommendations, or experiences discussed online, bring these findings to a physician for personal evaluation. Medical needs vary considerably, and a medical approach or therapy for one individual could be entirely misguided for another. Final medical advice and a plan of action must come only from a physician.

# 3

# The Science of Bioterrorism: Department of Health and Human Services (HHS) Preparedness

Testimony

Before the Committee on Science

United States House of Representatives

**The Science of Bioterrorism: HHS Preparedness**

*Statement of*

**D.A. Henderson, M.D.**
*Director,*

*Office of Public Health Preparedness*

*Department of Health and Human Services*

Mr. Chairman and Members of the Committee, thank you for inviting me here today. The Department of Health and Human Services (HHS) welcomes your interest in our efforts to respond to terrorist events, including uses of biological weapons against the civilian population. I am Dr. D. A. Henderson, Director of the newly created HHS Office of Public Health Preparedness, which will coordinate the Department-wide response to public health emergencies. To that end, I look forward to working with the Office of Homeland Security and our other partners at the Federal, state, and local level to protect the American people from acts of terrorism.

# HHS READINESS TO RESPOND TO MASS CASUALTY EVENTS

Although the Department of Defense (DoD) has developed defenses for biological warfare, there are additional concerns that need to be addressed to provide an adequate civilian defense from a bioterrorist attack. The potential list of microbial pathogens that threaten civilian populations is larger than that of classical biological warfare threats. HHS's identification of the major bioterrorism threat agents—a list developed in collaboration with experts in medicine and public health, law enforcement, and national security—is included as an Appendix to this testimony. Moreover, the populations to be protected are different from those generally involved in combat situations because the civilian community includes people of all ages and health status.

As you know, local and state governments bear much of the initial burden and responsibility for providing an effective response by medical and public health professionals to a terrorist attack on the civilian population. If the disease outbreak reaches any significant magnitude, however, local resources will be overwhelmed, and the federal government will be required to provide protective and responsive measures for the affected populations. HHS is working on a number of fronts to assist our partners at the state and local level, including local hospitals and medical practitioners, to deal with the effects of biological, chemical, and other terrorist acts.

## METROPOLITAN MEDICAL RESPONSE SYSTEM

Since Fiscal Year 1995, for example, HHS through its Office of Emergency Preparedness (OEP) has been developing local Metropolitan Medical Response Systems (MMRS). Through contractual relationships, the MMRS uses existing emergency response systems—emergency management, medical and mental health providers, public health departments, law enforcement, fire departments, EMS, and the National Guard—to provide an integrated, unified response to a mass casualty event. As of September 30, 2001, OEP has contracted with 97 municipalities to develop MMRSs. During FY 2002, we intend to invest $20 million in 25 additional cities (for a total of 122) for bioterrorism-related planning through the MMRS and to help them improve their medical response capabilities.

# National Disaster Medical System (NDMS)

As HHS's action agent for responding to requests for assistance and resources, OEP also manages the National Disaster Medical System (NDMS), which was established in partnership with DoD, the Department of Veterans Affairs (VA), the Federal Emergency Management Agency (FEMA), and the Public Health Service Commissioned Corps Readiness Force. The NDMS can be called into action, depending upon the severity of the event, to assist in providing needed services to ensure the continued health and well-being of disaster victims.

The National Disaster Medical System is a group of more than 7,000 volunteer health and support professionals who can be deployed anywhere in the country to assist communities in which local response systems are overwhelmed or incapacitated. Organized into 44 Disaster Medical Assistance Teams, these volunteers would provide on-site medical triage, patient care, and transportation to medical facilities. Four National Medical Response Teams (NMRTs), which travel with their own caches of pharmaceuticals, have capabilities to detect illness-causing agents, decontaminate victims, provide medical care, and remove victims from the scene. Three of the four NMRTs can be mobilized and deployed anywhere in the nation; the fourth is permanently stationed in the Washington, D.C., area. The NDMS also includes Disaster Mortuary Operations Response Teams that handle the disposition of the remains of victims of major disasters, as well as provide for victim identification and assistance to their families.

The Department of Veterans Affairs is one of the largest purchasers of pharmaceuticals and medical supplies in the world. Capitalizing on this buying power, HHS and VA have entered into an agreement under which the VA manages and stores specialized pharmaceutical caches for OEP's National Medical Response Teams. The VA has purchased many of the items in the pharmaceutical stockpile. The VA is also responsible for maintaining the inventory, ensuring its security, and rotating the stock to ensure that the caches are ready for deployment with the specialized National Medical Response Teams.

# National Pharmaceutical Stockpile

HHS has also developed the National Pharmaceutical Stockpile Program (NPS) into a major national security asset. The purpose of the NPS is to be able to rapidly respond to a domestic biological or chemical terrorist event with antibiotics, antidotes, vaccines, and medical material to help save lives and prevent further spread of disease resulting from the terrorist threat agent. Operated by HHS's Centers for Disease Control and Prevention (CDC), the NPS Program would provide an initial, broad-based response within 12 hours of the federal authorization to deploy, followed by a prompt and more targeted response as dictated by the specific nature of the biological or chemical agent that is used.

One of the NPS "12-hour Push Packages" was brought to operational status on September 11th. CDC delivered a 12-hour Push Package of pharmaceuticals and medical supplies by ground, vendor managed inventory by air, and a technical advisory team in New York City, all within 7 hours of the order to deploy. Three out of the four non-military aircraft in United States airspace on the night of September 11th were carrying National Pharmaceutical Stockpile assets and personnel to New York City.

The Stockpile Program was developed as a supplementary response asset mainly to address biological and chemical terrorism. But following the events of September 11th, the program is now being expanded for response to an all-hazards event. The Stockpile presently is able to provide a full course of anthrax postexposure prophylaxis to more than 2 million persons. Secretary Thompson has directed that the Stockpile development be accelerated to provide increased anthrax prophylaxis capacity for 12 million persons, and CDC will reach that level of response within the next 12 months. We will also add four more push packs to the eight already located across the country, making more emergency supplies available and augmenting our existing supplies of 400 tons by another 200 tons.

But we must accelerate the production of vaccines and antibiotics and invest in essential programs to ensure the speedy and orderly distribution of antibiotics and other supplies in the event of a biological event. That is why the President has called for an additional $1.5 billion in federal funding for those areas most critical to our ability to respond to bioterrorist threats. His proposal includes $643 million to expand the National Pharmaceutical Stockpile and $509 million to speed the development and purchase of smallpox vaccine.

Just last week, Secretary Thompson announced that Acambis Inc., with support from its subcontractor, Baxter International Inc., has been awarded a $428 million contract to produce 155 million doses of smallpox vaccine by the end of 2002. Production of the vaccine under the new contract could begin as soon as this month and, once completed, will bring the total number of vaccine doses in the nation's stockpile to 286 million by the end of next year, enough to protect every United States citizen, if needed. In light of increasing concerns regarding the possible use of biological agents such as smallpox in acts of terrorism or war,

HHS is undertaking efforts to stockpile as much vaccine as needed to protect the nation in the event of an outbreak of smallpox.

## CDC SURVEILLANCE AND PREVENTION EFFORTS

As our nation's premier prevention agency, CDC's top priority is to protect the Nation's health. To do this, CDC focuses on building a solid public health infrastructure—at CDC, as well as at the state and local level to protect the health of all citizens. CDC has used funds provided by Congress to begin the process of improving the expertise, facilities, and procedures of state and local health departments and within CDC itself related to bioterrorism. CDC has a dedicated anti-bioterrorism staff of more than 100 full-time professionals comprising expertise in epidemiology, surveillance, secure communications, and laboratory diagnostics.

Over the last three years, CDC has awarded more than $130 million in cooperative agreements to 50 states, one territory, and four major metropolitan health departments to support,

(1) Preparedness planning and readiness assessment;

(2) Epidemiology and surveillance;

(3) Laboratory capacity for biological or chemical agents; and

(4) The Health Alert Network (a nationwide electronic communications system).

Since September 11, almost 500 CDC staff have been sent to the field. For example, at the height of the anthrax response in the Nation's Capital, there were 85 staff in Washington, D.C., alone. These experts included epidemiologists, industrial hygienists involved in environmental sampling and clean up, laboratorians, communications specialists to assist with media relations, and logistics and management staff. CDC not only investigated cases that proved to be anthrax in four states and the District of Columbia, but also investigated suspicious cases in six other states. These cases proved not to be anthrax, but required CDC assistance to go through the process of ruling them out. CDC experts were needed to augment the staff of state and local health departments, who would have been severely overtaxed without our help. The Administration has requested $20 million to support additional expert epidemiology teams that can be sent to states and cities to help them respond quickly to infectious disease outbreaks and other public health risks. And let me reiterate Secretary Thompson's conviction that every state should have at least one federally funded epidemiologist who has been trained in the CDC's Epidemic Intelligence Service (EIS) training program. The President's budget will accomplish this goal.

## CDC and ATSDR Remediation Support Activities

Since the intentional release of anthrax spores, one of the areas on which CDC and HHS's Agency for Toxic Substances and Disease Registry (ATSDR) have focused is the identification and cleanup of contaminated facilities. We have refined methods for environmental sampling to assess whether anthrax contamination had occurred. In buildings, that has meant sampling of air and surfaces. CDC and ATSDR have issued recommendations on how to conduct environmental sampling and how laboratories should analyze those samples. We also recommended environmental sampling strategies to characterize the extent of exposure and to guide cleanup. We issued recommendations to protect first responders, investigators, and cleanup personnel. As buildings were identified as contaminated, we provided technical input to EPA and others tasked with cleanup to determine where remediation was necessary. These recommendations have been widely disseminated to federal, state, and local health and environmental agencies, and are available at CDC's bioterrorism website (http://www.bt.cdc.gov).

EPA has devised strategies for remediation and has gained much experience through its activities to date. Disease experts at CDC are developing strategies to prevent the spread of disease during and after bioterrorist attacks. Although there are some data on chemical disinfectants in the scientific literature, there are no historical data that indicate the best way to eliminate spores from an office building, or to disinfect a sorting machine. The ability of a disinfectant to kill an anthrax spore is dependent upon time of contact and concentration and is mitigated by the amount and composition of material through which it must penetrate to get to the spore. For many of the cleanup methods being used to kill anthrax spores, we will not know their effectiveness until we go through the process. EPA understands this and has sought help from a variety of sources, including CDC and ATSDR, to ensure that the appropriate indicators are used and that post-sampling strategies are adequate.

With regard to the effectiveness of cleaning, even our most exhaustive sampling strategies will not identify every spore. It is unlikely that any cleaning strategy will kill every spore. However, the EPA should be able to clean and re-test to the point where we all are comfortable that spores have been killed or removed from surfaces where human contact is likely to occur. A range of sampling methods and strategies should be used to ensure the safety of building occupants.

In heavily contaminated areas, such as Senator Daschle's suite and the Brentwood postal facility, fumigation is being proposed as the method of cleanup. The use of fumigants is a potential hazard for cleanup workers, those in areas adjacent to the buildings, and those that must re-occupy the building. A fumigant that is effective at killing spores is, of necessity, a highly toxic agent. The protection of workers during the fumigation process is a matter of good industrial hygiene. EPA, CDC, and ATSDR are working together to ensure remediation workers are protected during the fumigation processes. EPA works with local public health agencies to ensure that people in the area but outside of the building being fumigated are notified and kept at a safe distance.

With regard to the safety of those who will re-occupy the building, it is important to determine both that the area is clear of the fumigant and that there is no health risk. Again, CDC, ATSDR, and the Occupational Safety and Health Administration (OSHA) have developed exposure limits for fumigants, and detection methods are available to determine when any residual fumigant is well below established limits. After buildings are cleaned and post-cleaning environmental sampling has been conducted, CDC and ATSDR are committed to providing technical input to the incident command and other experts to determine whether the building is ready for re-occupancy.

## HHS ROLE IN VACCINE AND DRUG RESEARCH AND DEVELOPMENT

With the support of Congress, the President has implemented a government-wide emergency response package to help deal with the tragic events of September 11th and subsequent anthrax attacks. This complements efforts already underway to prepare our nation against such heinous attacks, including threats of bioterrorism. For example, CDC, the Food and Drug Administration (FDA), and the National Institutes of Health (NIH), all within HHS, are collaborating with the DoD and other agencies to support and encourage research to address scientific issues related to bioterrorism. The capability to detect and counter bioterrorism depends to a substantial degree on the state of relevant medical science. In some cases, new vaccines, antitoxins, or innovative drug treatments need to be developed, manufactured (or produced), and/or stocked. Moreover, we need to learn more about the pathogenesis and epidemiology of the infectious diseases that do not affect the U.S. population currently. We have only limited knowledge about how artificial methods of dispersion may affect the infection rate, virulence, or impact of these biological agents. HHS's continuing, collaborative, research agenda at CDC, FDA, NIH, and with DoD, is critical to overall preparedness.

Let me briefly outline the vital role that HHS agencies, particularly the FDA and NIH, play in our Nation's research and development agenda for vaccines and other drugs.

## Food and Drug Administration

Even before the events of September 11, HHS's Food and Drug Administration actively cooperated with DoD in the operation of DoD's vaccine development program and the maintenance of their stockpile program. Any vaccine or drug development, whether by a government agency or private industry, must be in accordance with FDA requirements that ensure the safety, effectiveness, and manufacturing quality of the finished product. FDA provides regulatory guidance to DoD, CDC, and others regarding the studies required to develop new vaccines and drugs, as well as assistance during all phases of development. FDA also works with DoD's office that screens new and unusual ideas for development of products to treat diseases and develop diagnostic tools.

The scope of FDA's regulatory responsibility extends to both approved (licensed) products and investigational products (unlicensed) products. FDA's Center for Biologics Evaluation Research (CBER) is responsible for evaluating the safety, purity, and potency of biological products such as vaccines, antitoxins, and blood products. FDA's Center for Drug Evaluation and Research (CDER) is responsible for a similar regulatory process for drugs. Bio-warfare defense vaccines and drugs undergo the same FDA review process as any other vaccines or drugs.

FDA will work with potential sponsors of experimental therapies at all stages of the product development process in order to stimulate scientific interchange and clarify FDA regulatory requirements. A sponsor of a vaccine or drug under review must also provide adequate product labeling to allow healthcare providers to understand the product's proper use, including its potential benefits and risks, to communicate with patients, and to safely deliver the product to the public.

When all of the clinical, chemistry, pre-approval inspection, manufacturing, labeling, and other issues have been adequately resolved, FDA will approve the application. Licensing or approving a new vaccine or drug is only one stage of FDA's oversight of medical product safety. Following issuance of the license, there is continued post-marketing surveillance of the product by monitoring adverse events through the Adverse Event Reporting System. Subsequent to the issuance of the license, FDA also monitors the manufacturer's production activities through FDA inspections to determine the manufacturer's compliance with good manufacturing practices (GMP) regulations. Because of the complex manufacturing processes for most biological products, manufacturers may be required to submit samples of each licensed vaccine lot, along with manufacturing testing results, to FDA for review and permission to release the lot for distribution.

# NATIONAL INSTITUTES OF HEALTH

The NIH bioterrorism research program, spearheaded by the National Institute of Allergy and Infectious Diseases (NIAID), includes both short- and long-term research targeted at the design, development, evaluation, and approval of diagnostics, therapies, and vaccines needed to control infections caused by microbes with potential for use as biological weapons. NIAID efforts have primarily focused on the bioterrorist threats posed by anthrax and smallpox, and many of these efforts are carried out in collaboration with other federal agencies.

NIAID formed a Working Group on Anthrax Vaccines (WGAV) in 1998 to develop and test a new vaccine that could be used in response to a bioterrorist event. Such a vaccine must be capable of generating protective immunity against inhalation spores within a relatively short period of time after 1-2 immunizing doses. Through an Inter-Agency Agreement, NIAID is collaborating with the Department of Defense's U.S. Army Medical Research Institute of Infectious Diseases (USAMRIID) on a research plan to develop a new vaccine based on the use of recombinant protective antigen vaccine (rPA) to protect all ages of the American public, including military personnel. In preparation for Phase 1 clinical trials of rPA vaccines, NIH is working with CDC, FDA, and DoD to refine standard serological tests to assess the effectiveness of anthrax vaccines. These tests would enable comparison of new rPA vaccines to the currently licensed anthrax (or AVA) vaccine. If the new vaccine is capable of generating a rapid immune response, it may provide a quick transition to protective immunity to those individuals undergoing treatment with antibiotics due to an anthrax exposure.

NIAID also has expanded the national research capacity substantially over the past few years on those bioterrorist threat agents of greatest concern. First, NIAID has solicited from the scientific community research proposals on anthrax and other bacterial pathogens, in an effort to further encourage research that may lead to better means of diagnosis, prevention, and treatment.

Second, NIAID recently awarded administrative supplements to several active research grants to further studies on how anthrax causes disease, which could expedite the development and implementation of novel, more effective therapeutic intervention strategies. NIAID also anticipates funding several new research proposals on the molecular mechanisms involved in the germination of anthrax spores in vivo; such work may provide the basis for a novel and very promising post-attack strategy, one that would be more acceptable than the widespread use of antimicrobial drugs which are not specific for anthrax and, when given to large groups of exposed individuals, may promote the development of antibiotic resistant strains of other bacteria.

Through an Inter-Agency Agreement with the Office of Naval Research, NIAID has provided funding to help complete work on sequencing the DNA of the chromosome of anthrax; additional funds were also provided by the Department of Energy for this purpose. The information derived from this genome-sequencing project should be of great value in developing rapid diagnostic tests, as well as new vaccines and antibiotic therapies against mutant strains of anthrax.

NIAID research on smallpox focuses on extending existing vaccine stocks to increase the number of available doses, developing new vaccines and treatments, as well as diagnostic tools to detect the disease quickly. Although a worldwide immunization program eradicated smallpox disease decades ago, small quantities of smallpox virus still exist under guarded conditions at CDC and in Russia, and several rogue nations may have samples. NIAID, in collaboration with DoD, CDC, and the Department of Energy, funds increased research to:

- Develop and evaluate at least three antiviral drugs with preclinical activity against smallpox and vaccinia viruses and acceptable clinical safety;

- Extend the usefulness of the currently available, older vaccine by doing human studies to see if we can "stretch" available stocks by diluting it;

- Help develop a safe, sterile smallpox vaccine grown in cell cultures using modern technology;

- Explore development of a vaccine that can be used in all segments of the civilian population (i.e., the immune-suppressed, pregnant mothers, etc.); and

- Increase our knowledge of the genome of smallpox and related viruses.

NIAID recently launched a Phase 2 clinical trial to further evaluate the effectiveness of different strengths of vaccine in order to possibly expand the use of the limited smallpox vaccine supply; CDC and FDA have cooperated to ensure that the NIH study is carried out as expeditiously as possible.

In addition, NIAID and DoD's Defense Advanced Research Projects Agency (DARPA) have funded a collaborative effort involving those two agencies along with four academic centers, the CDC, USAMRIID, and the American Type Culture Collection that will focus on designing and implementing an "Orthopoxvirus Genomics and Bioinformatics Resource Center." This Center will conduct sequence and functional comparisons of genes to provide insights for the selection of targets for the design of antivirals and vaccines. The Center will design and maintain relational databases to store, display, annotate, and query genome sequences, structural information, phenotypic data, and bibliographic information. Part of the effort will include development and maintenance of a "Poxvirus Bioinformatics Resource Center" website to facilitate the availability of this data for other researchers.

## CONCLUSION

Mr. Chairman, let me again emphasize that the Administration is taking aggressive steps to make sure that our country is well protected from bioterrorism. Moreover, the government—at all levels—is responding to bioterrorist threats, and responding well.

Contemplating bioterrorism is unpleasant, but it is imperative. Under the leadership of President Bush, Secretary Thompson, and Homeland Security Director Ridge, we are taking all the steps necessary to keep America safe in an era when biological and chemical attacks are as possible as they are unthinkable.

Thank you, Mr. Chairman, for letting me speak about this matter of critical importance. I will be happy to answer any questions which you or members of the Committee may have.

# APPENDIX
# CRITICAL BIOLOGICAL AGENTS

The U.S. Public Health system and primary healthcare providers must be prepared to address varied biological agents, including pathogens that are rarely seen in the United States. The critical agents are listed below in priority order:

## Category A

High-priority agents include organisms that pose a risk to national security because they can be easily disseminated or transmitted person-to-person; cause high mortality, with potential for major public health impact; might cause public panic and social disruption; and require special action for public health preparedness.

## Category A Agents:

- variola major (smallpox)
- *Bacillus anthracis* (anthrax)
- *Yersinia pestis* (plague)
- *Clostridium botulinum* toxin (botulism)
- *Francisella tularensis* (tularemia)
- filoviruses
- Ebola hemorrhagic fever
- Marburg hemorrhagic fever
- arenaviruses
- Lassa (Lassa fever)
- Junin (Argentine hemorrhagic fever) and related viruses

## Category B

Second-highest priority agents include those that are moderately easy to disseminate; cause moderate morbidity and low mortality; and require specific enhancements of CDC's diagnostic capacity and enhanced disease surveillance.

## Category B Agents

- *Coxiella burnetti* (Q fever)
- *Brucella* species (brucellosis)
- *Burkholderia mallei* (glanders)
- alphaviruses

- Venezuelan encephalomyelitis
- eastern and western equine encephalomyelitis
- ricin toxin from *Ricinus communis* (castor beans)
- epsilon toxin of *Clostridium perfringens*
- *Staphylococcus* enterotoxin B

A subset of List B agents includes pathogens that are food or waterborne. These pathogens include but are not limited to:

- *Salmonella* species
- *Shigella dysenteriae*
- *Escherichia coli* O157:H7
- *Vibrio cholerae*
- *Cryptosporidium parvum*

## Category C

Third-highest priority agents include emerging pathogens that could be engineered for mass dissemination in the future because of availability; ease of production and dissemination; and potential for high morbidity and mortality and major health impact.

**Category C Agents**

- Nipah virus
- hantaviruses
- tickborne hemorrhagic fever viruses
- tickborne encephalitis viruses
- yellow fever
- multidrug-resistant tuberculosis

# 4

# FREQUENTLY ASKED QUESTIONS: BIOTERRORISM CONCERNS AFTER SEPTEMBER 11

## *The Johns Hopkins Center for Civilian Biodefense Strategies*

Since the terrorist attacks of September 11, public concern regarding a potential biological attack has heightened. The Johns Hopkins Center for Civilian Biodefense Strategies received a steady stream of phone calls from the general public seeking more information about bioterrorism and ways to protect themselves. In response, the Center prepared the following "Frequently Asked Questions" (FAQ) fact sheet. Individuals may also want to contact their local health department and physician for additional information.

### Should I buy a gas mask?

No. A mask would only protect you if you were wearing it at the exact moment a bioterrorist attack occurred. Unfortunately, a release of a biological agent is most likely to be done "covertly," that is, without anyone knowing it. That means you would not know ahead of time to put on your mask. To wear a mask continuously, or "just in case" a bioterrorist attack occurs, is impractical, if not impossible.

To work effectively, masks must be specially fitted to the wearer, and wearers must be trained in their use. This is usually done for the military and for workers in industries and laboratories who face routine exposure to chemicals and germs on the job. Gas masks purchased at an Army surplus store or off the Internet carry no guarantees that they will work. In fact, one national chain of surplus stores provides the following statement: "(X) has been selling gas masks as a novelty item since 1948. We have never been able to warrant their effectiveness and we cannot do so at this time...We do not know what each type of gas mask we sell might or might not be effective against...We do not know the age of each gas mask...."

In brief, no guarantees whatsoever are provided. More serious is the fact that the masks can be dangerous. There are reports of accidental suffocation when people have worn masks incorrectly, as happened to some Israeli civilians during the Persian Gulf War.

### Should I have my own supply of antibiotics?

There are a number of different germs a bioterrorist might use to carry out an attack. Many antibiotics are effective for a variety of diseases, but there is no antibiotic that is effective against all diseases. Thus, no single pill can protect against all types of biological weapon attacks. Keeping a supply of antibiotics on hand poses other problems because the antibiotics have a limited "shelf life" before they lose their strength.

There is currently no justification for taking antibiotics. Also, it should be known that antibiotics can cause side effects. They should only be taken with medical supervision.

### Is it safe for me to drink water from the tap?

It would be extremely difficult for a bioterrorist to contaminate our drinking water supplies to cause widespread illness. There are two reasons. First of all, huge amounts of water are pumped daily from our reservoirs, most of which is used for industrial and other purposes; very little is actually consumed. Thus, anything deliberately put into the water supply would be greatly diluted. Secondly, water treatment facilities routinely filter the water supply and add chlorine in order to kill harmful germs.

### What is smallpox?

Smallpox is a disease caused by the Variola virus. Historically, 1 out of 3 people who contracted the disease died. The disease can spread from person to person. Transmission usually occurs only after the patient develops a fever and rash. Although there is no treatment for the disease, a vaccine against smallpox provides excellent protection and serves to stop the spread of the disease. While many vaccines must be given weeks or months before a person is exposed to infection, smallpox vaccine is different. It protects a person even when given 2 to 3 days after exposure to the disease and may prevent a fatal outcome even when given as late as 4 to 5 days after exposure.

Smallpox was stamped out globally by 1980 and vaccination stopped everywhere in the world. However, the Centers for Disease Control and Prevention (CDC) maintain an emergency supply of smallpox vaccine. Currently there are 12-15 million doses in storage, and a program to produce more vaccine began a year ago.

**If smallpox is a potential threat to the U.S., why shouldn't we all get vaccinated?**

The vaccine may cause serious side effects. In 1972, the U.S. decided to stop routinely vaccinating its citizens because many people were experiencing side effects, while they had almost no risk of getting smallpox. By 1972, the disease was present only in a few countries of Asia and Africa. Today, health authorities would only recommend vaccination if there was clear evidence that the disease had resurfaced and those in the U.S. were at risk of acquiring infection.

Many people over age 30 have a vaccination scar. Vaccination consists of introducing the virus into the top layers of the skin. Over the following few days, a blister forms at the site of vaccination (usually the upper arm). The arm is sore, and there is fever. Very rarely, some people get a vaccine-related infection of the brain (about 1 case per 300,000 vaccinations); one fourth of these cases are fatal. Other potential negative effects of the vaccine are a severe skin reaction, spread of the vaccine virus (known as Vaccinia) to other parts of the body, and spread of the Vaccinia virus to other people.

**If I was vaccinated against smallpox before 1980, am I still protected?**

Probably not. Vaccination has been shown to wear off in most people after 10 years but may last longer if the person has been successfully vaccinated on multiple occasions. If health authorities determine that you have been exposed to smallpox or are at risk of infection, they would recommend that you be re-vaccinated immediately.

**What is anthrax?**

Anthrax is a disease caused by bacteria called *Bacillus anthracis*. The form of the disease that health authorities are concerned that a bioterrorist attack might produce is inhalational anthrax. Inhalational anthrax occurs when a person breathes in anthrax spores. As early as a day or two after exposure or as late as seven weeks afterward, the spores begin to grow rapidly and the victim develops fever, has difficulty breathing, and feels miserable. Death typically occurs within a few days after these symptoms if the person doesn't receive medical treatment. It is believed that antibiotics can stop the disease if they are taken at the time the anthrax spores begin to grow or very soon thereafter.

In the event of a bioterrorist attack, health authorities would conduct a rapid investigation, determine the place and time of the release, and identify individuals who need antibiotics. The federal government has stockpiled antibiotics for large-scale distribution in the event of a bioterrorist attack.

## Is anthrax contagious?

No. Anthrax is not contagious. It does not spread from person to person. Healthy people who come into contact with persons sick with anthrax cannot acquire the disease.

## What is the National Pharmaceutical Stockpile (NPS)?

The NPS is a large reserve of antibiotics, chemical antidotes, and other medical supplies set aside for emergencies. The CDC reports that it has the capacity to move these stockpiled materials to affected areas in the U.S. within 12 hours of notification. There are a number of different stockpiles, strategically located around the country. In addition to the medical supplies already set aside, the federal government has made agreements with drug manufacturers to make large amounts of additional emergency medicine. For more information on the NPS, go to http://www.cdc.gov/nceh/nps/default.htm.

## What can I do to protect myself and my family?

Unfortunately, there is presently little that individuals can do in advance to protect themselves from a bioterrorist attack. However, there is much that government agencies, healthcare institutions and public health departments can and should be doing to improve the capacity to protect the public following a bioterrorist attack. Medical institutions and public health agencies, in particular, have not received adequate attention and resources to cope with disasters like bioterrorism.

You can express your concern regarding adequate protections against the potential threat of bioterrorism to your local leaders. In each area, local health departments have an important responsibility for helping protect your community against outbreaks of infectious disease, whether they occur in nature or because of a malicious terrorist act. They can assist you with additional bioterrorism-related concerns that are pertinent to your own community.

## What if my fear about bioterrorism is having a serious impact on my family and work life?

Given the attacks upon civilians that took place on September 11, it is reasonable for citizens to feel anxious about their personal safety. Should your fear get to the point that it stops you from doing the things you would normally do in a day, it might be helpful to talk with someone. Your healthcare provider can make a referral if you do not already have someone in mind. In the wake of the attack on New York City, we have learned how helpful it has been to many New Yorkers to speak with a counselor or to go to a mental health center.

# 5

# FUNDING FOR BIOTERRORISM PREPAREDNESS AND RESPONSE

**107TH CONGRESS**

**1ST SESSION S. RES. 171**

Expressing the sense of the Senate concerning the provision of funding for bioterrorism preparedness and response.

IN THE SENATE OF THE UNITED STATES

OCTOBER 11, 2001

Mr. FRIST (for himself, Mr. KENNEDY, Mr. HATCH, Mr. BREAUX, Mr. WARNER, Ms. MIKULSKI, Mr. MURKOWSKI, Mr. DORGAN, Mr. BOND, Mr. CLELAND, Mr. BURNS, Mr. REED, Mr. INHOFE, Mrs. LINCOLN, Mr. THOMPSON, Mr. SANTORUM, Mr. ALLARD, Ms. COLLINS, Mr. ENZI, Mr. HUTCHINSON, Mr. HAGEL, Mr. ROBERTS, Mr. SESSIONS, Mr. CHAFEE, Mrs. CLINTON, and Mr. DOMENICI) submitted the following resolution; which was referred to the Committee on Health, Education, Labor, and Pensions

## RESOLUTION

Expressing the sense of the Senate concerning the provision of funding for bioterrorism preparedness and response.

Whereas additional steps must be taken to better prepare the United States to respond to potential bioterrorism attacks;

Whereas the threat of a bioterrorist attack is still remote, but is increasing for a variety of reasons, including—

(1) public pronouncements by Osama bin Laden that it is his religious duty to acquire weapons of mass destruction, including chemical and biological weapons;

(2) the callous disregard for innocent human life as demonstrated by the terrorists' attacks of September 11, 2001;

(3)  the resources and motivation of known terrorists and their sponsors and supporters to use biological warfare;

(4)  recent scientific and technological advances in agent delivery technology such as aerosolization that have made weaponization of certain germs much easier; and

(5)  the increasing access to the technologies and expertise necessary to construct and deploy chemical and biological weapons of mass destruction;

Whereas coordination of Federal, State, and local terrorism research, preparedness, and response programs must be improved;

Whereas States, local areas, and public health officials must have enhanced resources and expertise in order to respond to a potential bioterrorist attack;

Whereas national, State, and local communication capacities must be enhanced to combat the spread of chemical and biological illness;

Whereas greater resources must be provided to increase the capacity of hospitals and local healthcare workers to respond to public health threats;

Whereas healthcare professionals must be better trained to recognize, diagnose, and treat illnesses arising from biochemical attacks;

Whereas additional supplies may be essential to increase the readiness of the United States to respond to a bio-attack;

Whereas improvements must be made in assuring the safety of the food supply;

Whereas new vaccines and treatments are needed to assure that we have an adequate response to a biochemical attack;

Whereas government research, preparedness, and response programs need to utilize private sector expertise and resources; and

Whereas now is the time to strengthen our public health system and ensure that the United States is adequately prepared to respond to potential bioterrorist attacks, natural infectious disease outbreaks, and other challenges and potential threats to the public health: Now, therefore, be it *Resolved,* That it is the sense of the Senate that the United States should make a substantial new investment this year toward the following:

(1)  Improving State and local preparedness capabilities by upgrading State and local surveillance epidemiology, assisting in the development of response plans, assuring adequate staffing and train-

ing of health professionals to diagnose and care for victims of bioterrorism, extending the electronics communications networks and training personnel, and improving public health laboratories.

(2)  Improving hospital response capabilities by assisting hospitals in developing plans for a bioterrorist attack and improving the surge capacity of hospitals.

(3)  Upgrading the bioterrorism capabilities of the Centers for Disease Control and Prevention through improving rapid identification and health early warning systems.

(4)  Improving disaster response medical systems, such as the National Disaster Medical System and the Metropolitan Medical Response System and Epidemic Intelligence Service.

(5)  Targeting research to assist with the development of appropriate therapeutics and vaccines for likely bioterrorist agents and assisting with expedited drug and device review through the Food and Drug Administration.

(6)  Improving the National Pharmaceutical Stockpile program by increasing the amount of necessary therapies (including smallpox vaccines and other postexposure vaccines) and ensuring the appropriate deployment of stockpiles.

(7)  Targeting activities to increase food safety at the Food and Drug Administration.

(8)  Increasing international cooperation to secure dangerous biological agents, increase surveillance, and retrain biological warfare specialists.

# Bioterrorism Public Health Advisories and Guidelines

## 6.1 FAQs about Anthrax

The following FAQs are provided by the Centers for Disease Control Office of Public Health Emergency Preparedness and Response.

### Definition

**What is anthrax?**
*Bacillus anthracis*, the etiologic agent of anthrax, is a large, gram-positive, non-motile, spore-forming bacterial rod. The three virulence factors of *B. anthracis* are edema toxin, lethal toxin, and a capsular antigen. Human anthrax has three major clinical forms: cutaneous, inhalation, and gastrointestinal. If left untreated, anthrax in all forms can lead to septicemia and death.

**What is the case definition for anthrax?**
A confirmed case of anthrax is defined as

1. a clinically compatible case of cutaneous, inhalational, or gastro-intestinal illness that is laboratory-confirmed by isolation of *B. anthracis* from an affected tissue or site, or

2. a clinically compatible case of cutaneous, inhalational, or gastro-intestinal disease with other laboratory evidence of *B. anthracis* infection based on at least two supportive laboratory tests.

## HISTORY

### How many anthrax cases have we had in the United States in the last 50 years?

From January 1955 to December 1999, there were 236 reported cases of anthrax, most of them cutaneous, in 30 states and the District of Columbia.

### When was the last case of inhalational anthrax in the United States?

The last case of inhalational anthrax in the United States, before 2001, was in 1976 in California. A home craftsman, who worked with yarn, died. *Bacillus anthracis* was isolated from some of the imported yarns used by the patient. (MMWR 1976;25:33,34.)

### When was the last case of cutaneous anthrax?

The last case of cutaneous anthrax, before 2001, occurred in North Dakota, in 2000. It was the only case since 1992. To find out more about this case, read the following article: "Human Anthrax Associated with an Epizootic Among Livestock—North Dakota, 2000" (MMWR 2000; 5[32]:677; Available at http://www.cdc.gov/mmwr/preview/mmwrhtml/mm5032a1.htm)

### Can you list the most recent cases of anthrax in the Southeast of the United States?

Before October 2001, the last cases of anthrax, all cutaneous, were

- Florida, 1973
- South Carolina, 1974
- North Carolina, 1987

## SIGNS AND SYMPTOMS

### What are the signs and symptoms of anthrax?

Symptoms of disease vary depending on how the disease was contracted, but symptoms usually occur within 7 days.

Cutaneous anthrax is the most common naturally occurring type of infection (>95%) and usually occurs after skin contact with contaminated meat, wool, hides, or leather from infected animals. The incubation period ranges from 1-12 days. The skin infection begins as a small papule, progresses to a vesicle in 1-2 days followed by a necrotic ulcer. The lesion is usually painless, but patients also may have fever, malaise, headache, and regional lymphadenopathy. Most (about 95%) anthrax infections occur when the bacterium enters a cut or abrasion on the skin. Skin infection begins as a raised bump that resembles a spider bite, but (within 1-2 days) it develops into a vesicle and then a painless ulcer, usually 1-3 cm in diameter, with a characteristic black necrotic (dying) area in the center. Lymph glands in the adjacent area may swell. About 20% of untreated cases of cutaneous anthrax will result in death. Deaths are rare if patients are given appropriate antimicrobial therapy.

Inhalational anthrax is the most lethal form of anthrax. Anthrax spores must be aerosolized in order to cause inhalational anthrax. The number of spores that cause human infection is unknown. The incubation period of inhalational anthrax among humans is unclear, but it is reported to range from 1 to 7 days, possibly ranging up to 60 days. It resembles a viral respiratory illness and initial symptoms include sore throat, mild fever, muscle aches, and malaise. These symptoms may progress to respiratory failure and shock, with meningitis frequently developing.

Gastrointestinal anthrax usually follows the consumption of raw or undercooked contaminated meat and has an incubation period of 1-7 days. It is associated with severe abdominal distress followed by fever and signs of septicemia. The disease can take an oropharyngeal or abdominal form. Involvement of the pharynx is usually characterized by lesions at the base of the tongue, sore throat, dysphagia, fever, and regional lymphadenopathy. Lower bowel inflammation usually causes nausea, loss of appetite, vomiting, and fever, followed by abdominal pain, vomiting blood, and bloody diarrhea.

## What specific symptoms should I watch for?
People should watch for the following symptoms:

- Fever (temperature greater than 100 degrees F). The fever may be accompanied by chills or night sweats.

- Flu-like symptoms

- Cough, usually a non-productive cough, chest discomfort, shortness of breath, fatigue, muscle aches

- Sore throat, followed by difficulty swallowing, enlarged lymph nodes, headache, nausea, loss of appetite, abdominal distress, vomiting, or diarrhea

- A sore, especially on your face, arms, or hands, that starts as a raised bump and develops into a painless ulcer with a black area in the center.

## Is anthrax contagious?

No. Anthrax is not contagious; the illness cannot be transmitted from person to person.

## What are the case fatality rates for the various forms of anthrax?

Early treatment of cutaneous anthrax is usually curative, and early treatment of all forms is important for recovery. Patients with cutaneous anthrax have reported case fatality rates of 20% without antibiotic treatment and less than 1% with it. Although case-fatality estimates for inhalational anthrax are based on incomplete information, the rate is extremely high, approximately 75%, even with all possible supportive care including appropriate antibiotics. Estimates of the impact of the delay in postexposure prophylaxis or treatment on survival are not known. For gastrointestinal anthrax, the case-fatality rate is estimated to be 25%-60% and the effect of early antibiotic treatment on that case-fatality rate is not defined.

## EXPOSURE

## What is the difference between exposure to anthrax and disease caused by anthrax?

A person can be said to be exposed to anthrax when that person comes in contact with the anthrax bacteria and a culture taken from that person is positive for anthrax. A person can be exposed without having disease. A person who might have come in contact with anthrax, but without a positive culture, would be said to be potentially exposed. Disease caused by anthrax occurs when there is some sign of illness, such as the skin lesion that occurs with cutaneous anthrax.

A person who is exposed to anthrax but is given appropriate antibiotics can avoid developing disease.

## Can I be exposed to anthrax via mail?

Letters containing *Bacillus anthracis* (anthrax) have been received by mail in several areas in the United States. In some instances, anthrax exposures have occurred, with several persons becoming infected. To prevent such exposures and subsequent infection, all persons should learn how to recognize a suspicious package or envelope and take appropriate steps to protect themselves and others.

## What kind of mail should be considered suspicious?
Identifying Suspicious Packages and Envelopes
*Some characteristics of suspicious packages and envelopes include the following:*

- Inappropriate or unusual labeling
  - Excessive postage
  - Handwritten or poorly typed addresses
  - Misspellings of common words
  - Strange return address or no return address
  - Incorrect titles or title without a name
  - Not addressed to a specific person
  - Marked with restrictions, such as "Personal," "Confidential," or "Do not X-ray"
  - Marked with any threatening language
  - Postmarked from a city or state that does not match the return address

- Appearance
  - Powdery substance felt through or appearing on the package or envelope
  - Oily stains, discolorations, or odor
  - Lopsided or uneven envelope
  - Excessive packaging material such as masking tape, string, etc.

- Other suspicious signs
  - Excessive weight
  - Ticking sound
  - Protruding wires or aluminum foil

If a package or envelope appears suspicious, DO NOT OPEN IT.

## What should people do who get a letter or package with powder?
Handling of Suspicious Packages or Envelopes*

- Do not shake or empty the contents of any suspicious package or envelope.

- Do not carry the package or envelope, show it to others or allow others to examine it.

- Put the package or envelope down on a stable surface; do not sniff, touch, taste, or look closely at it or at any contents which may have spilled.

- Alert others in the area about the suspicious package or envelope. Leave the area, close any doors, and take actions to prevent others from entering the area. If possible, shut off the ventilation system.

- WASH hands with soap and water to prevent spreading potentially infectious material to face or skin. Seek additional instructions for exposed or potentially exposed persons.

- If at work, notify a supervisor, a security officer, or a law enforcement official. If at home, contact the local law enforcement agency.

- If possible, create a list of persons who were in the room or area when this suspicious letter or package was recognized and a list of persons who also may have handled this package or letter. Give this list to both the local public health authorities and law enforcement officials.

*These recommendations were published on October 26, 2001, in "Update: Investigation of bioterrorism-related anthrax and interim guidelines for exposure management and antimicrobial therapy." MMWR 2001; 50:909-919

**Can anthrax spores be killed on letters in the mail by microwave, UV light, or ironing?**
While some of these methods may kill some spores, it is not known what procedures to use (e.g., length of time, temperature, etc.). Furthermore, because of insufficient data on the efficacy of these methods in inactivating anthrax spores, CDC does not recommend these techniques for reliable decontamination.

**What should I do to protect my family and myself if a dangerous chemical agent were released in my community?**
Emergency management teams would lead efforts in the event of a chemical attack and would let you know if you need to evacuate the area or seek some type of shelter.

**Should I purchase a gas mask as protection from any chemical agent release such as anthrax?**
No, CDC does not recommend purchasing gas masks. The likelihood that you would be involved in a chemical attack is low, and your protection is the responsibility of state and federal law enforcement officials. They are on high alert to ensure that such an event does not happen. In addition, CDC believes that purchasing a gas mask causes a false sense of

security and can do more harm than good. Masks that aren't used properly or that do not fit well will not give you adequate protection.

## TESTING

### Can I get screened or tested to find out whether I have been exposed to anthrax?

There is no screening test for anthrax; there is no test that a doctor can do for you that says you've been exposed to or carry it. The only way exposure can be determined is through a public health investigation. The tests that you hear or read about, such as nasal swabs and environmental tests, are not tests to determine whether an individual should be treated. These kinds of tests are used only to determine the extent of exposure in a given building or workplace.

### If the patient is suspected of being exposed to anthrax, should he/she be quarantined or should other family members be tested?

Direct person-to-person spread of anthrax is extremely unlikely and anthrax is not contagious. Therefore, there is no need to quarantine individuals suspected of being exposed to anthrax or to immunize or treat contacts of persons ill with anthrax, such as household contacts, friends, or coworkers, unless they were also exposed to the same source of infection.

### Does CDC collect samples to test the bacteria?

CDC is engaging its partners in the Laboratory Response Network (LRN) in states all across the United States. The LRN is a collaborative partnership and multilevel system linking state and local public health laboratories with advanced capacity laboratories —including clinical, military, veterinary, agricultural, water, and food-testing laboratories—to rapidly identify threat agents, including anthrax. Local clinical laboratory testing is confirmed at state and large metropolitan public health laboratories. CDC conducts the definitive or highly specialized testing for major threat agents. There are 100 laboratories in the network; none of them are commercial labs.

### What's the turnaround time for an anthrax test in an environmental sample—for example, the time it takes to confirm that a substance in an envelope was indeed anthrax?

Before testing can begin, samples must be collected and arrive in the laboratory in a form suitable for testing. Testing itself is a two-step process. The initial screening tests may be positive within two hours if the sample is large and the concentration of bacteria is high. The confirmation tests take much longer, depending in part on how fast the bacteria grow, but are usually available 24-36 hours after the sample is received in the laboratory.

## Does CDC recommend the use of home test kits for anthrax?

Hand-held assays (sometimes referred to as "Smart Tickets") are sold commercially for the rapid detection of *Bacillus anthracis*. These assays are intended only for the screening of environmental samples. First responder and law enforcement communities are using these as instant screening devices and should forward any positive samples to authorities for more sensitive and specialized confirmatory testing. The results of these assays should not be used to make decisions about patient management or prophylaxis. The utility and validity of these assays are unknown.

At this time, CDC does not have enough scientific data to recommend the use of these assays. The analytical sensitivity of these assays is limited by the technology, and data provided by manufacturers indicate that a minimum of 10,000 spores is required to generate a positive signal. This number of spores would suggest a heavy contamination of the area (sample). Therefore a negative result does not rule out a lower level of contamination. Data collected from field use also indicate specificity problems with some of these assays. Some positive results have been obtained with spores of the non-anthrax *Bacillus* bacteria that may be found in the environment.

For these reasons, CDC has been asked to evaluate the sensitivity and specificity of the commercially available rapid, hand-held assays for *B. anthracis*. When this study is completed, results will be made available. Conclusions from this study are not expected in the near future.

## Is a nasal swab test an approved diagnostic tool for determining whether a person has been exposed to anthrax?

No. At present, CDC does not recommend the use of nasal swab testing on a routine basis to determine whether a person has been exposed to *B. anthracis* or as a diagnostic tool. At best, a positive result may be interpreted only to indicate exposure; a negative result does not exclude the possibility of exposure. Nasal swab screening may be used by public health officials to assist in an epidemiological investigation of potentially exposed persons to evaluate the dispersion of spores. See also: http://www.bt.cdc.gov/DocumentsApp/faqanthrax.asp#Q602

## Are health department laboratories capable of conducting testing?

All state health departments are capable of obtaining results of tests on suspected infectious agents. Laboratories are usually classified as Level A,

B, C, or D. Level A laboratories are those typically found in community hospitals, and these laboratories should be able to perform initial testing on all clinical specimens (usually blood or some other body fluid). Public health laboratories are usually Level B; these laboratories are valuable for confirming or refuting preliminary test results and can usually perform antimicrobial susceptibility tests on bacteria and viruses. Level C laboratories, which are reference facilities and can be public health laboratories, can perform more rapid identification tests. Level D laboratories are designed to perform the most sophisticated tests and are located in federal facilities such as CDC. Every state has a Laboratory Response Network (LRN) contact. The LRN links state and local public health laboratories with advanced-capacity laboratories, including clinical, military, veterinary, agricultural, water, and food-testing laboratories. Laboratorians should contact their state public health laboratory to identify their local LRN representative. CDC's public bioterrorism Web site (http://www.bt.cdc.gov/) provides access to CDC's Centers for Public Health Preparedness, a national network of academic institutions and local health departments whose goal is to ensure that local public health workers are fully prepared to respond to current and emerging health threats, including bioterrorism.

## Diagnosis

### How is anthrax diagnosed?
Anthrax is diagnosed by isolating *B. anthracis* from the blood, skin lesions, or respiratory secretions or by measuring specific antibodies in the blood of persons with suspected cases.

In patients with symptoms compatible with anthrax, providers should confirm the diagnosis by obtaining the appropriate laboratory specimens based on the clinical form of anthrax that is suspected (i.e., cutaneous, inhalational, or gastrointestinal).

Cutaneous–vesicular fluid and blood
Inhalational—blood, cerebrospinal fluid (if meningeal signs are present) or chest X-ray
Gastrointestinal–blood
For more information read *Update: Investigation of Bioterrorism-Related Anthrax and Interim Guidelines for Clinical Evaluation of Persons with Possible Anthrax*

### What are the standard diagnostic tests used by the laboratories?
Presumptive identification to identify to Genus level (*Bacillus* family of organisms) requires Gram stain and colony identification.

Presumptive identification to identify to species level (*B. anthracis*) requires tests for motility, lysis by gamma phage, capsule production and visualization, hemolysis, wet mount, and malachite green staining for spores.

Confirmatory identification of *B. anthracis* carried out by CDC may include phage lysis, capsular staining, and direct fluorescent antibody (DFA) testing on capsule antigen and cell wall polysaccharide.

### When is a nasal swab indicated?

Nasal swabs and screening may assist in epidemiologic investigations, but should not be relied upon as a guide for prophylaxis or treatment. Epidemiologic investigation in response to threats of exposure to *B. anthracis* may employ nasal swabs of potentially exposed persons as an adjunct to environmental sampling to determine the extent of exposure.

### Why were nasal swabs used to screen individuals in the Florida investigation for anthrax?

The nasal swab test was used as a screening tool because, following initial recognition of the case of confirmed inhalational anthrax, there were no known sources of exposure. Determining whether anyone else associated with the case-patient might have been exposed was important. In this setting, the nasal swab method was used for a rapid assessment of exposure among people, and as a tool for rapid environmental assessment. When the source of exposure is not known, nasal swabs can help investigators determine that information. They are not used for diagnosing people with anthrax, and they are not 100 percent effective in determining all who may have been exposed. See also: http://www.bt.cdc.gov/DocumentsApp/faqanthrax.asp#Q602

### Is there an X-ray for detecting anthrax?

A chest X-ray can be used to help diagnose inhalation anthrax in people who have symptoms. It is not useful as a test for determining anthrax exposure or for people with no symptoms.

### Can someone get anthrax from contaminated mail, equipment, or clothing?

In the mail-handling/processing sites, *B. anthracis* spores may be aerosolized during the operation and maintenance of high-speed, mail-sorting machines potentially exposing workers. In addition, these spores could get into heating, ventilating, or air conditioning (HVAC) systems. CDC interim guidelines have been issued to advise workers on how best to protect themselves in the workplace.
http://www.bt.cdc.gov/DocumentsApp/Anthrax/10312001/han51.asp
http://www.cdc.gov/mmwr/preview/mmwrhtml/mm5043a6.htm

## Preventive Therapy

### What is the therapy for preventing inhalational anthrax?
Interim recommendations for postexposure prophylaxis for prevention of inhalational anthrax after intentional exposure to *B. anthracis* may be found in the MMWR issue cited below:

http://www.cdc.gov/mmwr/preview/mmwrhtml/mm5041a1.htm

### What is cipro (ciprofloxacin)?
Ciprofloxacin, or cipro as it is commonly known, is a broad-spectrum, synthetic antimicrobial agent active against several microorganisms. The use of ciprofloxacin is warranted only under the strict supervision of a physician.

### Does ciprofloxacin have an expiration date?
Yes. Antibiotics, just like all medicines, have expiration dates. If you received your ciprofloxacin through a pharmacist, the expiration date should be listed on the bottle. If you can't find it or have questions about the expiration date, contact your pharmacist directly.

### What are the side effects of Cipro?
Adverse health effects include vomiting, diarrhea, headaches, dizziness, sun sensitivity, and rash. Hypertension, blurred vision, and other central nervous system effects occur in <1% of patients and may be accentuated by caffeine or medications containing theophylline.

### What are the guidelines for changing from ciprofloxacin to another antibiotic?
Considerations for choosing an antimicrobial agent include effectiveness, resistance, side effects, and cost. As a measure to preserve the effectiveness of ciprofloxacin against anthrax and other infections, use of doxycycline for preventive therapy may be preferable. As always, the selection of the antimicrobial agent for an individual patient should be based on side-effect profiles, history of reactions, and the clinical setting. For more information about possible adverse reactions from taking antimicrobial prophylaxis see the following *Update: Investigation of Bioterrorism-Related Anthrax and Adverse Events from Antimicrobial Prophylaxis* (http://www.cdc.gov/mmwr/preview/mmwrhtml/mm5044a 1.htm)

### Should people buy and store antibiotics?

There is no need to buy or store antibiotics, and indeed, it can be detrimental to both the individual and to the community. First, only people who are exposed to anthrax should take antibiotics, and health authorities must make that determination. Second, individuals may not stockpile or store the correct antibiotics. Third, under emergency plans, the Federal government can ship appropriate antibiotics from its stockpile to wherever they are needed.

### Will antibiotics protect me from a bioterrorist event? Should I stockpile them?

CDC does not recommend using antibiotics unless a specific disease has been identified. There are several different agents that could be used for bioterrorism, such as bacteria, viruses, and toxins. Not a single antibiotic (or vaccine) works for all of these agents. Antibiotics only kill bacteria, not viruses or other agents that could also be used in a bioterrorist event. Antibiotics are not harmless drugs. They can cause serious side effects and drug interactions. National and state public health officials have large supplies of needed drugs and vaccines if a bioterrorism event should occur. These supplies can be sent anywhere in the United States within 12 hours.

### What drugs are FDA approved for PEP and treatment?

Ciprofloxacin and doxycycline are FDA approved for PEP, and ciprofloxacin, doxycycline, and amoxicillin are FDA approved for treatment. In the current situation of intentional anthrax distribution, doxycycline and ciprofloxacin are the recommended drugs for prophylaxis.

Inhalational anthrax treatment protocol for cases associated with this attack  http://www.cdc.gov/mmwr/preview/mmwrhtml/mm5042a1.htm  - (table 1)
Cutaneous anthrax treatment protocol for cases associated with this attack  http://www.cdc.gov/mmwr/preview/mmwrhtml/mm5042a1.htm  - (table 2)

## TREATMENT

### What is the treatment for patients with inhalational and cutaneous anthrax?

Treatment protocols for cases of inhalational and cutaneous anthrax associated with this bioterrorist attack are found in the MMWR, 10/26/2001; 50(42), 909-919.

## What if I develop side effects from the antibiotic?

If you develop side effects from the antibiotic, call your healthcare provider immediately. Depending on the type of side effects, you may be able to continue taking the medicine, or you may be switched to an alternative antibiotic. If necessary, your physician may contact your State Department of Health for consultation on possible alternate antibiotics.

## Has CDC tested the anthrax isolates for sensitivity to different antibiotics?

Yes. Antibiotic sensitivity testing performed at CDC has determined that the strain of anthrax was sensitive to a wide range of antibiotics, including penicillin and ciprofloxacin, giving public health officials important treatment information.

## What are the risks of using tetracyclines and fluoroquinolones in children; are alternatives available?

Risks of using tetracyclines and fluoroquinolones in children must be weighed carefully against the risk for developing a life-threatening disease due to *B. anthracis*. Both agents can have adverse health reactions in children. If adverse reactions are suspected, therapy may be changed to amoxicillin or penicillin.

## Are there special instructions for taking ciprofloxacin or doxycycline?

As with all antibiotics, take the medication according to the schedule you were instructed, and even if you begin to feel better, continue taking it for the full number of days. If you need an extension of the antibiotic at the end of your prescribed number of days, local emergency healthcare workers or your healthcare provider will inform and tell you how to get more medicine. They may also tell you to discontinue the antibiotic, or will change the type of antibiotic, depending on results of laboratory tests.

## After I have started taking ciprofloxacin to protect me from developing anthrax, what side effects could I get from taking this antibiotic?

Side effects which sometimes occur include nausea, mild diarrhea, stomach pain, headache, and dizziness. Talk with your doctor if you have any of these problems while you are taking the antibiotic. Certain foods and medications should not be taken with ciprofloxacin; this should be discussed at the time the antibiotic is prescribed, so that side effects will not occur from the combinations. Ciprofloxacin also can cause sun sensitivity which increases the chances of sunburn. More serious side effects include central nervous system side effects such as confusion, tremors, hallucinations, depression, and increased risk of seizures. High blood pressure and blurred vision are also possible. Allergic reactions could cause difficulty breathing; closing of the throat; swelling of the lips, tongue, or face; hives; or severe diarrhea. Pain, inflammation, or rupture of a tendon are possible and also severe tissue inflammation of the colon could occur. **Call your doctor or seek medical advice right away if you are having any of these side effects.** This list is NOT a complete list of side effects reported with ciprofloxacin. Your healthcare provider can discuss with you a more complete list of side effects.

### After I have started taking doxycycline to protect me from developing anthrax, what side effects could I get from taking this antibiotic?

Less serious side effects include diarrhea, upset stomach, nausea, sore mouth or throat, sensitivity to sunlight, vaginal yeast infection, or itching of the mouth lasting more than 2 days. You should talk with your doctor if you have any of these problems while taking doxycycline. Certain foods and medications should not be taken with doxycycline, and this should be discussed with your healthcare provider at the time the antibiotic is prescribed, so that side effects will not occur from the combinations. Doxycycline also causes sun sensitivity which increases the chances of sunburn. Serious side effects of doxycycline that are possible but uncommon include: life-threatening allergic reaction (symptoms are trouble breathing; closing of the throat; swelling of the lips, tongue, or face; hives), blood problems (symptoms are unusual bleeding or bruising), liver damage (symptoms are yellowing of the skin or eyes, dark urine, nausea, vomiting, loss of appetite, abdominal pain), irritation of the esophagus. **Call your doctor or seek medical attention right away if you are having any of these side effects.** This list is NOT a complete list of side effects reported with doxycycline. Your healthcare provider can discuss with you a more complete list of side effects.

### Why is CDC recommending doxycycline instead of ciprofloxacin for the treatment and prevention of anthrax?

Both doxycycline and ciprofloxacin are effective in treating the *Bacillus anthracis* that we are dealing with in these investigations. Although CDC first recommended the use of either drug for postexposure prophylaxis for the prevention of inhalational anthrax, we are now recommending doxycycline in order to prevent other bacteria from developing resistance to ciprofloxacin. Ciprofloxacin is part of the fluoroquinolones family of drugs, a relatively new class of antibiotics used to treat infections caused by organisms for which doctors do not have information about antimicrobial susceptibility. This kind of treatment is known as empiric therapy. Ciprofloxacin and other fluoroquinolones are used for empiric treatment for a variety of serious and common infections in the United States, including pneumonia, gastrointestinal infections, and urinary tract infections. The number of people who have been exposed to *B. anthracis* and need antibiotics has increased dramatically since CDC first issued guidelines for treatment. If all those people take ciprofloxacin, other bacteria they carry in their bodies may develop resistance to fluoroquinolones, potentially limiting the usefulness of these drugs as empiric therapy. Doxycycline is less frequently used for empiric treatment than ciprofloxacin; therefore, we have fewer concerns regarding this drug and the emergence of new resistant bacteria.

### Why are people who have been exposed to *B. anthracis* being given antibiotics for different amounts of time?

The initial number of people placed on prophylaxis may reflect conservative estimates with wide safety margins based on limited preliminary information. As the investigation progresses, and a clearer picture of exposure develops, the number of people advised to continue prophylaxis may be reduced. As of the last week of October 2001, when preliminary tests show that people have been exposed to *Bacillus anthracis*, those exposed may be provided with a starter packet of antibiotics; the number of days for which antibiotics are prescribed can vary according to the specific situation and person. Additional tests are then conducted of the area where exposure occurred and to determine the extent of exposure. Based on the results of these additional tests, those exposed may be instructed to return to a centralized location for additional care or to seek additional care from their primary care providers; additional antibiotics may be prescribed based on the particular situation and person. Lastly, it is recommended that people found to be at risk of inhalation anthrax be prescribed 60 days of antibiotics. These general procedures may change at any time as new information is gathered.

### Are there different strains of *B. anthracis*? Do they all respond to antibiotics?

Yes, there are different strains of *Bacillus anthracis*. Some strains of *B. anthracis* may be naturally resistant to certain antibiotics and not others. In addition, there may be biologically mutant strains that are engineered to be resistant to various antibiotics. A laboratory analysis can help to define which strain of *B. anthracis* is present and which antibiotic would be the most effective in treating the resulting anthrax.

### What is the FDA telling physicians and other health professionals about prescriptions for ciprofloxacin?

Although FDA does not regulate the practice of medicine, the agency is strongly recommending that physicians not prescribe ciprofloxacin for individual patients to have on hand for possible use against inhaled anthrax. Indiscriminate and widespread use of ciprofloxacin could hasten the development of drug-resistant organisms and lessen the effects of these agents against many infections.

### Can other fluoroquinolones be used instead of ciprofloxacin for PEP/treatment for anthrax?
Other fluoroquinolones, such as ofloxacin and levofloxacin, are not specifically recommended as alternatives to ciprofloxacin because of a lack of sufficient efficacy data.

## VACCINE

### Is the anthrax vaccine available to the public?
A vaccine has been developed for anthrax that is protective against invasive disease, but it is currently only recommended for high-risk populations. CDC and academic partners are continuing to support the development of the next generation of anthrax vaccines.

### Who should be vaccinated against anthrax?
The Advisory Committee on Immunization Practices (ACIP) has recommend anthrax vaccination for the following groups:

- Persons who work directly with the organism in the laboratory.

- Persons who work with imported animal hides or furs in areas where standards are insufficient to prevent exposure to anthrax spores.

- Persons who handle potentially infected animal products in high-incidence areas; while incidence is low in the United States, veterinarians who travel to work in other countries where incidence is higher should consider being vaccinated.

- Military personnel deployed to areas with high risk for exposure to the organism.

### What is the protocol for anthrax vaccination?
The immunization consists of three subcutaneous injections given 2 weeks apart, followed by three additional subcutaneous injections given at 6, 12, and 18 months. Annual booster injections of the vaccine are recommended thereafter.

**Are there adverse reactions to the anthrax vaccine?**
Mild local reactions occur in 30% of recipients and consist of slight tenderness and redness at the injection site. Severe local reactions are infrequent and consist of extensive swelling of the forearm in addition to the local reaction. Systemic reactions occur in fewer than 0.2% of recipients.

**Is there a vaccination for anthrax?**
A protective vaccine has been developed for anthrax; however, it is primarily given to military personnel. Vaccination is recommended only for those at high risk, such as workers in research laboratories that handle anthrax bacteria routinely. The antibiotics used in postexposure prophylaxis are very effective in preventing anthrax disease from occurring after an exposure.

## REPORTING

**What is the protocol for investigating and reporting possible anthrax exposures?**
Physicians should report any suspected cases of *B. anthracis* to their local or state public health officials IMMEDIATELY. Subsequent notification procedures for these officials may be found on this Web site at:
http://www.bt.cdc.gov/EmContact/Protocols.asp

**How should healthcare workers respond to suspected exposure to a bioterrorist agent? Who should healthcare workers call first, second, third? CDC, FBI, local police, local health department?**
Healthcare providers, clinical laboratory personnel, and infection control professionals who notice illness patterns and diagnostic clues that might indicate an unusual infectious disease outbreak associated with intentional release of a biologic agent should report any clusters or findings to their local or state health department. (Guidelines for recognizing a number of biologic agents, including anthrax, plague, botulism, smallpox, inhalational tularemia, and hemorrhagic fever, are described in CDC's Morbidity and Mortality Weekly Report, Vol. 50, No. 41, dated October 19, 2001.
http://www.cdc.gov/mmwr/preview/mmwrhtml/mm5041a2.htm )

## RESPONSE

### How is CDC responding to the anthrax reports?

The Federal government is coordinating the overall response to the anthrax reports. CDC continues to work with state and local health departments and other federal agencies to protect the public's health and facilitate the epidemiologic investigations.

CDC has deployed a large number of epidemiologists, laboratorians, and other program staff to areas with possible anthrax exposures to assist local health professionals conducting these investigations. CDC also has professional staff in Atlanta working around the clock to track the exposures, process specimens, answer questions, and provide technical assistance and support.

As CDC learns of an emerging situation involving a possible exposure to anthrax, the agency works with state and local health departments and other federal agencies to determine an appropriate response.

### What is CDC's role on "rapid response teams"?

CDC teams are on stand-by and available to assist with investigations into outbreaks, confirmation of cases and exposures, and cleanup of *B. anthracis* and other biologic and chemical agents. These teams work closely with local health officials in the areas of laboratory capacity, epidemiologic response, disease surveillance, and communication.

### What is the approach to cleanup of buildings?

The Environmental Protection Agency (EPA) has lead responsibility for issues related to environmental cleanup of hazardous materials and weapons of mass destruction with the assistance of 16 different federal agencies and departments including HHS/CDC working with the State and local agencies. The decision for a most efficient approach to cleanup will be defined based upon the sampling results, review of cleanup options, environmental media, etc.

### Does CDC cooperate with international health organizations like the World Health Organization (WHO) to help in other countries with anthrax cases?

CDC has assisted authorities in other countries investigating cases of bioterrorism-related anthrax. During October 12—November 13, 2001, CDC received 111 requests from 66 countries. Of these, 47 requests were laboratory related; 43 were general requests for bioterrorism informa-tion; 13 were for environmental or occupational health guidelines; and eight were about developing bioterrorism preparedness plans. The largest proportion of requests were from Central and South America (26%). Of the 66 countries, 15 received laboratory assistance, including testing or arrangements for testing of suspected isolates at a CDC-supported laboratory or a reference laboratory in another country. Forty-two countries received telephone or e-mail consultation regarding specific tests for suspected *B. anthracis* isolates. Requests for information regarding bioterrorism-related issues outside the United States should be directed to the International Team of CDC's Emergency Operations Center (e-mail, eocinternational@cdc.gov). Read more about the Investigation of Bioterrorism-Related Anthrax, 2001(http://www.cdc.gov/mmwr/preview/mmwrhtml/mm5047a1.htm).

## How can I recognize a bioterrorism hoax?

If you are not sure whether a bioterrorism report is true or not, check with credible sources, such as CDC's Health-Related Hoaxes and Rumors Web site at http://www.cdc.gov/hoax_rumors.htm. A number of Internet sites are available regarding urban legends and hoaxes, such as the Urban Legend Reference Page at http://www.snopes2.com and the Computer Incident Advisory Committee and Department of Energy's HoaxBusters site at http://hoaxbusters.ciac.org. The HoaxBuster's site also offers a guide for recognizing an Internet hoax at http://hoax busters.ciac.org/HBHoaxInfo.html#identify .

## Are other public health programs being neglected due to the focus on anthrax and other bioterrorism issues?

CDC continues to carry out its vision for the 21st Century: "Healthy People in a Healthy World—Through Prevention." Because anthrax and bioterrorism remain in the media spotlight, it might appear that all of CDC's attention has been shifted to these issues. CDC is paying a great deal of attention to the current bioterrorism event, however, CDC staff continue to implement important public health programs to protect our nation's communities. For information on other CDC programs, please visit http://www.cdc.gov .

## Does CDC have a system for monitoring all samples of anthrax that come into state laboratories?

CDC supports a network of state laboratories through routine quality assurance, training, and random testing. In addition, the state laboratories send CDC samples for confirmation. Other questions concerning state public health labs should be directed to your state public health department.

## How is CDC responding to the anthrax reports?

CDC continues to work with state and local health departments and other federal agencies to conduct public health investigations stemming from the recent bioterrorism attacks with *B. anthracis* spores. Dozens of CDC epidemiologists, laboratory scientists, and other program staff are working in Florida, New York, Washington, D.C., and New Jersey to assist local health professionals in conducting these investigations. CDC staff members in Atlanta are also responding to the bioterrorism attacks. More than 50 laboratory scientists are working around the clock to process hundreds of specimens CDC is receiving. CDC has set up a 24-hour a day emergency operations center equipped with state-of-the-art communications equipment to help coordinate these public health investigations. The operations center includes telephone hotlines for both the public and for health professionals, where staff members are receiving hundreds of calls each day.

## What is CDC's role in an anthrax field investigation?

CDC is using traditional public health strategies in its approach to these investigations. In this situation, the primary intervention has been to rapidly identify people at risk and to treat them with appropriate postexposure antibiotics in an effort to prevent the development of anthrax. The structure of the investigation evolves into at least five teams that coordinate various aspects of the investigation or intervention.

- An intervention team ensures that the people who have suspected exposure to anthrax are identified and receive antibiotics.

- A surveillance team looks for persons who develop anthrax.

- A clinical team, which is led by infectious disease specialists, rapidly assesses any possible case of anthrax revealed by surveillance.

- An environmental assessment team coordinates the sampling of environments associated with the investigation for *Bacillus anthracis*, and coordinates the movement of those samples to appropriate laboratories.

- An epidemiology team gathers available information in an effort to try and better understand the circumstances of exposure and persons at risk for infection. The leader of the investigation manages these teams and communicates with local, state, and public health authorities; media; and community and political leaders. The leader also works with the FBI and the U.S. Postal Service and makes sure laboratory test results and other new information are incorporated into the investigation.

## LABORATORY SAFETY

### How are microbiological materials, such as bacterial cultures, kept safe for legitimate laboratory use only?

On June 10, 1996, CDC and the Department of Health and Human Services (HHS) issued a Notice of Proposed Rulemaking (NPRM) to implement Section 511 of Public Law 104-132, "The Antiterrorism and Effective Death Penalty Act of 1996," which requires the Secretary of HHS to regulate the transfer of select agents. Current regulations specify requirements for the packaging, labeling, and transport of select agents shipped in interstate commerce. This final rule places additional shipping and handling requirements on facilities that transfer or receive select agents listed in the rule that are capable of causing substantial harm to human health. For more information on these regulations, see http://www.cdc.gov/od/ohs/lrsat/42cfr72.htm - Registration of Facilities.

## WORKER SAFETY

### What are CDC's recommendations for protecting mail handlers?

CDC and the U.S. Postal Service are collaborating to ensure that all mail handlers and postal workers are protected against exposure to anthrax. Detailed guidelines may be found on these Web sites:
http://www.bt.cdc.gov/DocumentsApp/Anthrax/10312001/han51.asp
http://www.cdc.gov/mmwr/preview/mmwrhtml/mm5043a6.htm

### Does CDC have recommendations to help workers who handle mail protect themselves from anthrax exposure?

Yes, CDC has published interim recommendations that are intended to assist personnel responsible for occupational health and safety in developing a comprehensive program to reduce potential cutaneous or inhalational exposures to *Bacillus anthracis* spores among workers, including maintenance and custodial workers, in work sites where mail is handled or processed. Such work sites include post offices, mail distribution/handling centers, bulk mail centers, airmail facilities, priority mail processing centers, public and private mailrooms, and other settings in which workers are responsible for the handling and processing of mail. CDC and the U.S. Postal Service are collaborating to ensure that all mail handlers and postal workers are protected against exposure to anthrax. Detailed guidelines may be found on these Web sites:

http://www.bt.cdc.gov/DocumentsApp/Anthrax/10312001/han51.asp
http://www.cdc.gov/mmwr/preview/mmwrhtml/mm5043a6.htm

### If these recommendations are followed does it mean workers will stop getting sick with anthrax?

The interim recommendations that have been developed are based on the limited information available on ways to avoid infection and the effectiveness of various prevention strategies. As new information becomes available the guidelines will be updated. These recommendations do not address instances where a known or suspected exposure has occurred. Workers should be trained in how to recognize and handle a suspicious piece of mail http://www.bt.cdc.gov/DocumentsApp/Anthrax/0312001/han51.asp). In addition, each work site should develop an emergency plan describing appropriate actions to be taken when a known or suspected exposure to *B. anthracis* occurs.

### What kinds of anthrax worker safety guidelines are being issued?

The recommendations are divided into four categories. They are engineering controls, administrative controls, housekeeping controls, and personal protective equipment for workers. The guidelines describe measures that should be implemented in mail-handling/processing sites to prevent potential exposures to *B. anthracis* spores.

http://www.bt.cdc.gov/DocumentsApp/Anthrax/10312001/han51.asp
http://www.cdc.gov/mmwr/preview/mmwrhtml/mm5043a6.htm

### Is CDC telling all mail-handling operations to adopt these anthrax worker safety guidelines immediately?

Every facility is different and should be evaluated based on the recommendations in the guidelines, and the recommendations implemented should be selected on the basis of an initial evaluation of the work site. This evaluation should focus on determining which processes, operations, jobs, or tasks would be most likely to result in an exposure should a contaminated envelope or package enter the work site. Many of these measures (e.g., administrative controls, use of HEPA filter-equipped vacuums, wet-cleaning, use of protective gloves) can be implemented immediately; implementation of others will require additional time and efforts.

### What kinds of engineering controls should mail-handling/processing operations consider implementing for detecting anthrax spores?

*B. anthracis* spores can be aerosolized during the operation and maintenance of high-speed, mail-sorting machines, potentially exposing workers and possibly entering heating, ventilation, or air-conditioning (HVAC) systems. Engineering controls can provide the best means of preventing worker exposure to potential aerosolized particles, thereby reducing the risk for inhalational anthrax, the most severe form of the disease. In settings where such machinery is in use, the following engineering controls should be considered:

- An industrial vacuum cleaner equipped with a high-efficiency particulate air (HEPA) filter for cleaning high-speed, mail-sorting machinery.

- Local exhaust ventilation at pinch roller areas.

- HEPA-filtered exhaust hoods installed in areas where dust is generated (e.g., areas with high-speed, mail-sorting machinery).

- Air curtains (using laminar air flow) installed in areas where large amounts of mail are processed.

- HEPA filters installed in the building's HVAC systems (if feasible) to capture aerosolized spores. Note: Machinery should not be cleaned using compressed air (i.e., "blowdown/blowoff").

**What administrative controls should mail-handling/processing sites consider implementing to protect workers from exposure to *B. anthracis* spores?**
Strategies should be developed to limit the number of people working at or near sites where aerosolized particles may be generated, such as mail-sorting machinery and places where mailbags are unloaded or emptied. In addition, restrictions should be in place to limit the number of people including support staff and nonemployees entering areas where aerosolized particles may be generated. This recommendation applies to contractors, business visitors, and support staff.

**What housekeeping controls in mail-handling/processing sites are recommended to protect workers from exposure to *B. anthracis* spores?**
In the mail-handling work-site, dry sweeping and dusting should be avoided. Instead, the area should be wet-cleaned and vacuumed with HEPA-equipped vacuum cleaners.

### What personal protective equipment for workers in mail-handling/processing sites is recommended to protect workers from exposure to *B. anthracis* spores?

Personal protective equipment for workers in mail-handling/processing work sites must be selected on the basis of the potential for cutaneous or inhalational exposure to *B. anthracis* spores. Handling packages or envelopes may result in skin exposure. In addition, because certain machinery such as electronic mail sorters can generate aerosolized particles, people who operate, maintain, or work near such machinery may be exposed through inhalation. People who hand sort mail or work at other sites where airborne particles may be generated such as where mailbags are unloaded or emptied may also be exposed through inhalation.

### What are some examples of personal protective equipment and clothing that could be used to protect workers who handle mail from exposure to *B. anthracis* spores?

Protective, impermeable gloves should be worn by all workers who handle mail. In some cases, workers may need to wear cotton gloves under their protective gloves for comfort and to prevent dermatitis. Skin rashes and other dermatological conditions are a potential hazard of wearing gloves. Latex gloves should be avoided because of the risk of developing skin sensitivity or allergy.

- Gloves should be provided in a range of sizes to ensure proper fit.

- The choice of glove material such as nitrile or vinyl should be based on safety, fit, durability, and comfort. Sterile gloves such as surgical gloves are not necessary.

- Different gloves or layers of gloves may be needed depending on the task, the dexterity required, and the type of protection needed. Protective gloves can be worn under heavier gloves such as leather, heavy cotton for operations where gloves can easily be torn or if more protection against hand injury is needed.

- For workers involved in situations where a gloved hand presents a hazard such as those who work close to moving machine parts, the risk for potential injury resulting from glove use should be measured against the risk for potential exposure to *B. anthracis*.

- Workers should avoid touching their skin, eyes, or other mucous membranes since contaminated gloves may transfer *B. anthracis* spores to other body sites.

- Workers should consider wearing long-sleeved clothing and long pants to protect exposed skin.

- Gloves and other personal protective clothing and equipment can be discarded in regular trash once they are removed or if they are visibly torn, unless a suspicious piece of mail is recognized and handled. If a suspicious piece of mail is recognized and handled for anthrax, the worker's protective gear should be handled as potentially contaminated material (See "Guideline for Handwashing and Hospital Environmental Control," 1985, available at http://www.cdc.gov/ncidod/hip/guide/handwash.htm)

- Workers should wash their hands thoroughly with soap and water when gloves are removed, before eating, and when replacing torn or worn gloves. Soap and water will wash away most spores that may have contacted the skin; disinfectant solutions are not needed.

**Are there some areas in the postal setting that present a greater risk to some workers than others for anthrax exposure?**

- People working with or near machinery capable of generating aerosolized particles, such as electronic mail sorters, or at other work sites where such particles may be generated should be fitted with NIOSH-approved respirators that are at least as protective as an N95 respirator.

- People working in areas where oil mist from machinery is present should be fitted with respirators equipped with P-type filters.

- Because facial hair interferes with the fit of protective respirators, workers with facial hair like beards and or large moustaches may require alternative respirators such as powered air-purifying respirators [PAPRs] with loose-fitting hoods.

- Workers who cannot be fitted properly with a half-mask respirator based on a fit test may require the use of alternative respirators, such as full facepiece, negative-pressure respirators, PAPRs equipped with HEPA filters, or supplied-air respirators.

- If a worker is medically unable to wear a respirator, the employer should consider reassigning that worker to a job that does not require respiratory protection.

- In addition, the use of disposable aprons or goggles by persons working with or near machinery capable of generating aerosolized particles may provide an extra margin of protection.

### How can I recognize suspicious packages that have anthrax?

Only specially trained personnel can distinguish between a real bioterrorism attack and a false one. If you suspect that a package, letter, or anything else contains a harmful biological agent, call 911 to activate the local emergency response system; in communities without 911 systems, notify local law enforcement authorities. Guidance on identifying suspicious packages and letters and what to do until the authorities arrive are available on CDC's Web site at:
http://www.bt.cdc.gov/DocumentsApp/Anthrax/10312001/han50.asp

### What can the consumer buy to protect against "germ" or "chemical warfare" such as anthrax?

Currently, the CDC does not recommend consumers buy any particular product to protect against biological or chemical attacks.

### What should be done with clothing contaminated with anthrax? Is washing in a regular home washer and dryer ok? Does CDC recommend adding bleach to the wash?

Contact your state or local public health department for advice. Clothing can be decontaminated using soap and water, and 0.5% hypochlorite solution (one part household bleach to 9 parts water).

### Are other solutions used at hospitals for cleaning blood spills also effective against anthrax?

(Source: Interim Recommendation for Firefighters and other First Responders) The recommendation for decontaminating equipment is a 0.5% hypochlorite solution (1 part household bleach to ten parts water).
http://www.bt.cdc.gov/DocumentsApp/
Anthrax/Protective/10242001Protect.asp

## Sources

### How long do anthrax spores live?

Anthrax spores can survive for decades in soil.

**What is the importance of knowing the genetic information about anthrax?**
Genetic information about B. *anthracis*, particularly to determine genetic similarity among strains, is an important part of a disease investigation, but it is not immediately required for taking action to prevent or treat anthrax in those who may have been exposed to or infected by *B. anthracis*. Genetic information is often used to determine the similarity of strains if a common source is suspected.

**Does the similarity in strains from Florida, New York, and Washington, D.C., mean that they came from the same source or are these just the most common strains?**
The strains of anthrax identified in Florida, New York, and Washington, D.C., are similar and consistent with a naturally occurring strain that shows no evidence of genetic alteration or bioengineering. All are sensitive and susceptible to the antibiotics recommended by CDC for those who have been exposed to or infected with B. *anthracis*.

## 6.2 BIOLOGICAL AND CHEMICAL TERRORISM: STRATEGIC PLAN FOR PREPAREDNESS AND RESPONSE

The following CDC staff members prepared this report:

Ali S. Khan, M.D.
Alexandra M. Levitt, M.A., Ph.D.
*National Center for Infectious Diseases*

Michael J. Sage, M.P.H.
*National Center for Environment Health*

in collaboration with the CDC Strategic Planning Workgroup

Samuel L. Groseclose, D.V.M., M.P.H.
*Epidemiology Program Office*

Edwin Kent Gray
Elaine W. Gunter
Alison B. Johnson, M.P.A.
Anne L. Wilson, M.S.
*National Center for Environmental Health*

David A. Ashford, D.V.M., M.P.H., D.Sc.
Robert B. Craven, M.D.
Robert P. Gaynes, M.D.
Stephen A. Morse, Ph.D.
Clarence J. Peters, M.D.
Richard A. Spiegel, D.V.M., M.P.H.
David L. Swerdlow, M.D.
*National Center for Infectious Diseases*

Scott D. Deitchman, M.D., M.P.H.
*National Institute for Occupational Safety and Health*

Paul K. Halverson, Dr.P.H., M.H.S.A.
*Public Health Practice Program Office*

Joseph Hughart, M.P.H.
*Agency for Toxic Substances and Disease Registry*

Patricia Quinlisk, M.D.
*Iowa Department of Health*
*Des Moines, Iowa*

# RECOMMENDATIONS OF THE CDC
# STRATEGIC PLANNING WORKGROUP

*". . . and he that will not apply new remedies must expect new evils; for time is the greatest innovator. . . ."*

*-The Essays by Sir Francis Bacon, 1601*

### Summary

*The U.S. national civilian vulnerability to the deliberate use of biological and chemical agents has been highlighted by recognition of substantial biological weapons development programs and arsenals in foreign countries, attempts to acquire or possess biological agents by militants, and high-profile terrorist attacks. Evaluation of this vulnerability has focused on the role public health will have detecting and managing the probable covert biological terrorist incident with the realization that the U.S. local, state, and federal infrastructure is already strained as a result of other important public health problems. In partnership with representatives for local and state health departments, other federal agencies, and medical and public health professional associations, CDC has developed a strategic plan to address the deliberate dissemination of biological or chemical agents. The plan contains recommendations to reduce U.S. vulnerability to biological and chemical terrorism—preparedness planning, detection and surveillance, laboratory analysis, emergency response, and communication systems. Training and research are integral components for achieving these recommendations. Success of the plan hinges on strengthening the relationships between medical and public health professionals and on building new partnerships with emergency management, the military, and law enforcement professionals.*

## INTRODUCTION

An act of biological or chemical terrorism might range from dissemination of aerosolized anthrax spores to food product contamination, and predicting when and how such an attack might occur is not possible. However, the possibility of biological or chemical terrorism should not be ignored, especially in light of events during the past 10 years (e.g., the sarin gas attack in the Tokyo subway [1] and the discovery of military bioweapons programs in Iraq and the former Soviet Union [2]). Preparing the nation to address this threat is a formidable challenge, but the consequences of being unprepared could be devastating.

The public health infrastructure must be prepared to prevent illness and injury that would result from biological and chemical terrorism, especially a covert terrorist attack. As with emerging infectious diseases, early detection and control of biological or chemical attacks depends on a strong and flexible public health system at the local, state, and federal levels. In addition, primary healthcare providers throughout the United States must be vigilant because they will probably be the first to observe and report unusual illnesses or injuries.

This report is a summary of the recommendations made by CDC's Strategic Planning Workgroup in *Preparedness and Response to Biological and Chemical Terrorism: A Strategic Plan* (CDC, unpublished report, 2000), which outlines steps for strengthening public health and healthcare capacity to protect the United States against these dangers. This strategic plan marks the first time that CDC has joined with law enforcement, intelligence, and defense agencies in addition to traditional CDC partners to address a national security threat.

As a reflection of the need for broad-based public health involvement in terrorism preparedness and planning, staff from CDC's centers, institute, and offices participated in developing the strategic plan, including the

- National Center for Infectious Diseases,
- National Center for Environmental Health,
- Public Health Practice Program Office,
- Epidemiology Program Office,
- National Institute for Occupational Safety and Health,
- Office of Health and Safety,
- National Immunization Program, and
- National Center for Injury Prevention and Control.

The Agency for Toxic Substances and Disease Registry (ATSDR) is also participating with CDC in this effort and will provide expertise in the area of industrial chemical terrorism. In this report, the term *CDC* includes ATSDR when activities related to chemical terrorism are discussed. In addition, colleagues from local, state, and federal agencies; emergency medical services (EMS); professional societies; universities and medical centers; and private industry provided suggestions and constructive criticism.

Combating biological and chemical terrorism will require capitalizing on advances in technology, information systems, and medical sciences. Preparedness will also require a re-examination of core public health activities (e.g., disease surveillance) in light of these advances. Preparedness efforts by public health agencies and primary healthcare providers to detect and respond to biological and chemical terrorism will have the added benefit of strengthening the U.S. capacity for identifying and controlling injuries and emerging infectious diseases.

## U.S. VULNERABILITY TO
## BIOLOGICAL AND CHEMICAL TERRORISM

Terrorist incidents in the United States and elsewhere involving bacterial pathogens (3), nerve gas (1), and a lethal plant toxin (i.e., ricin) (4), have demonstrated that the United States is vulnerable to biological and chemical threats as well as explosives. Recipes for preparing "homemade" agents are readily available (5), and reports of arsenals of military bioweapons (2) raise the possibility that terrorists might have access to highly dangerous agents, which have been engineered for mass dissemination as small-particle aerosols. Such agents as the variola virus, the causative agent of smallpox, are highly contagious and often fatal. Responding to large-scale outbreaks caused by these agents will require the rapid mobilization of public health workers, emergency responders, and private healthcare providers. Large-scale outbreaks will also require rapid procurement and distribution of large quantities of drugs and vaccines, which must be available quickly.

## OVERT VERSUS COVERT TERRORIST ATTACKS

In the past, most planning for emergency response to terrorism has been concerned with overt attacks (e.g., bombings). Chemical terrorism acts are likely to be overt because the effects of chemical agents absorbed through inhalation or by absorption through the skin or mucous membranes are usually immediate and obvious. Such attacks elicit immediate response from police, fire, and EMS personnel.

In contrast, attacks with biological agents are more likely to be covert. They present different challenges and require an additional dimension of emergency planning that involves the public health infrastructure (Box 1). Covert dissemination of a biological agent in a public place will not have an immediate impact because of the delay between exposure and onset of illness (i.e., the incubation period). Consequently, the first casualties of a covert attack probably will be identified by physicians or other primary healthcare providers. For example, in the event of a covert release of the contagious variola virus, patients will appear in doctors' offices, clinics, and emergency rooms during the first or second week, complaining of fever, back pain, headache, nausea, and other symptoms of what initially might appear to be an ordinary viral infection. As the disease progresses, these persons will develop the papular rash characteristic of early-stage smallpox, a rash that physicians might not recognize immediately. By the time the rash becomes pustular and patients begin to die, the terrorists would be far away and the disease disseminated through the population by person-to-person contact. Only a short window of opportunity will exist between the time the first cases are identified and a second wave of the population becomes ill. During that brief period, public health officials will need to determine that an attack has occurred, identify the organism, and prevent more casualties through prevention strategies (e.g., mass vaccination or prophylactic treatment). As person-to-person contact continues, successive waves of transmission could carry infection to other worldwide localities. These issues might also be relevant for other person-to-person transmissible etiologic agents (e.g., plague or certain viral hemorrhagic fevers).

Certain chemical agents can also be delivered covertly through contaminated food or water. In 1999, the vulnerability of the food supply was illustrated in Belgium, when chickens were unintentionally exposed to dioxin-contaminated fat used to make animal feed (6). Because the contamination was not discovered for months, the dioxin, a cancer-causing chemical that does not cause immediate symptoms in humans, was probably present in chicken meat and eggs sold in Europe during early 1999. This incident underscores the need for prompt diagnoses of unusual or suspicious health problems in animals as well as humans, a lesson that was also demonstrated by the recent outbreak of mosquito-borne West Nile virus in birds and humans in New York City in 1999. The dioxin episode also demonstrates how a covert act of foodborne biological or chemical terrorism could affect commerce and human or animal health.

## FOCUSING PREPAREDNESS ACTIVITIES

Early detection of and response to biological or chemical terrorism are crucial. Without special preparation at the local and state levels, a large-scale attack with variola virus, aerosolized anthrax spores, a nerve gas, or a foodborne biological or chemical agent could overwhelm the local and perhaps national public health infrastructure. Large numbers of patients, including both infected persons and the "worried well," would seek medical attention, with a corresponding need for medical supplies, diagnostic tests, and hospital beds. Emergency responders, healthcare workers, and public health officials could be at special risk, and everyday life would be disrupted as a result of widespread fear of contagion.

Preparedness for terrorist-caused outbreaks and injuries is an essential component of the U.S. public health surveillance and response system, which is designed to protect the population against any unusual public health event (e.g., influenza pandemics, contaminated municipal water supplies, or intentional dissemination of *Yersinia pestis*, the causative agent of plague [7]). The epidemiologic skills, surveillance methods, diagnostic techniques, and physical resources required to detect and investigate unusual or unknown diseases, as well as syndromes or injuries caused by chemical accidents, are similar to those needed to identify and respond to an attack with a biological or chemical agent. However, public health agencies must prepare also for the special features a terrorist attack probably would have (e.g., mass casualties or the use of rare agents) (Boxes 2-5). Terrorists might use combinations of these agents, attack in more than one location simultaneously, use new agents, or use organisms that are not on the critical list (e.g., common, drug-resistant, or genetically engineered pathogens). Lists of critical biological and chemical agents will need to be modified as new information becomes available. In addition, each state and locality will need to adapt the lists to local conditions and preparedness needs by using the criteria provided in CDC's strategic plan.

Potential biological and chemical agents are numerous, and the public health infrastructure must be equipped to quickly resolve crises that would arise from a biological or chemical attack. However, to best protect the public, the preparedness efforts must be focused on agents that might have the greatest impact on U.S. health and security, especially agents that are highly contagious or that can be engineered for wide-spread dissemination via small-particle aerosols. Preparing the nation to address these dangers is a major challenge to U.S. public health systems and healthcare providers. Early detection requires increased biological and chemical terrorism awareness among front-line healthcare providers because they are in the best position to report suspicious illnesses and injuries. Also, early detection will require improved communication systems between those providers and public health officials. In addition, state and local healthcare agencies must have enhanced capacity to investigate unusual events and unexplained illnesses, and diagnostic laboratories must be equipped to identify biological and chemical agents that rarely are seen in the United States. Fundamental to these efforts is comprehensive, integrated training designed to ensure core competency in public health preparedness and the highest levels of scientific expertise among local, state, and federal partners.

## KEY FOCUS AREAS

CDC's strategic plan is based on the following five focus areas, with each area integrating training and research:

- preparedness and prevention;

- detection and surveillance;

- diagnosis and characterization of biological and chemical agents;

- response; and

- communication.

## Preparedness and Prevention

Detection, diagnosis, and mitigation of illness and injury caused by biological and chemical terrorism is a complex process that involves numerous partners and activities. Meeting this challenge will require special emergency preparedness in all cities and states. CDC will provide public health guidelines, support, and technical assistance to local and state public health agencies as they develop coordinated preparedness plans and response protocols. CDC also will provide self-assessment tools for terrorism preparedness, including performance standards, attack simulations, and other exercises. In addition, CDC will encourage and support applied research to develop innovative tools and strategies to prevent or mitigate illness and injury caused by biological and chemical terrorism.

## Detection and Surveillance

Early detection is essential for ensuring a prompt response to a biological or chemical attack, including the provision of prophylactic medicines, chemical antidotes, or vaccines. CDC will integrate surveillance for illness and injury resulting from biological and chemical terrorism into the U.S. disease surveillance systems, while developing new mechanisms for detecting, evaluating, and reporting suspicious events that might represent covert terrorist acts. As part of this effort, CDC and state and local health agencies will form partnerships with front-line medical personnel in hospital emergency departments, hospital care facilities, poison control centers, and other offices to enhance detection and reporting of unexplained injuries and illnesses as part of routine surveillance mechanisms for biological and chemical terrorism.

## Diagnosis and Characterization
## of Biological and Chemical Agents

CDC and its partners will create a multilevel laboratory response network for bioterrorism (LRNB). That network will link clinical labs to public health agencies in all states, districts, territories, and selected cities and counties and to state-of-the-art facilities that can analyze biological agents (<u>Figure 1</u>). As part of this effort, CDC will transfer diagnostic technology to state health laboratories and others who will perform initial testing. CDC will also create an in-house rapid-response and advanced technology (RRAT) laboratory. This laboratory will provide around-the-clock diagnostic confirmatory and reference support for terrorism response teams. This network will include the regional chemical laboratories for diagnosing human exposure to chemical agents and provide links with other departments (e.g., the U.S. Environmental Protection Agency, which is responsible for environmental sampling).

## Response

A comprehensive public health response to a biological or chemical terrorist event involves epidemiologic investigation, medical treatment and prophylaxis for affected persons, and the initiation of disease prevention or environmental decontamination measures. CDC will assist state and local health agencies in developing resources and expertise for investigating unusual events and unexplained illnesses. In the event of a confirmed terrorist attack, CDC will coordinate with other federal agencies in accord with Presidential Decision Directive (PDD) 39. PDD 39 designates the Federal Bureau of Investigation as the lead agency for the crisis plan and charges the Federal Emergency Management Agency with ensuring that the federal response management is adequate to respond to the consequences of terrorism (8). If requested by a state health agency, CDC will deploy response teams to investigate unexplained or suspicious illnesses or unusual etiologic agents and provide on-site consultation regarding medical management and disease control. To ensure the availability, procurement, and delivery of medical supplies, devices, and equipment that might be needed to respond to terrorist-caused illness or injury, CDC will maintain a national pharmaceutical stockpile.

## Communication Systems

U.S. preparedness to mitigate the public health consequences of biological and chemical terrorism depends on the coordinated activities of well-trained healthcare and public health personnel throughout the United States who have access to up-to-the-minute emergency information. Effective communication with the public through the news media will also be essential to limit terrorists' ability to induce public panic and disrupt daily life. During the next 5 years, CDC will work with state and local health agencies to develop a) a state-of-the-art communication system that will support disease surveillance; b) rapid notification and information exchange regarding disease outbreaks that are possibly related to bioterrorism; c) dissemination of diagnostic results and emergency health information; and d) coordination of emergency response activities. Through this network and similar mechanisms, CDC will provide terrorism-related training to epidemiologists and laboratorians, emergency responders, emergency department personnel and other front-line healthcare providers, and health and safety personnel.

## PARTNERSHIPS AND IMPLEMENTATION

Implementation of the objectives outlined in CDC's strategic plan will be coordinated through CDC's Bioterrorism Preparedness and Response Program. Program personnel are charged with a) helping build local and state preparedness, b) developing U.S. expertise regarding potential threat agents, and c) coordinating response activities during actual bioterrorist events. Program staff have established priorities for 2000-2002 regarding the focus areas (Box 6).

Implementation will require collaboration with state and local public health agencies, as well as with other persons and groups, including

- public health organizations,
- medical research centers,
- healthcare providers and their networks,
- professional societies,
- medical examiners,
- emergency response units and responder organizations,
- safety and medical equipment manufacturers,
- the U.S. Office of Emergency Preparedness and other Department of Health and Human Services agencies,
- other federal agencies, and
- international organizations.

## RECOMMENDATIONS

Implementing CDC's strategic preparedness and response plan by 2004 will ensure the following outcomes:

U.S. public health agencies and healthcare providers will be prepared to mitigate illness and injuries that result from acts of biological and chemical terrorism.

Public health surveillance for infectious diseases and injuries—including events that might indicate terrorist activity—will be timely and complete, and reporting of suspected terrorist events will be integrated with the evolving, comprehensive networks of the national public health surveillance system.

The national laboratory response network for bioterrorism will be extended to include facilities in all 50 states. The network will include CDC's environmental health laboratory for chemical terrorism and four regional facilities.

State and federal public health departments will be equipped with state-of-the-art tools for rapid epidemiological investigation and control of suspected or confirmed acts of biological or chemical terrorism, and a designated stock of terrorism-related medical supplies will be available through a national pharmaceutical stockpile.

A cadre of well-trained healthcare and public health workers will be available in every state. Their terrorism-related activities will be coordinated through a rapid and efficient communication system that links U.S. public health agencies and their partners.

## CONCLUSION

Recent threats and use of biological and chemical agents against civilians have exposed U.S. vulnerability and highlighted the need to enhance our capacity to detect and control terrorist acts. The U.S. must be protected from an extensive range of critical biological and chemical agents, including some that have been developed and stockpiled for military use. Even without threat of war, investment in national defense ensures preparedness and acts as a deterrent against hostile acts. Similarly, investment in the public health system provides the best civil defense against bioterrorism. Tools developed in response to terrorist threats serve a dual purpose. They help detect rare or unusual disease outbreaks and respond to health emergencies, including naturally occurring outbreaks or industrial injuries that might resemble terrorist events in their unpredictability and ability to cause mass casualties (e.g., a pandemic influenza outbreak or a large-scale chemical spill). Terrorism-preparedness activities described in CDC's plan, including the development of a public health communication infrastructure, a multilevel network of diagnostic laboratories, and an integrated disease surveillance system, will improve our ability to investigate rapidly and control public health threats that emerge in the twenty first century.

## References

1. Okumura T, Suzuki K, Fukuda A, et al. Tokyo subway sarin attack; disaster management, Part 1: community emergency response. Acad Emerg Med 1998;5:613-7.

2. Davis, CJ. Nuclear blindness: an overview of the biological weapons programs of the former Soviet Union and Iraq. Emerg Infect Dis 1999;5:509-12.

3. Török TJ, Tauxe RV, Wise RP, et al. Large community outbreak of Salmonellosis caused by intentional contamination of restaurant salad bars. JAMA 1997;278:389-95.

4. Tucker JB. Chemical/biological terrorism: coping with a new threat. Politics and the Life Sciences 1996;15:167-184.

5. Uncle Fester. Silent death. 2nd ed. Port Townsend, WA: Loompanics Unlimited, 1997.

6. Ashraf H. European dioxin-contaminated food crisis grows and grows [news]. Lancet 1999;353:2049.

7. Janofsky M. Looking for motives in plague case. New York Times. May 28, 1995:A18.

8. Federal Emergency Management Agency. Federal response plan. Washington, DC: Government Printing Office, 1999. Available at http://www.fema.gov/r-n-r/frp. Accessed February 3, 2000.

## Figure 1. Multilevel laboratory response network for bioterrorism that will link clinical labs to public health agencies

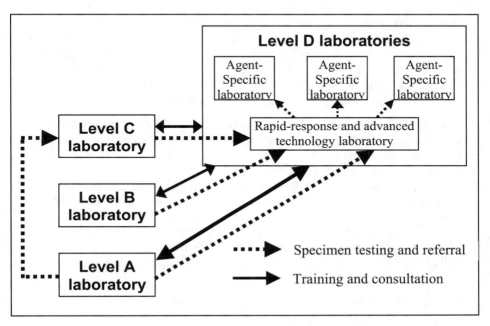

## Functional levels of the Laboratory Response Network for Bioterrorism

**Level A:** Early detection of intentional dissemination of biological agents—Level A laboratories will be public health and hospital laboratories with low-level biosafety facilities. Level A laboratories will use clinical data and standard microbiological tests to decide which specimens and isolates should be forwarded to higher level biocontainment laboratories. Level A laboratory staff will be trained in the safe collection, packaging, labeling, and shipping of samples that might contain dangerous pathogens.

**Level B:** Core capacity for agent isolation and presumptive-level testing of suspect specimens—Level B laboratories will be state and local public health agency laboratories that can test for specific agents and forward organisms or specimens to higher level biocontainment laboratories. Level B laboratories will minimize false positives and protect Level C laboratories from overload. Ultimately, Level B laboratories will maintain capacity to perform confirmatory testing and characterize drug susceptibility.

**Level C:** Advanced capacity for rapid identification—Level C laboratories, which could be located at state health agencies, academic research centers, or federal facilities, will perform advanced and specialized testing. Ultimately, Level C laboratories will have the capacity to perform toxicity testing and employ advanced diagnostic technologies (e.g., nucleic acid amplification and molecular fingerprinting). Level C laboratories will participate in the evaluation of new tests and reagents and determine which assays could be transferred to Level B laboratories.

**Level D:** Highest level containment and expertise in the diagnosis of rare and dangerous biological agents—Level D laboratories will be specialized federal laboratories with unique experience in diagnosis of rare diseases (e.g., smallpox and Ebola). Level D laboratories also will develop or evaluate new tests and methods and have the resources to maintain a strain bank of biological agents. Level D laboratories will maintain the highest biocontainment facilities and will be able to conduct all tests performed in Level A, B, and C laboratories, as well as additional confirmatory testing and characterization, as needed. They will also have the capacity to detect genetically engineered agents.

**BOX 1.** Local public health agency preparedness

> - Because the initial detection of a covert biological or chemical attack will probably occur at the local level, disease surveillance systems at state and local health agencies must be capable of detecting unusual patterns of disease or injury, including those caused by unusual or unknown threat agents.
>
> - Because the initial response to a covert biological or chemical attack will probably be made at the local level, epidemiologists at state and local health agencies must have expertise and resources for responding to reports of clusters of rare, unusual, or unexplained illnesses.

**BOX 2.** Preparing public health agencies for biological attacks

**Steps in Preparing for Biological Attacks**

- Enhance epidemiologic capacity to detect and respond to biological attacks.
- Supply diagnostic reagents to state and local public health agencies.
- Establish communication programs to ensure delivery of accurate information.
- Enhance bioterrorism-related education and training for healthcare professionals.
- Prepare educational materials that will inform and reassure the public during and after a biological attack.
- Stockpile appropriate vaccines and drugs.
- Establish molecular surveillance for microbial strains, including unusual or drug-resistant strains.
- Support the development of diagnostic tests.
- Encourage research on antiviral drugs and vaccines.

**BOX 3.** Critical biological agents

**Category A**

The U.S. public health system and primary healthcare providers must be prepared to address varied biological agents, including pathogens that are rarely seen in the United States. High-priority agents include organisms that pose a risk to national security because they

- can be easily disseminated or transmitted person-to-person;
- cause high mortality, with potential for major public health impact;
- might cause public panic and social disruption; and
- require special action for public health preparedness (Box 2).

Category A agents include

- variola major (smallpox);
- *Bacillus anthracis* (anthrax);

- *Yersinia pestis* (plague);
- *Clostridium botulinum* toxin (botulism);
- *Francisella tularensis* (tularaemia);
- filoviruses,
  - o Ebola hemorrhagic fever,
  - o Marburg hemorrhagic fever; and
- arenaviruses,
  - o Lassa (Lassa fever),
  - o Junin (Argentine hemorrhagic fever) and related viruses.

## Category B

Second highest priority agents include those that

- are moderately easy to disseminate;
- cause moderate morbidity and low mortality; and
- require specific enhancements of CDC's diagnostic capacity and enhanced disease surveillance.

Category B agents include

- *Coxiella burnetti* (Q fever);
- *Brucella* species (brucellosis);
- *Burkholderia mallei* (glanders);
- alphaviruses,
  - o Venezuelan encephalomyelitis,
  - o eastern and western equine encephalomyelitis;
- ricin toxin from *Ricinus communis* (castor beans);
- epsilon toxin of *Clostridium perfringens*; and
- *Staphylococcus* enterotoxin B.

A subset of List B agents includes pathogens that are food- or waterborne.
These pathogens include but are not limited to

- *Salmonella* species,
- *Shigella dysenteriae*,
- *Escherichia coli* O157:H7,
- *Vibrio cholerae*, and
- *Cryptosporidium parvum*.

## Category C

Third highest priority agents include emerging pathogens that could be engineered for mass dissemination in the future

because of
- availability;
- ease of production and dissemination; and
- potential for high morbidity and mortality and major health impact.

Category C agents include
- Nipah virus,
- hantaviruses,
- tickborne hemorrhagic fever viruses,
- tickborne encephalitis viruses,
- yellow fever, and
- multidrug-resistant tuberculosis.

Preparedness for List C agents requires ongoing research to improve disease detection, diagnosis, treatment, and prevention. Knowing in advance which newly emergent pathogens might be employed by terrorists is not possible; therefore, linking bioterrorism preparedness efforts with ongoing disease surveillance and outbreak response activities as defined in CDC's emerging infectious disease strategy is imperative.*

* CDC. Preventing emerging infectious diseases: a strategy for the 21st century. Atlanta, Georgia: U.S. Department of Health and Human Services, 1998.

**BOX 4.** Preparing public health agencies for chemical attacks

**Steps in Preparing for Chemical Attacks**
- Enhance epidemiologic capacity for detecting and responding to chemical attacks.
- Enhance awareness of chemical terrorism among emergency medical service personnel, police officers, firefighters, physicians, and nurses.
- Stockpile chemical antidotes.
- Develop and provide bioassays for detection and diagnosis of chemical injuries.
- Prepare educational materials to inform the public during and after a chemical attack

**BOX 5.** Chemical agents

Chemical agents that might be used by terrorists range from warfare agents to toxic chemicals commonly used in industry. Criteria for determining priority chemical agents include

- chemical agents already known to be used as weaponry;

- availability of chemical agents to potential terrorists;

- chemical agents likely to cause major morbidity or mortality;

- potential of agents for causing public panic and social disruption; and

- agents that require special action for public health preparedness (Box 4).

Categories of chemical agents include

- nerve agents,

  o tabun (ethyl N,N-dimethylphosphoramidocyanidate),

  o sarin (isopropyl methylphosphanofluoridate),

  o soman (pinacolyl methyl phosphonofluoridate),

  o GF (cyclohexylmethylphosphonofluoridate),

  o VX (o-ethyl-[S]-[2-diisopropylaminoethyl]-methylphosphonothiolate);

- blood agents,

  o hydrogen cyanide,

  o cyanogen chloride;

- blister agents,

  o lewisite (an aliphatic arsenic compound, 2-chlorovinyldichloroarsine),

- o   nitrogen and sulfur mustards,
- o   phosgene oxime;
- heavy metals,
  - o   arsenic,
  - o   lead,
  - o   mercury;
- volatile toxins,
  - o   benzene,
  - o   chloroform,
  - o   trihalomethanes;
- pulmonary agents,
  - o   phosgene,
  - o   chlorine,
  - o   vinyl chloride;
- incapacitating agents,
  - o   BZ (3-quinuclidinyl benzilate);
- pesticides, persistent and nonpersistent;
- dioxins, furans, and polychlorinated biphenyls (PCBs);
- explosive nitro compounds and oxidizers,
  - o   ammonium nitrate combined with fuel oil;
- flammable industrial gases and liquids,
  - o   gasoline,
  - o   propane;
- poison industrial gases, liquids, and solids,
  - o   cyanides,
  - o   nitriles; and
- corrosive industrial acids and bases,
  - o   nitric acid,
  - o   sulfuric acid.

Because of the hundreds of new chemicals introduced internationally each month, treating exposed persons by clinical syndrome rather than by specific agent is more useful for public health planning and emergency medical response purposes. Public health agencies and first responders might render the most aggressive, timely, and clinically relevant treatment possible by using treatment modalities based on syndromic categories (e.g., burns and trauma, cardiorespiratory failure, neurologic damage, and shock). These activities must be linked with authorities responsible for environmental sampling and decontamination.

**BOX 6.** Implementation Priorities Regarding Focus Areas for 2000-2002

**Preparedness and Prevention**

- Maintain a public health preparedness and response cooperative agreement that provides support to state health agencies who are working with local agencies in developing coordinated bioterrorism plans and protocols.

- Establish a national public health distance-learning system that provides biological and chemical terrorism preparedness training to healthcare workers and to state and local public health workers.

- Disseminate public health guidelines and performance standards on biological and chemical terrorism preparedness planning for use by state and local health agencies.

**Detection and Surveillance**

- Strengthen state and local surveillance systems for illness and injury resulting from pathogens and chemical substances that are on CDC's critical agents list.

- Develop new algorithms and statistical methods for searching medical databases on a real-time basis for evidence of suspicious events.

- Establish criteria for investigating and evaluating suspicious clusters of human or animal disease or injury and triggers for notifying law enforcement of suspected acts of biological or chemical terrorism.

**Diagnosis and Characterization of Biological and Chemical Agents**

- Establish a multilevel laboratory response network for bioterrorism that links public health agencies to advanced capacity facilities for the identification and reporting of critical biological agents.

- Establish regional chemical terrorism laboratories that will provide diagnostic capacity during terrorist attacks involving chemical agents.

- Establish a rapid-response and advanced technology laboratory within CDC to provide around-the-clock diagnostic support to bioterrorism response teams and expedite molecular characterization of critical biological agents.

**Response**

- Assist state and local health agencies in organizing response capacities to rapidly deploy in the event of an overt attack or a suspicious outbreak that might be the result of a covert attack.

- Ensure that procedures are in place for rapid mobilization of CDC terrorism response teams that will provide on-site assistance to local health workers, security agents, and law enforcement officers.

- Establish a national pharmaceutical stockpile to provide medical supplies in the event of a terrorist attack that involves biological or chemical agents.

- Establish a national electronic infrastructure to improve exchange of emergency health information among local, state, and federal health agencies.

- Implement an emergency communication plan that ensures rapid dissemination of health information to the public during actual, threatened, or suspected acts of biological or chemical terrorism.

- Create a Web site that disseminates bioterrorism preparedness and training information, as well as other bioterrorism-related emergency information, to public health and healthcare workers and the public.

## 6.3  CHILDREN AND ANTHRAX:
## A FACT SHEET FOR CLINICIANS

Anthrax is an acute infectious disease caused by the bacterium *Bacillus anthracis*. Children, like adults, may be affected by three clinical forms: cutaneous, inhalational, or gastrointestinal.

The symptoms and signs of anthrax infection in children older than 2 months of age are similar to those in adults. The clinical presentation of anthrax in young infants is not well defined.  When children become ill and present for treatment, making a diagnosis may be more difficult than in adults because young children have difficulty reporting what has happened to them or telling a doctor exactly how they feel.  Because respiratory illnesses are much more common in children than adults, the examining clinician should have an understanding of disease manifestations in children.

The following are clinical descriptions (based on experience with adults) of the three forms of anthrax (MMWR 2001; 50(41):889-893).

### INHALATIONAL
Inhalational anthrax begins with a brief prodrome resembling an influenza-like viral respiratory illness followed by development of dyspnea, systemic symptoms, and shock, with radiographic evidence of mediastinal widening and pleural effusion. Inhalational anthrax is the most lethal form of anthrax. The incubation period of inhalational anthrax among humans typically ranges from 1 to 7 days but may be up to 60 days. Host factors, dose of exposure, and chemoprophylaxis may affect the duration of the incubation period. Patients frequently develop meningitis. Case-fatality estimates for inhalational anthrax are extremely high; the risk for death is high even if patients are provided with supportive care, including appropriate antimicrobial treatment.

### CUTANEOUS
Cutaneous anthrax is characterized by a skin lesion evolving from a papule, through a vesicular stage, to a depressed black eschar. The incubation period ranges from 1 to 12 days. The lesion is usually painless, but patients also may have fever, malaise, headache, and regional lymphadenopathy. The case fatality rate for cutaneous anthrax is 20% without, and <1% with, antimicrobial treatment.

## GASTROINTESTINAL

Gastrointestinal anthrax is characterized by severe abdominal pain followed by fever and signs of septicemia. This form of anthrax usually results from eating raw or undercooked meat containing B. *anthracis,* and the incubation period is usually 1 to 7 days. An oropharyngeal and an abdominal form of the disease have been described. Involvement of the pharynx is usually characterized by lesions at the base of the tongue, dysphagia, fever, and regional lymphadenopathy. Lower bowel inflammation typically causes nausea, loss of appetite, and fever followed by abdominal pain, hematemesis, and bloody diarrhea. The case-fatality rate is estimated to be between 25% and 60%. The effect of early antibiotic treatment on the case-fatality rate has not been established.

Neither CDC nor the American Academy of Pediatrics (AAP) recommend dispensing antibiotics for parents to have on hand in case of a possible exposure to *Bacillus anthracis.* CDC and its partner organizations will dispense antibiotics through the National Pharmaceutical Stockpile (NPS) program if exposure occurs. The NPS was designed to ensure the availability of lifesaving pharmaceuticals; antimicrobials; chemical interventions; and medical, surgical, and patient-support supplies, as well as equipment for prompt delivery to disaster sites. Disasters include a possible biological or chemical terrorist event anywhere in the United States. For more detailed information about the NPS, see CDC's Web site at http://www.bt.cdc.gov.

## VACCINATION

At this time, anthrax vaccine is not recommended for people younger than 18 years of age. Military personnel and civilians at high risk for repeated exposure (e.g., laboratory workers handling powders containing *Bacillus anthracis*) may benefit from the vaccine.

## PROPHYLAXIS

Post-exposure prophylaxis is indicated to prevent inhalational anthrax after a confirmed or suspected aerosol exposure to *Bacillus anthracis.* Consultation with public health authorities is strongly encouraged to identify people who should receive prophylaxis. When no information is available about the antimicrobial susceptibility of the implicated strain of *Bacillus anthracis*, CDC recommends initial therapy with either ciprofloxacin or doxycycline for children, as follows:

**Ciprofloxacin:**

- 10–15 mg/kg/dose po Q12 hours (not to exceed 1 gram per day) for 60 days.

**Doxycycline:**

- ✓ 8 years or older and weighing more than 45 kg: 100 mg po BID for 60 days.

- ✓ 8 years or older and weighing 45 kg or less: 2.2 mg/kg/dose po BID for 60 days.

- ✓ 8 years or younger: 2.2 mg/kg/dose po BID for 60 days

Reference: CDC. Update: Investigation of anthrax associated with intentional exposure and interim public health guidelines, October, 2001. MMWR 2001; 50 (41):889-893.

The National Pharmaceutical Stockpile (NSP) contains oral and liquid types of both drugs for use by children who are too small to tolerate pills. Both tetracyclines and fluoroquinolones can cause adverse health effects in children. These risks must be weighed carefully against the risk of developing a life-threatening disease due to *Bacillus anthracis*. As soon as the penicillin susceptibility of the organism has been confirmed, prophylactic therapy for children should be changed to oral amoxicillin 80 mg/kg of body mass per day divided every 8 hours (not to exceed 500 mg three times daily). The NSP also includes amoxicillin suspension for children. *Bacillus anthracis* is not susceptible to cephalosporins or to trimethoprim/sulfamethoxazole, and these agents should not be used for prophylaxis.

## DRUG RECOMMENDATIONS

## FOR PEDIATRIC ANTHRAX CASES

Some antibiotics and other treatments that have proven effective against anthrax in adults have not been studied as extensively in children. Therefore, CDC provides the following recommendations for treating anthrax in children:

**For inhalational anthrax:**

| Initial Therapy (intravenous) | Duration |
|---|---|
| Ciprofloxacin* 10–15 mg/kg/dose every 12 hours<br><br>OR<br><br>Doxycycline: ¶<br><br>> 8 years and > 45 kg: 100 mg every 12 hours<br><br>> 8 years and 45 kg or less: 2.2 mg/kg/dose every 12 hours<br><br>8 years or younger: 2.2 mg/kg/dose every 12 hours<br><br>AND<br><br>One or two additional antimicrobials§ | IV treatment initially. Switch to oral antimicrobial therapy when clinically appropriate:<br><br>Ciprofloxacin 10–15 mg/kg/dose po every 12 hours<br><br>OR<br><br>Doxycycline: ¶<br><br>> 8 years and > 45 kg: 100 mg po BID<br><br>> 8 years and 45 kg or less: 2.2 mg/kg/dose po BID<br><br>8 years or younger: 2.2 mg/kg/dose po BID<br><br>Continue for 60 days (IV and po combined) |

Antimicrobial therapy should be continued for 60 days because of the potential persistence of spores after an aerosol exposure. Initial therapy may be altered on the basis of the clinical course of the patient; one or two antimicrobial agents (e.g., ciprofloxacin or doxycycline) may be adequate as the patient improves.

*If intravenous ciprofloxacin is not available, oral ciprofloxacin may be acceptable because it is rapidly and well absorbed from the gastrointestinal tract with no substantial loss by first-pass metabolism. Maximum serum concentrations are attained 1 to 2 hours after oral dosing but may not be achieved if vomiting or ileus is present. In children, ciprofloxacin dosage should not exceed 1 g/day.

¶ The AAP recommends treatment of young children with tetracyclines for serious infections (e.g., Rocky Mountain spotted fever). If meningitis is suspected, doxycycline may be less optimal because of poor central nervous system penetration.

§ Other agents with *in vitro* activity include rifampin, vancomycin, penicillin, ampicillin, chloramphenicol, imipenem, clindamycin, and clarithromycin. Because of concerns of constitutive and inducible beta-lactamases in *Bacillus anthracis* isolates involved in the current bioterrorist attack, penicillin and ampicillin should not be used alone. Consultation with an infectious disease specialist is advised.

**For cutaneous anthrax:**

| Initial Therapy (oral) | Duration |
|---|---|
| Ciprofloxacin: 10–15 mg/kg/dose every 12 hours (not to exceed 1 g/day) | 60 days |
| **OR** | |
| Doxycycline: <br><br> ➤   8 years and > 45 kg: 100 mg every 12 hours <br><br> ➤   8 years and 45 kg or less: 2.2 mg/kg/dose every 12 hours <br><br> ➤   8 years or younger: 2.2 mg/kg/dose every 12 hours | 60 days |

Cutaneous anthrax with signs of systemic involvement, extensive edema, or lesions on the head or neck requires intravenous therapy, and a multidrug approach is recommended. Ciprofloxacin or doxycycline should be considered first-line therapy. Amoxicillin 80 mg/kg/day divided every 8 hours is an option for completion of therapy after clinical improvement, if the organism is susceptible.

Previous guidelines have suggested treating cutaneous anthrax for 7 to 10 days, but 60 days is recommended in the setting of this attack, given the likelihood of exposure to aerosolized *Bacillus anthracis*.

**For gastrointestinal and oropharyngeal anthrax**, use regimens recommended for inhalational anthrax.

Children are more likely than adults to suffer side effects from some antibiotics used to prevent or treat the disease. If a child does develop side effects, testing should be done to determine whether the bacteria to which the child was exposed are susceptible to other drugs with fewer side effects, such as amoxicillin.

**For additional information**

The American Academy of Pediatrics offers more extensive information about children and anthrax at its Web site, http://www.aap.org/advocacy/releases/smlpoxanthrax.htm. For information related to preparedness and bioterrorism, see CDC's Web site at http://www.bt.cdc.gov.

*Sources:* MMWR 50(41); October 19, 2001; MMWR 50(42); October 26, 2001; American Academy of Pediatrics fact sheet at: http://www.aap.org/advocacy/releases/smlpoxanthrax.htm.

## 6.4 Considerations for Distinguishing Influenza-Like Illness from Inhalational Anthrax

CDC has issued guidelines on the evaluation of persons with a history of exposure to *Bacillus anthracis* spores or who have an occupational or environmental risk for anthrax exposure (1). This notice describes the clinical evaluation of persons who are not known to be at increased risk for anthrax but who have symptoms of influenza-like illness (ILI). Clinicians evaluating persons with ILI should consider a combination of epidemiologic, clinical, and, if indicated, laboratory and radiographic test results to evaluate the likelihood that inhalational anthrax is the basis for ILI symptoms.

ILI is a nonspecific respiratory illness characterized by fever, fatigue, cough, and other symptoms. The majority of ILI cases are not caused by influenza but by other viruses (e.g., rhinoviruses and respiratory syncytial virus [RSV]), adenoviruses, and parainfluenza viruses). Less common causes of ILI include bacteria such as *Legionella* spp., *Chlamydia pneumoniae*, *Mycoplasma pneumoniae*, and *Streptococcus pneumoniae*. Influenza, RSV, and certain bacterial infections are particularly important causes of ILI because these infections can lead to serious complications requiring hospitalization (2-4). Yearly, adults and children can average one to three and three to six ILI, respectively (5).

### Epidemiologic Considerations

To date, 10 confirmed cases of inhalational anthrax have been identified (1). The epidemiologic profile of these 10 cases caused by bioterrorism can guide the assessment of persons with ILI. All but one case have occurred among postal workers, persons exposed to letters or areas known to be contaminated by anthrax spores, and media employees. The 10 confirmed cases have been identified in a limited number of communities. Inhalational anthrax is not spread from person to person. In comparison, millions of ILI cases associated with other respiratory pathogens occur each year and in all communities. Respiratory infections associated with bacteria can occur throughout the year; pneumococcal disease peaks during the winter, and mycoplasma and legionellosis are more common during the summer and fall (4). Cases of ILI resulting from influenza and RSV infection generally peak during the winter; rhinoviruses and parainfluenza virus infections usually peak during the fall and spring; and adenoviruses circulate throughout the year. All of these viruses are highly communicable and spread easily from person to viruses are highly communicable and spread easily from person to person.

## Clinical Considerations

Although many different illnesses might present with ILI symptoms, the presence of certain signs and symptoms might help to distinguish other causes of ILI from inhalational anthrax. Nasal congestion and rhinorrhea are features of most ILI cases not associated with anthrax (Table 1) (6, 7). In comparison, rhinorrhea was reported in one of the 10 persons who had inhalational anthrax diagnosed since September, 2001. All 10 persons with inhalational anthrax had abnormal chest radiographs on initial presentation; seven had mediastinal widening, seven had infiltrates, and eight had pleural effusion. Findings might be more readily discernable on posteroanterior with lateral views, compared with anteroposterior views (i.e., portable radiograph alone) (1). Most cases of ILI are not associated with radiographic findings of pneumonia, which occurs most often among the very young, elderly, or those with chronic lung disease (2, 3). Influenza associated pneumonia occurs in approximately 1%-5% of community-dwelling adults with influenza and can occur in >20% of influenza-infected elderly (2). Influenza-associated pneumonia might be caused by the primary virus infection or, more commonly, by bacterial infection occurring coincident with or following influenza illness (2).

## Testing

No rapid screening test is available to diagnose inhalational anthrax in the early stages. Blood cultures grew *B. anthracis* in all seven patients with inhalational anthrax who had not received previous antimicrobial therapy. However, blood cultures should not be obtained routinely on all patients with ILI symptoms who have no probable exposure to anthrax but should be obtained for persons in situations in which bacteremia is suspected.

Rapid tests for influenza and RSV are available, and, if used, should be conducted within the first 3-4 days of a person's illness when viral shedding is most likely. RSV antigen detection tests have a peak sensitivity of 75%-95% in infants but do not have enough sensitivity to warrant their routine use among adults (8).

Among the influenza tests available for point-of-care testing, the reported sensitivities and specificities range from 45%-90% and 60%-95%, respectively (9). Two tests (Quidel Quickvue Influenza test and ZymeTx Zstatflu test®) can be performed in any physician's office, and three are classified as moderately complex tests (Biostar FLU OIA; Becton-Dickinson Directigen Flu A+B; and Becton-Dickinson Directigen Flu A™).

The clinical usefulness of rapid influenza tests for the diagnosis of influenza in individual patients is limited because the sensitivity of the influenza rapid tests is relatively low (45%-90%), and a large proportion of persons with influenza might be missed with these tests. Therefore, the rapid influenza tests should not be done on every person presenting with ILI. However, rapid influenza testing used with viral culture can help indicate whether influenza viruses are circulating among specific populations, (e.g., nursing home residents or patients attending a clinic). This type of epidemiologic information on specific populations can aid in diagnosing ILI.

Vaccination against influenza is the best means to prevent influenza and its severe complications. The influenza vaccine is targeted towards persons aged >65 years and to persons aged 6 months to 64 years who have a high-risk medical condition because these groups are at increased risk for influenza-related complications. The vaccine also is targeted towards healthcare workers to prevent transmission of influenza to high-risk persons. In addition, vaccination is recommended for household members of high-risk persons and for healthy persons aged 50-64 years. The vaccine can prevent 70%-90% of influenza infections in healthy adults. However, the vaccine does not prevent ILI caused by infectious agents other than influenza, and many persons vaccinated against influenza will still get ILI. Therefore, receipt of vaccine will not definitely exclude influenza from the differential diagnosis of ILI or increase the probability of inhalational anthrax as a cause, especially among persons who have no probable exposure to anthrax. Frequent handwashing can reduce the number of respiratory illnesses (10) and pneumococcal polysaccharide vaccine can reduce the risk for serious pneumococcal disease.

Additional information about anthrax is available at http://www.hhs.gov/hottopics/healing/biological.html and http://www.bt.cdc.gov/DocumentsApp/FactsAbout/FactsAbout.asp. Additional information about influenza, RSV and other viral respiratory infections, and pneumococcal disease is available at http://www.cdc.gov/ncidod/diseases/flu/fluvirus.htm, http://www.cdc.gov/nip/flu/default.htm, http://www.cdc.gov/ncidod/dvrd/revb/index.htm, http://www.cdc.gov/ncidod/dbmd/diseaseinfo/streppneum_t.htm, and http://www.cdc.gov/nip/diseases/Pneumo/vac-chart.htm.

# References

1. CDC. Update: investigation of bioterrorism-related anthrax and interim guidelines for clinical evaluation of persons with possible anthrax. MMWR 2001; 50: 941-8.

2. Nicholson KG. Human influenza. In: Nicholson KG, Webster RG, Hay AJ, eds. Textbook of influenza. Malden, Massachusetts: Blackwell Science 1998: 219-64.

3. Hall CB. Medical progress: respiratory syncytial virus and parainfluenza virus. N Engl J Med 2001; 344: 1917-28.

4. Bartlett JG, Dowell SF, Mandell LA, File TM Jr, Musher DM, Fine MJ. Practice guidelines for the management of community-acquired pneumonia in adults. Clin Infect Dis 2000; 31: 347-82.

5. Monto AS. Viral respiratory infections in the community: epidemiology, agents, and interventions. Am J Med 1995; 99: 6B24S-6B27S.

6. Carrat F, Tachet A, Rouzioux C, Housset B, Valleron A-J. Evaluation of clinical case definitions of influenza: detailed investigation of patients during the 1995-1996 epidemic in France. Clin Infect Dis 1999; 28: 283-90.

7. Monto AS, Gravenstein S, Elliott M, Colopy M, Schweinle J. Clinical signs and symptoms predicting influenza infection. Arch Intern Med 2000; 160: 3243-7.

8. Kellogg JA. Culture vs. direct antigen assays for detection of microbial pathogens from lower respiratory tract specimens suspected of containing the respiratory syncytial virus. Arch Pathol Lab Med 1991; 115: 451-8.

9. Munoz FM, Galasso GJ, Gwaltney JM, et al. Current research on influenza and other respiratory viruses: II International Symposium. Antiviral Res 2000; 46: 91-124.

10. Ryan MAK, Christian RS, Wohlrabe J. Handwashing and respiratory illness among young adults in military training. Am J Prevent Med 2001; 21: 79-83.

## Table 1

| Symptom/Sign | Inhalational Anthrax (n=10) | Lab-confirmed Influenza | ILI from other causes |
|---|---|---|---|
| Elevated temperature | 70% | 68%-77% | 40%-73% |
| Fever or chills | 100% | 83%-90% | 75%-89% |
| Fatigue/malaise | 100% | 75%-94% | 62%-94% |
| Cough (minimal or nonproductive) | 90% | 84%-93% | 72%-80% |
| Shortness of breath | 80% | 6% | 6% |
| Chest discomfort or pleuritic chest pain | 60% | 35% | 23% |
| Headache | 50% | 84%-91% | 74%-89% |
| Myalgias | 50% | 67%-94% | 73%-94% |
| Sore throat | 20% | 64%-84% | 64%-84% |
| Rhinorrhea | 10% | 79% | 68% |
| Nausea or vomiting | 80% | 12% | 12% |
| Abdominal pain | 30% | 22% | 22% |

## 6.5    EPIDEMIOLOGY OF BIOTERRORISM

**Julie A. Pavlin**
**Walter Reed Army Institute of Research,**
**Washington, D.C., USA**

Since the discovery of Iraq's biological weapons program, concern regarding the threat of biological warfare has increased (1). Anthrax immunizations; increased nuclear, biological, and chemical defense training; improved detection systems and protective gear; and increased vigilance have been instituted to protect the military.

However, the military is not the only population at risk for biological attack. To effectively counter the potentially devastating effects of an attack, we need to understand the basic epidemiologic principles of biological agents used as weapons.

A biological agent is commonly portrayed as a genetically engineered organism resistant to all known vaccines and drugs, highly contagious, and able to harm thousands of people. However, alleged attacks by the Aum Shinrikyo did not result in a single illness from a biological agent (2), and the successful 1984 contamination of salad bars in The Dalles, Oregon, by a religious cult involved a common salmonella strain that was not lethal or contagious and was susceptible to antibiotics (3).

Therefore, our level of suspicion and diligence in identifying and reacting to a biological attack must remain high, since the attack may not follow an expected pattern. Furthermore, a small outbreak of illness could be an early warning of a more serious attack, and recognition and prompt institution of preventive measures (such as effective vaccines and antibiotics) could save thousands of lives.

To facilitate the rapid identification of a bioterrorist attack, all healthcare providers and public health personnel should have basic epidemiologic skills and knowledge of what to expect in such a setting.

### DIFFERENTIAL DIAGNOSIS

Any small or large outbreak of disease should be evaluated as a potential bioterrorist attack. This initial investigation does not have to be time consuming or involve law enforcement. A look at the facts surrounding the outbreak to determine if anything seems unusual or indicative of bioterrorism should suffice. Since a disease outbreak can be the result of intentional contamination, the differential diagnosis of an outbreak should first be considered. The possibilities include a spontaneous outbreak of a known endemic disease, a spontaneous outbreak of a new or reemerging disease, a laboratory accident, or an intentional attack with a biological agent. Epidemiologic tools can assist in differentiating between these possibilities.

The cause of a disease or even the occurrence of something unusual may be very difficult to determine, especially if the initial cases are few. Surveillance needs to be more than routine. Not only unusually high rates of illness but also unusual diseases should signal a warning. For example, even one case of inhalation anthrax should cause immediate concern and action.

Unlike chemical terrorism, biological terrorism is not immediately obvious but may appear insidiously, with primary-care providers witnessing the first cases. However, it may not even be emergency room personnel who first detect a problem. The first to notice could be a hospital laboratory seeing unusual strains of organisms, or the county epidemiologist keeping track of hospital admissions, or even pharmacists distributing more antibiotics than usual, 911 operators noticing an increase in respiratory distress calls, or funeral directors with increased business. All epidemiologic data should be tracked and aggressively followed to ensure the most rapid recognition and response.

## EPIDEMIOLOGIC APPROACH

The basic epidemiologic approach in the evaluation of a potential bioterrorist or biowarfare attack is not different from any standard epidemiologic investigation. The first step is to use laboratory and clinical findings to confirm that a disease outbreak has occurred. A case definition should be constructed to determine the number of cases and the attack rate. The use of objective criteria in the development of a case definition is very important in determining an accurate case number, as both additional cases may be found and some may be excluded, especially as the potential exists for hysteria to be confused with actual disease. The estimated rate of illness should be compared with rates during previous years to determine if the rate constitutes a deviation from the norm.

Once the case definition and attack rate have been determined, the outbreak can be characterized in the conventional context of time, place, and person. These data will provide crucial information in determining the potential source of the outbreak.

## EPIDEMIC CURVE

Using data gathered on cases over time, an epidemic curve can be calculated. The disease pattern is an important factor in differentiating between a natural outbreak and an intentional attack. In most naturally occurring outbreaks, numbers of cases gradually increase as a progressively larger number of people come in contact with other patients, fomites, and vectors that can spread disease. Eventually, most of the population has been exposed and is immune to further disease, and the number of cases, or epidemic curve, gradually decreases. Conversely, a bioterrorism attack is most likely to be caused by a point source, with everyone coming in contact with the agent at approximately the same time. The epidemic curve in this case would be compressed, with a peak in a matter of days or even hours, even with physiologic and exposure differences. If the biological agent is contagious, it is possible to see a second curve peak after the first, as original cases expose originally unexposed persons to the agent. The steep epidemic curve expected in a bioterrorism attack is similar to what would be seen with other point source exposures, such as foodborne outbreaks. Therefore, the compressed epidemic curve is still not pathognomonic for an intentional bioterrorism attack.

If a specific group has been exposed, the epidemic curve may indicate the time of exposure. From this information, a possible incubation period can be calculated, which can assist in determining the potential cause of illness, as well as suggesting a possible intentional attack (if the incubation period is shorter than usual as a result of an unusually high inoculum or more effective exposure route). Calculating the incubation period may also help determine if the disease is spread from person to person, which is extremely important to effective disease control measures.

## EPIDEMIOLOGIC CLUES

As steep epidemic curves can be seen in natural point-source exposures, additional characteristics of the outbreak should be investigated in determining whether it is the result of a biological attack (4, 5). None of the following clues alone constitute proof of intentional use of a biological agent, but together they can assist greatly in determining if further investigation is warranted. 1) The presence of a large epidemic, with greater case loads than expected, especially in a discrete population. 2) More severe disease than expected for a given pathogen, as well as unusual routes of exposure, such as a preponderance of inhalational disease as was seen in Sverdlovsk after the accidental release of aerosolized *Bacillus anthracis* spores (6). 3) A disease that is unusual for a given geographic area, is found outside the normal transmission season, or is impossible to transmit naturally in the absence of the normal vector for transmission. 4) Multiple simultaneous epidemics of different diseases. 5) A disease outbreak with zoonotic as well as human consequences, as many of the potential threat agents are pathogenic to animals. 6) Unusual strains or variants of organisms or antimicrobial resistance patterns disparate from those circulating. 7) Higher attack rates in those exposed in certain areas, such as inside a building if the agent was released indoors, or lower rates in those inside a sealed building if an aerosol was released outdoors. 8) Intelligence that an adversary has access to a particular agent or agents. 9) Claims by a terrorist of the release of a biologic agent. 10) Direct evidence of the release of an agent, with findings of equipment, munitions, or tampering.

Even with the presence of more than one of the above indicators, it may not be easy to determine that an attack occurred through nefarious means. For example, it took months to determine that the outbreak of salmonellosis in Oregon was caused by intentional contamination of salad bars (3). Other outbreaks, such as the hantavirus outbreak in the Four Corners area of the United States, have been thought of as possible results of intentional contamination (7). Even if no conclusive answer can be derived quickly, the means employed in determining the cause of an attack will still provide medical personnel with information that may prevent illness and death.

## RECOMMENDATIONS FOR PREPAREDNESS

Improved awareness and readiness should a bioterrorism attack occur include education of all medical personnel, especially primary-care providers and emergency personnel first to see patients affected by a biological attack. Training should include basic epidemiologic principles as well as clinical information on diagnosing and treating agents that pose the highest threat. Training should be refreshed periodically to ensure that skills remain current.

Improved surveillance efforts should be instituted with as close to real-time data gathering as possible. All facets of surveillance should be used, to include emergency visits, laboratory data, pharmacy use, school absenteeism, or any other data that correlate with an increase in infectious disease. Robust surveillance systems are essential to detecting any emerging or reemerging disease. Quick recognition of any change in disease patterns will facilitate determining the source and preventing further exposure, which should be the key driving force behind any epidemiologic investigation. Through strong epidemiologic training, a close attention to disease patterns, and a healthy respect for the threat of biological terrorism, potential problems can be discovered rapidly, and actions can be taken to decrease the impact of disease, regardless of its origin.

Major Pavlin is chief of the Field Studies Department, Division of Preventive Medicine, Walter Reed Army Institute of Research. She has worked in the area of medical biodefense education. Currently she is developing national and international surveillance systems for emerging diseases with the Department of Defense's Global Emerging Infections Surveillance and Response System.

Address for correspondence: Julie A. Pavlin, Department of Field Studies, Division of Preventive Medicine, Walter Reed Army Institute of Research, Washington, D.C. 20307-5100, USA; fax: 202-782-0613; e-mail: pavlinj@wrsmtp-ccmail.army.mil.

## References

1. Proliferation: threat and response. Office of the Secretary of Defense; November 1997.

2. Broad WJ, Miller J. The threat of germ weapons is rising. Fear, too. New York Times 1998 Dec 27; sec. 4, col. 1, pg. 1.

3. Torok TJ, Tauxe RV, Wise RP, Livengood JR, Sokolow R, Mauvais S, et al. A large community outbreak of salmonellosis caused by intentional contamination of restaurant salad bars. JAMA 1997; 278: 389-95.

4. Weiner SL. Strategies of biowarfare defense. Mil Med 1987; 152: 25-8.

5. Noah DL, Sobel AL, Ostroff SM, Kildew JA. Biological warfare training: infectious disease outbreak differentiation criteria. Mil Med 1998; 163: 198-201.

6. Meselson M, Guillemin J, Hugh-Jones M, Langmuir A, Popova I, Shelokov A, et al. The Sverdlovsk anthrax outbreak of 1979. Science 1994; 266: 1202-8.

7. Horgan J. Were Four Corners victims biowar casualties? Sci Am 1993; 269: 16.

## 6.6 Health Advisory: How to Recognize and Handle a Suspicious Package or Envelope

This is an official CDC Health Advisory

Distributed via the Health Alert Network,
October 31, 2001, 21:25 EST (9:25 PM, EST)
CDCHAN-00050-01-10-31-ADV-N

This information supplements CDC's recommendations for recognizing and handling suspicious packages or envelopes that were published as a CDC Health Advisory on October 27, 2001, and replaces information about identifying suspicious packages that was published as a Health Advisory on October 12, 2001.

Letters containing *Bacillus anthracis* (anthrax) have been received by mail in several areas in the United States. In some instances, anthrax exposures have occurred, with several persons becoming infected. To prevent such exposures and subsequent infection, all persons should learn how to recognize a suspicious package or envelope and take appropriate steps to protect themselves and others.

### Identifying Suspicious Packages and Envelopes

*Some characteristics of suspicious packages and envelopes include the following:*

- Inappropriate or unusual labeling
  - Excessive postage
  - Handwritten or poorly typed addresses
  - Misspellings of common words
  - Strange return address or no return address
  - Incorrect titles or title without a name
  - Not addressed to a specific person
  - Marked with restrictions, such as "Personal," "Confidential," or "Do not X-ray"
  - Marked with any threatening language
  - Postmarked from a city or state that does not match the return address
- Appearance
  - Powdery substance felt through or appearing on the package or envelope
  - Oily stains, discolorations, or odor

- Lopsided or uneven envelope
- Excessive packaging material such as masking tape, string, etc.
- Other suspicious signs
    - Excessive weight
    - Ticking sound
    - Protruding wires or aluminum foil

**If a package or envelope appears suspicious, DO NOT OPEN IT.**

**Handling of Suspicious Packages or Envelopes\***

- Do not shake or empty the contents of any suspicious package or envelope.

- Do not carry the package or envelope, show it to others or allow others to examine it.

- Put the package or envelope down on a stable surface; do not sniff, touch, taste, or look closely at it or at any contents which may have spilled.

- Alert others in the area about the suspicious package or envelope. Leave the area, close any doors, and take actions to prevent others from entering the area. If possible, shut off the ventilation system.

- WASH hands with soap and water to prevent spreading potentially infectious material to face or skin. Seek additional instructions for exposed or potentially exposed persons.

- If at work, notify a supervisor, a security officer, or a law enforcement official. If at home, contact the local law enforcement agency.

- If possible, create a list of persons who were in the room or area when this suspicious letter or package was recognized and a list of persons who also may have handled this package or letter. Give this list to both the local public health authorities and law enforcement officials.

\*These recommendations were published on October 26, 2001, in "Update: Investigation of bioterrorism-related anthrax and interim guidelines for exposure management and antimicrobial therapy." MMWR 2001; 50:909-919

## 6.7   HEALTH ADVISORY: RECOMMENDATIONS FOR PROTECTING WORKERS FROM EXPOSURE TO *BACILLUS ANTHRACIS* IN WORK SITES WHERE MAIL IS HANDLED OR PROCESSED

This is an official CDC Health Advisory

Distributed via the Health Alert Network
October 31, 2001, 21:30 EST (9:30 PM, EST)
CDCHAN-00051-01-10-31-ADV-N

CDC Interim* Recommendations for Protecting Workers from Exposure to *Bacillus anthracis* in Work Sites Where Mail Is Handled or Processed (*Updated from CDC Health Advisory 45 issued 10/24/01)

These interim recommendations are intended to assist personnel responsible for occupational health and safety in developing a comprehensive program to reduce potential cutaneous or inhalational exposures to *Bacillus anthracis* spores among workers, including maintenance and custodial workers, in work sites where mail is handled or processed. Such work sites include post offices, mail distribution/handling centers, bulk mail centers, air mail facilities, priority mail processing centers, public and private mailrooms, and other settings in which workers are responsible for the handling and processing of mail. These interim recommendations are based on the limited information available on ways to avoid infection and the effectiveness of various prevention strategies and will be updated as new information becomes available. These recommendations do not address instances where a known or suspected exposure has occurred. Workers should be trained in how to recognize and handle a suspicious piece of mail (http://www.phppo.cdc.gov). In addition, each work site should develop an emergency plan describing appropriate actions to be taken when a known or suspected exposure to *B. anthracis* occurs.

These recommendations are divided into the following hierarchical categories describing measures that should be implemented in mail-handling/processing sites to prevent potential exposures to *B. anthracis* spores:

1. Engineering controls
2. Administrative controls
3. Housekeeping controls
4. Personal protective equipment for workers

These measures should be selected on the basis of an initial evaluation of the work site. This evaluation should focus on determining which processes, operations, jobs, or tasks would be most likely to result in an exposure should a contaminated envelope or package enter the work site. Many of these measures (e.g., administrative controls, use of HEPA filter-equipped vacuums, wet-cleaning, use of protective gloves) can be implemented immediately; implementation of others will require additional time and efforts.

## Engineering Controls in Mail-handling/processing Sites

*B. anthracis* spores can be aerosolized during the operation and maintenance of high-speed, mail-sorting machines, potentially exposing workers and possibly entering heating, ventilation, or air-conditioning (HVAC) systems. Engineering controls can provide the best means of preventing worker exposure to potential aerosolized particles, thereby reducing the risk for inhalational anthrax, the most severe form of the disease. In settings where such machinery is in use, the following engineering controls should be considered:

An industrial vacuum cleaner equipped with a high-efficiency particulate air (HEPA) filter for cleaning high-speed, mail-sorting machinery

Local exhaust ventilation at pinch roller areas

HEPA-filtered exhaust hoods installed in areas where dust is generated (e.g., areas with high-speed, mail-sorting machinery)

Air curtains (using laminar air flow) installed in areas where large amounts of mail are processed

HEPA filters installed in the building's HVAC systems (if feasible) to capture aerosolized spores
**Note: Machinery should not be cleaned using compressed air (i.e., "blowdown/blowoff").**

## Administrative Controls in Mail-handling/processing Sites

Strategies should be developed to limit the number of persons working at or near sites where aerosolized particles may be generated (e.g., mail-sorting machinery, places where mailbags are unloaded or emptied). In addition, restrictions should be in place to limit the number of persons (including support staff and non-employees, e.g., contractors, business visitors) entering areas where aerosolized particles may be generated. This includes contractors, business visitors, and support staff.

## HOUSEKEEPING CONTROLS IN MAIL-HANDLING/PROCESSING SITES

Dry sweeping and dusting should be avoided. Instead, areas should be wet-cleaned and vacuumed with HEPA-equipped vacuum cleaners.

## PERSONAL PROTECTIVE EQUIPMENT FOR WORKERS IN MAIL-HANDLING/PROCESSING SITES

Personal protective equipment for workers in mail-handling/processing work sites must be selected on the basis of the potential for cutaneous or inhalational exposure to *B. anthracis* spores. Handling packages or envelopes may result in cutaneous exposure. In addition, because certain machinery (e.g., electronic mail sorters) can generate aerosolized particles, persons who operate, maintain, or work near such machinery may be exposed through inhalation. Persons who hand sort mail or work at other sites where airborne particles may be generated (e.g., where mailbags are unloaded or emptied) may also be exposed through inhalation.

### Recommendations for Workers Who Handle Mail

Protective, impermeable gloves should be worn by all workers who handle mail. In some cases, workers may need to wear cotton gloves under their protective gloves for comfort and to prevent dermatitis. Skin rashes and other dermatological conditions are a potential hazard of wearing gloves. Latex gloves should be avoided because of the risk of developing skin sensitivity or allergy.

Gloves should be provided in a range of sizes to ensure proper fit.

The choice of glove material (e.g., nitrile, vinyl) should be based on safety, fit, durability, and comfort. Sterile gloves (e.g., surgical gloves) are not necessary.

Different gloves or layers of gloves may be needed depending on the task, the dexterity required, and the type of protection needed. Protective gloves can be worn under heavier gloves (e.g., leather, heavy cotton) for operations where gloves can easily be torn or if more protection against hand injury is needed.

For workers involved in situations where a gloved hand presents a hazard (e.g., close to moving machine parts), the risk for potential injury resulting from glove use should be measured against the risk for potential exposure to *B. anthracis*.

Workers should avoid touching their skin, eyes, or other mucous membranes since contaminated gloves may transfer *B. anthracis* spores to other body sites.

Workers should consider wearing long-sleeved clothing and long pants to protect exposed skin.

Gloves and other personal protective clothing and equipment can be discarded in regular trash once they are removed or if they are visibly torn, unless a suspicious piece of mail is recognized and handled. If a suspicious piece of mail is recognized and handled, the worker's protective gear should be handled as potentially contaminated material (See "Guideline for Hand Washing and Hospital Environmental Control," 1985, available at http://www.cdc.gov/ncidod/hip/guide/handwash.htm.)

Hands should be thoroughly washed with soap and water when gloves are removed, before eating, and when replacing torn or worn gloves. Soap and water will wash away most spores that may have contacted the skin; disinfectant solutions are not needed.

### Additional Recommendations for Workers Who May Be Exposed through Inhalation

Persons working with or near machinery capable of generating aerosolized particles (e.g., electronic mail sorters) or at other work sites where such particles may be generated should be fitted with NIOSH-approved respirators that are at least as protective as an N95 respirator.

Persons working in areas where oil mist from machinery is present should be fitted with respirators equipped with P-type filters.

Because facial hair interferes with the fit of protective respirators, workers with facial hair (beards and or large moustaches) may require alternative respirators (such as powered air-purifying respirators [PAPRS] with loose-fitting hoods).

Workers who cannot be fitted properly with a half-mask respirator based on a fit test may require the use of alternative respirators, such as full facepiece, negative-pressure respirators, PAPRs equipped with HEPA filters, or supplied-air respirators. If a worker is medically unable to wear a respirator, the employer should consider reassigning that worker to a job that does not require respiratory protection.

In addition, the use of disposable aprons or goggles by persons working with or near machinery capable of generating aerosolized particles may provide an extra margin of protection.

In work sites where respirators are worn, a respiratory-protection program that complies with the provisions of OSHA [29 CFR 1910.134] should be in place. Such a program includes provisions for obtaining medical clearance for wearing a respirator and conducting a respirator fit-test to ensure that the respirator fits properly. Without fit testing, persons unknowingly may have poor face seals, allowing aerosols to leak around the mask and be inhaled. (See December 11, 1998, MMWR, available at http://www.cdc.gov/mmwr/preview/mmwrhtml/00055954.htm.)

## 6.8 HEALTH ADVISORY: USE OF CIPROFLOXACIN OR DOXYCYCLINE FOR POSTEXPOSURE PROPHYLAXIS FOR PREVENTION OF INHALATION ANTHRAX

This is an official CDC Health Advisory

Distributed via the Health Alert Network
October 31, 2001, 21:30 EST (9:30 PM, EST)
CDCHAN-00049-01-10-31-ADV-N

Interim recommendations, MMWR 50(no 41):893 Oct 19, 2001, for postexposure prophylaxis to prevent inhalational anthrax after exposure to *B. anthracis* spores recommend **ciprofloxacin or doxycycline** as initial therapy in situations associated with the current bioterrorist attack in the United States.

**EFFECTIVENESS**: There is no evidence which demonstrates that ciprofloxacin is more or less effective than doxycycline for postexposure prophylaxis for prevention of infection with *B. anthracis*.

**RESISTANCE**: Widespread use of any antibiotic will promote resistance. Many common pathogens are already resistant to tetracyclines such as doxycycline. However, ciprofloxacin resistance is not yet common in these same organisms. To preserve the effectiveness of ciprofloxacin against other infections, use of doxycycline for prevention of *B. anthracis* infection is reasonable. Ciprofloxacin is an effective antimicrobial for a variety of other bacterial infections. Thus, the wide use of this drug in thousands of individuals may lead to increased resistance of other bacterial pathogens to ciprofloxacin and other fluoroquinolones, and limit the usefulness of these agents.

**SIDE EFFECTS**: On the basis of side-effect profiles (see below), the history of reactions, or the clinical setting, either doxycycline or cipro-floxacin may be preferable for an individual patient.

**Patient Information on Ciprofloxacin**
(http://www.bt.cdc.gov/DocumentsApp/Anthrax/10312001/cipro.asp)

**Patient Information on Doxycycline**
(http://www.bt.cdc.gov/DocumentsApp/Anthrax/10312001/doxy.asp)

## 6.9 INTERIM GUIDELINES FOR INVESTIGATION OF AND RESPONSE TO *BACILLUS ANTHRACIS* EXPOSURES

### ENVIRONMENTAL SAMPLING

Environmental testing to detect *B. anthracis* on surfaces or in the air can be used to investigate known or suspected exposure events. The highest priority of an investigation is to evaluate the risk for exposure to aerosolized *B. anthracis* spores. Persons collecting and testing samples should 1) obtain adequate samples, 2) avoid cross-contamination during processing, and 3) ensure proficient laboratory testing and interpretation of test results. A positive laboratory test for *B. anthracis* from a sample of an environmental surface may be caused by cross-contamination from an exposure vehicle (e.g., contact with an envelope containing *B. anthracis*), background occurrence of *B. anthracis* spores in the environment, or previously aerosolized *B. anthracis* that has settled onto environmental surfaces. Laboratory test results of environmental surface samples should not be the only criterion for starting, continuing, or stopping antimicrobial prophylaxis for inhalational disease.

Environmental sampling can be directed, prospective, or random. In directed sampling, air and/or surface samples are obtained as part of an investigation of a specific threat, a known exposure, or of persons with bioterrorism-related anthrax. Directed environmental sampling may play a critical role in characterizing potential exposures and guiding public health action.

Prospective environmental sampling is defined as ongoing sampling and testing of air or surfaces for *B. anthracis* spores. The value of prospective sampling is not known. Current technologies for monitoring air for *B. anthracis* and other agents are not validated and their performance has not been assessed during bioterrorism events. Prospective environmental sampling of surfaces may have a role in detecting *B. anthracis* contamination, especially at facilities or events determined to be at high risk for bioterrorism.

The testing of random environmental samples (i.e., sampling air or surfaces of facilities that are not directly associated with confirmed anthrax disease or a known *B. anthracis* exposure) is of uncertain utility in detecting past exposures. Random positive tests for *B. anthracis* spores may represent cross-contamination from an exposure vehicle (e.g., letter) that poses negligible risks for inhalational anthrax. These positive test results may prompt more extensive evaluation to direct cleanup, if needed.

## Nasal Swab Cultures

Nasal swab cultures should not be used to diagnose cases of anthrax or to evaluate whether a person had been exposed. Nasal swab cultures may be useful in the investigation of known or suspected airborne *B. anthracis*. Because the sensitivity of nasal swab cultures decreases over time, cultures should be obtained within 7 days of the exposure. The presence of *B. anthracis* from a nasal swab culture cannot be determined by gram stain or colony characteristics alone and requires confirmatory testing by qualified laboratories.

## Antimicrobial Prophylaxis

Antimicrobial prophylaxis is used to prevent cases of inhalational anthrax. Public health authorities often start prophylaxis before the extent of exposure is known. Subsequent epidemiologic and laboratory test data may indicate that some persons started on prophylaxis were not exposed. These persons should stop antimicrobial prophylaxis. Persons who were exposed should complete 60 days of therapy. No shorter course of antimicrobial prophylaxis exists. The choice of an antimicrobial agent should be based on antimicrobial susceptibility, the drug's effectiveness, adverse events, and cost. *B. anthracis* isolates from patients with bioterrorism-related anthrax have been susceptible to ciprofloxacin, doxycycline, and other agents; the use of doxycycline may be preferable to prevent development of ciprofloxacin resistance in more common bacteria (1). Respiratory transmission of *B. anthracis* from person to person does not occur; no antimicrobial prophylaxis is indicated.

## Closing Facilities

The decision to close a facility is made to prevent cases of inhalational anthrax. The facility should remain closed until the risk for inhalational disease is eliminated.

**Reference**
CDC. Update: Investigation of Bioterrorism-Related Anthrax and Interim Guidelines for Exposure Management and Antimicrobial Therapy, October 2001. MMWR 2001; 50: 909-19.

## INTERIM GUIDELINES FOR INVESTIGATION OF AND RESPONSE TO *B. ANTHRACIS* EXPOSURES

### ENVIRONMENTAL SAMPLING

**Directed sampling of environmental surfaces may be indicated:**

- To identify a site or source of *Bacillus anthracis* exposure that has resulted in a case(s) of anthrax

- To trace the route of an exposure vehicle (e.g., a powder-containing letter)

- To obtain the *B. anthracis* strain when isolates from patients are not available

- To guide cleanup activities in a contaminated area or building

- To assess biosafety procedures in laboratories processing *B. anthracis* specimens

**Prospective sampling of environmental surfaces may be indicated:**

- To identify receipt of a contaminated exposure vehicle in high risk facilities (e.g., mailrooms of targeted persons or groups)

- To detect aerosolized *B. anthracis* in high risk areas or events

*Laboratory testing of environmental surface samples should not be the only means to determine the need for antimicrobial prophylaxis.*

### NASAL SWAB CULTURES

**Collection of nasal swabs for culture of *B. anthracis* may be useful:**

- To help define an area of exposure to aerosolized *B. anthracis*

- To help ascertain where a person with inhalational anthrax was exposed if the time and place of exposure are not already known

**Collection of nasal swabs for culture of *B. anthracis* is not indicated:**

- To diagnose anthrax

- To determine a person's risk of exposure and the need for antimicrobial prophylaxis

- To determine when antimicrobial prophylaxis should be stopped

- To supplement random environmental sampling

## Antimicrobial Prophylaxis

**Antimicrobial prophylaxis may be initiated pending additional information when:**

- A person is exposed to an air space where a suspicious material may have been aerosolized (e.g., near a suspicious powder-containing letter during opening)

- A person has shared the air space likely to be the source of an inhalational anthrax case

**Antimicrobial prophylaxis should be continued for 60 days for:**

- Persons exposed to an air space known to be contaminated with aerosolized *B. anthracis*

- Persons exposed to an air space known to be the source of an inhalational anthrax case

- Persons along the transit path of an envelope or other vehicle containing *B. anthracis* that may have been aerosolized (e.g., a postal sorting facility in which an envelope containing *B. anthracis* was processed)

- Unvaccinated laboratory workers exposed to confirmed *B. anthracis* cultures

**Antimicrobial prophylaxis is not indicated:**

- For prevention of cutaneous anthrax

- For autopsy personnel examining bodies infected with anthrax when appropriate isolation precautions and procedures are followed

- For hospital personnel caring for patients with anthrax

- For persons who routinely open or handle mail in the absence of a suspicious letter or credible threat

*A positive test for B. anthracis from a randomly collected specimen does not require implementation of antimicrobial prophylaxis or the closing of a facility.*

## CLOSING A FACILITY

**Closing a facility or a part of a facility may be indicated:**

- After an inhalational anthrax case is detected and a probable site of exposure in the facility is identified

- When there is a known aerosolization of *B. anthracis* in the facility

- When evidence strongly suggests an aerosolization of *B. anthracis* in the facility

- As determined by law enforcement authorities in a criminal investigation

**Closing a facility is not indicated:**

- Based only on the identification of *B. anthracis* from samples of environmental surfaces

- Based only on the identification of a cutaneous anthrax case

## 6.10 Protecting Investigators Performing Environmental Sampling for *Bacillus anthracis*: Personal Protective Equipment

Workers conducting environmental sampling that places them at risk for exposure to *Bacillus anthracis*, the organism causing anthrax, should wear protective personal equipment (PPE), including respiratory devices, protective clothing, and gloves. The items described below are similar to those used by emergency personnel responding to incidents involving letters or packages. Emergency responders need to use greater levels of protection in responding to incidents involving unknown conditions or those involving aerosol-generating devices.

### Powered Air-Purifying Respirator with Full Facepiece and High-Efficiency Particulate Air (HEPA) Filters

- The constant flow of clean air into the facepieces is an important feature of this respirator because contaminated air cannot enter gaps in the face-to-facepiece seal. These respirators also give wearers needed mobility and field of vision.

- Respirators should be used in accordance with a respiratory-protection program that complies with the OSHA respiratory-protection standard (29 CFR 1910.134).

- Respiratory facepieces for investigators should be assigned on the basis of results of quantitative fit testing.

- Wearing a properly functioning and powered air-purifying respirator with a full facepiece that is assigned to the wearer on the basis of quantitative fit testing will reduce inhalation exposures by 98% of what they would be without wearing this type of respirator.

### Disposable Protective Clothing with Integral Hood and Booties

- Wearing protective clothing not only protects the skin but also can eliminate the likelihood of transferring contaminated dust to places away from the work site.

- Wearing disposable rubber shoe coverings with ridged soles made of slip-resistant material over the booties of the disposable suit will reduce the likelihood of slipping on wet or dusty surfaces.

- All PPE should be decontaminated immediately after leaving a potentially contaminated area.

- Protective clothing should be removed and discarded before removing the respirator.

## Disposable Gloves

- Disposable gloves made of lightweight nitrile or vinyl protect hands from contact with potentially contaminated dusts without compromising needed dexterity.

- A thin cotton glove can be worn inside a disposable glove to protect against dermatitis, which can occur from prolonged exposure of the skin to moisture in gloves caused by perspiration.

## 6.11 Recognition of Illness Associated with the Intentional Release of a Biologic Agent

On September 11, 2001, following the terrorist incidents in New York City and Washington, D.C., CDC recommended heightened surveillance for any unusual disease occurrence or increased numbers of illnesses that might be associated with the terrorist attacks. Subsequently, cases of anthrax in Florida and New York City have demonstrated the risks associated with intentional release of biologic agents (1). This report provides guidance for healthcare providers and public health personnel about recognizing illnesses or patterns of illness that might be associated with intentional release of biologic agents.

### Healthcare Providers

Healthcare providers should be alert to illness patterns and diagnostic clues that might indicate an unusual infectious disease outbreak associated with intentional release of a biologic agent and should report any clusters or findings to their local or state health department. The covert release of a biologic agent may not have an immediate impact because of the delay between exposure and illness onset, and outbreaks associated with intentional releases might closely resemble naturally occurring outbreaks. Indications of intentional release of a biologic agent include 1) an unusual temporal or geographic clustering of illness (e.g., persons who attended the same public event or gathering) or patients presenting with clinical signs and symptoms that suggest an infectious disease outbreak (e.g., $\geq 2$ patients presenting with an unexplained febrile illness associated with sepsis, pneumonia, respiratory failure, or rash or a botulism-like syndrome with flaccid muscle paralysis, especially if occurring in otherwise healthy persons); 2) an unusual age distribution for common diseases (e.g., an increase in what appears to be a chicken-pox-like illness among adult patients, but which might be smallpox); and 3) a large number of cases of acute flaccid paralysis with prominent bulbar palsies, suggestive of a release of *botulinum* toxin.

CDC defines three categories of biologic agents with potential to be used as weapons, based on ease of dissemination or transmission, potential for major public health impact (e.g., high mortality), potential for public panic and social disruption, and requirements for public health preparedness (2). Agents of highest concern are *Bacillus anthracis* (anthrax), *Yersinia pestis* (plague), variola major (smallpox), *Clostridium botulinum* toxin (botulism), *Francisella tularensis* (tularemia), filoviruses (Ebola hemorrhagic fever, Marburg hemorrhagic fever); and arenaviruses

(Lassa [Lassa fever], Junin [Argentine hemorrhagic fever], and related viruses). The following summarizes the clinical features of these agents (3-6).

**Anthrax.** A nonspecific prodrome (i.e., fever, dyspnea, cough, and chest discomfort) follows inhalation of infectious spores. Approximately 2-4 days after initial symptoms, sometimes after a brief period of improvement, respiratory failure and hemodynamic collapse ensue. Inhalational anthrax also might include thoracic edema and a widened mediastinum on chest radiograph. Gram-positive bacilli can grow on blood culture, usually 2-3 days after onset of illness. Cutaneous anthrax follows deposition of the organism onto the skin, occurring particularly on exposed areas of the hands, arms, or face. An area of local edema becomes a pruritic macule or papule, which enlarges and ulcerates after 1-2 days. Small, 1-3 mm vesicles may surround the ulcer. A painless, depressed, black eschar usually with surrounding local edema subsequently develops. The syndrome also may include lymphangitis and painful lymphadenopathy.

**Plague.** Clinical features of pneumonic plague include fever, cough with muco-purulent sputum (gram-negative rods may be seen on gram stain), hemoptysis, and chest pain. A chest radiograph will show evidence of bronchopneumonia.

**Botulism.** Clinical features include symmetric cranial neuropathies (i.e., drooping eyelids, weakened jaw clench, and difficulty swallowing or speaking), blurred vision or diplopia, symmetric descending weakness in a proximal to distal pattern, and respiratory dysfunction from respiratory muscle paralysis or upper airway obstruction without sensory deficits. Inhalational botulism would have a similar clinical presentation as foodborne botulism; however, the gastrointestinal symptoms that accompany foodborne botulism may be absent.

**Smallpox (variola).** The acute clinical symptoms of smallpox resemble other acute viral illnesses, such as influenza, beginning with a 2-4 day nonspecific prodrome of fever and myalgias before rash onset. Several clinical features can help clinicians differentiate varicella (chickenpox) from smallpox. The rash of varicella is most prominent on the trunk and develops in successive groups of lesions over several days, resulting in lesions in various stages of development and resolution. In comparison, the vesicular/pustular rash of smallpox is typically most prominent on the face and extremities, and lesions develop at the same time.

**Inhalational tularemia.** Inhalation of *F. tularensis* causes an abrupt onset of an acute, nonspecific febrile illness beginning 3-5 days after exposure, with pleuropneumonitis developing in a substantial proportion of cases during subsequent days (7).

**Hemorrhagic fever** (such as would be caused by Ebola or Marburg viruses). After an incubation period of usually 5-10 days (range: 2-19 days), illness is characterized by abrupt onset of fever, myalgia, and headache. Other signs and symptoms include nausea and vomiting, abdominal pain, diarrhea, chest pain, cough, and pharyngitis. A maculo-papular rash, prominent on the trunk, develops in most patients approximately 5 days after onset of illness. Bleeding manifestations, such as petechiae, ecchymoses, and hemorrhages, occur as the disease progresses (8).

## CLINICAL LABORATORY PERSONNEL

Although unidentified gram-positive bacilli growing on agar may be considered as contaminants and discarded, CDC recommends that these bacilli be treated as a "finding" when they occur in a suspicious clinical setting (e.g., febrile illness in a previously healthy person). The laboratory should attempt to characterize the organism, such as motility testing, inhibition by penicillin, absence of hemolysis on sheep blood agar, and further biochemical testing or species determination.

An unusually high number of samples, particularly from the same biologic medium (e.g., blood and stool cultures), may alert laboratory personnel to an outbreak. In addition, central laboratories that receive clinical specimens from several sources should be alert to increases in demand or unusual requests for culturing (e.g., uncommon biologic specimens such as cerebrospinal fluid or pulmonary aspirates).

When collecting or handling clinical specimens, laboratory personnel should 1) use Biological Safety Level II (BSL-2) or Level III (BSL-3) facilities and practices when working with clinical samples considered potentially infectious; 2) handle all specimens in a BSL-2 laminar flow hood with protective eyewear (e.g., safety glasses or eye shields), use closed-front laboratory coats with cuffed sleeves, and stretch the gloves over the cuffed sleeves; 3) avoid any activity that places persons at risk for infectious exposure, especially activities that might create aerosols or droplet dispersal; 4) decontaminate laboratory benches after each use and dispose of supplies and equipment in proper receptacles; 5) avoid touching mucosal surfaces with their hands (gloved or ungloved), and never eat or drink in the laboratory; and 6) remove and reverse their gloves before leaving the laboratory and dispose of them in a biohazard container, and wash their hands and remove their laboratory coat.

When a laboratory is unable to identify an organism in a clinical specimen, it should be sent to a laboratory where the agent can be characterized, such as the state public health laboratory or, in some large metropolitan areas, the local health department laboratory. Any clinical specimens suspected to contain variola (smallpox) should be reported to local and state health authorities and then transported to CDC. All variola diagnostics should be conducted at CDC laboratories. Clinical laboratories should report any clusters or findings that could indicate intentional release of a biologic agent to their state and local health departments.

## INFECTION-CONTROL PROFESSIONALS

Heightened awareness by infection-control professionals (ICPs) facilitates recognition of the release of a biologic agent. ICPs are involved with many aspects of hospital operations and several departments and with counterparts in other hospitals. As a result, ICPs may recognize changing patterns or clusters in a hospital or in a community that might otherwise go unrecognized.

ICPs should ensure that hospitals have current telephone numbers for notification of both internal (ICPs, epidemiologists, infectious diseases specialists, administrators, and public affairs officials) and external (state and local health departments, Federal Bureau of Investigation field office, and CDC Emergency Response office) contacts and that they are distributed to the appropriate personnel (9). ICPs should work with clinical microbiology laboratories, on- or off-site, that receive specimens for testing from their facility to ensure that cultures from suspicious cases are evaluated appropriately.

## STATE HEALTH DEPARTMENTS

State health departments should implement plans for educating and reminding healthcare providers about how to recognize unusual illnesses that might indicate intentional release of a biologic agent. Strategies for responding to potential bioterrorism include 1) providing information or reminders to healthcare providers and clinical laboratories about how to report events to the appropriate public health authorities; 2) implementing a 24-hour-a-day, 7-day-a-week capacity to receive and act on any positive report of events that suggest intentional release of a biologic agent; 3) investigating immediately any report of a cluster of illnesses or other event that suggests an intentional release of a biologic agent and requesting CDC's assistance when necessary; 4) implementing a plan, including accessing the Laboratory Response Network for Bioterrorism, to collect and transport specimens and to store them appropriately before laboratory analysis; and 5) reporting immediately to CDC if the results of an investigation suggest release of a biologic agent.

*Reported by: National Center for Infectious Diseases; Epidemiology Program Office; Public Health Practice Program Office; Office of the Director, CDC.*

**Editorial Note:**

Healthcare providers, clinical laboratory personnel, infection control professionals, and health departments play critical and complementary roles in recognizing and responding to illnesses caused by intentional release of biologic agents. The syndrome descriptions, epidemiologic clues, and laboratory recommendations in this report provide basic guidance that can be implemented immediately to improve recognition of these events.

After the terrorist attacks of September 11, state and local health departments initiated various activities to improve surveillance and response, ranging from enhancing communications (between state and local health departments and between public health agencies and healthcare providers) to conducting special surveillance projects. These special projects have included active surveillance for changes in the number of hospital admissions, emergency department visits, and occurrence of specific syndromes. Activities in bioterrorism preparedness and emerging infections over the past few years have better positioned public health agencies to detect and respond to the intentional release of a biologic agent. Immediate review of these activities to identify the most useful and practical approaches will help refine syndrome surveillance efforts in various clinical situations.

Information about clinical diagnosis and management can be found elsewhere (1-9). Additional information about responding to bioterrorism is available from CDC at http://www.bt.cdc.gov; the U.S. Army Medical Research Institute of Infectious Diseases at http://www.usamrii d.army.mil/education/bluebook.html; the Association for Infection Control Practitioners at http://www.apic.org; and the Johns Hopkins Center for Civilian Biodefense Strategies at http://www.hopkins-bio defense.org.

## References

1. CDC. Update: investigation of anthrax associated with intentional exposure and interim public health guidelines, October 2001. MMWR 2001; 50: 889-93.

2. CDC. Biological and chemical terrorism: strategic plan for preparedness and response. MMWR 2000; 49(no. RR-4).

3. Arnon SS, Schechter R, Inglesby TV, et al. Botulinum toxin as a biological weapon: medical and public health management. JAMA 2001; 285:1059-70.

4. Inglesby TV, Dennis DT, Henderson DA, et al. Plague as a biological weapon: medical and public health management. JAMA 2000; 283:2281-90.

5. Henderson DA, Inglesby TV, Bartlett JG, et al. Smallpox as a biological weapon: medical and public health management. JAMA 1999; 281:2127-37.

6. Inglesby TV, Henderson DA, Bartlett JG, et al. Anthrax as a biological weapon: medical and public health management. JAMA 1999; 281:1735-963.

7. Dennis DT, Inglesby TV, Henderson DA, et al. Tularemia as a biological weapon: medical and public health management. JAMA 2001; 285:2763-73.

8. Peters CJ. Marburg and Ebola virus hemorrhagic fevers. In: Mandell GL, Bennett JE, Dolin R, eds. Principles and practice of infectious diseases. 5th ed. New York, New York: Churchill Livingstone 2000; 2:1821-3.

9. APIC Bioterrorism Task Force and CDC Hospital Infections Program Bioterrorism Working Group. Bioterrorism readiness plan: a template for healthcare facilities. Available at http://www.cdc.gov/ncidod/hip/Bio/bio.htm. Accessed October 2001.

## 6.12 Updated Recommendations for Antimicrobial Prophylaxis among Asymptomatic Pregnant Women after Exposure to *Bacillus Anthracis*

The antimicrobial of choice for initial prophylactic therapy among asymptomatic pregnant women exposed to *Bacillus anthracis* is ciprofloxacin, 500 mg twice a day for 60 days. In instances in which the specific *B. anthracis* strain has been shown to be penicillin-sensitive, prophylactic therapy with amoxicillin, 500 mg three times a day for 60 days, may be considered. Isolates of *B. anthracis* implicated in the current bioterrorist attacks are susceptible to penicillin in laboratory tests, but may contain penicillinase activity (2). Pencillins are not recommended for treatment of anthrax, where such penicillinase activity may decrease their effectiveness. However, penicillins are likely to be effective for preventing anthrax, a setting where relatively few organisms are present. Doxycycline should be used with caution in asymptomatic pregnant women and only when contraindications are indicated to the use of other appropriate antimicrobial drugs.

Pregnant women are likely to be among the increasing number of persons receiving antimicrobial prophylaxis for exposure to *B. anthracis*. Clinicians, public health officials, and women who are candidates for treatment should weigh the possible risks and benefits to the mother and fetus when choosing an antimicrobial for postexposure anthrax prophylaxis. Women who become pregnant while taking antimicrobial prophylaxis should continue the medication and consult a healthcare provider or public health official to discuss these issues.

No formal clinical studies of ciprofloxacin have been performed during pregnancy. Based on limited human information, ciprofloxacin use during pregnancy is unlikely to be associated with a high risk for structural malformations in fetal development. Data on ciprofloxacin use during pregnancy from the Teratogen Information System indicate that therapeutic doses during pregnancy are unlikely to pose a substantial teratogenic risk, but data are insufficient to determine that there is no risk (1). Doxycycline is a tetracycline antimicrobial. Potential dangers of tetracyclines to fetal development include risk for dental staining of the primary teeth and concern about possible depressed bone growth and defective dental enamel. Rarely, hepatic necrosis has been reported in pregnant women using tetracyclines. Penicillins generally are considered safe for use during pregnancy and are not associated with an increased risk for fetal malformation. Pregnant women should be advised that congenital malformations occur in approximately 2%-3% of births, even in the absence of known teratogenic exposure.

Additional information about the treatment of anthrax infection is available at http://www.cdc.gov/mmwr/preview/mmwrhtml/mm5042a1.htm.

## Reference

1. Friedman JM, Polifka JE. Teratogenic effects of drugs: a resource for clinicians (TERIS). Baltimore, Maryland: Johns Hopkins University Press, 2000:149-95.

2. CDC. Update: investigation of bioterrorism-related anthrax and interim guidelines for exposure management and antimicrobial therapy, October 2001. MMWR 2001; 50:909-19.

## 6.13 Use of Onsite Technologies for Rapidly Assessing Environmental *Bacillus anthracis* Contamination on Surfaces in Buildings

Environmental sampling to ascertain the presence of *Bacillus anthracis* spores in buildings is an important tool for assessing risk for exposure. Similar to diagnostic testing, culture with positive identification of *B. anthracis* (CDC culture method) is the confirmatory test. Laboratory-based polymerase chain reaction (PCR) methods for detecting genetic material of *B. anthracis* can be used in preliminary assessments and as adjuncts to microbiologic methods. Although these tests are consistent with culture results, PCR methods are not approved by the Food and Drug Administration, and results should not be the basis for clinical decisions.

Rapid-assay devices that can provide results within minutes are used for onsite detection of environmental contamination. Some of these devices are PCR-based assays, and others are immune-based assays for *B. anthracis*. CDC has not obtained validation data for rapid-assay devices. A recent CDC evaluation of *B. anthracis* contamination at the Brentwood postal facility in the District of Columbia included use of one onsite PCR-based device and CDC culture method. Of 107 samples analyzed using CDC culture method and the PCR-based device, 95 (89%) were negative by both methods. Of six samples identified as positive by CDC culture method, two were positive using the PCR-based device. Of eight samples identified as positive by the PCR-based device, two were positive by CDC culture method. Although these results indicate a poor agreement between results from the onsite PCR-based device and CDC culture method, this assessment was not intended as a formal validation test because of limited capacity to implement adequate quality-control measures and the small number of *B. anthracis* positive samples.

The apparently poor agreement of the onsite PCR-based device could be attributed to several factors such as the concentration of spores on contaminated surfaces, sample collection and preparation procedures, sample splitting, and the methods used for removing the sample from collection material. Furthermore, PCR- or immune-based tests do not distinguish viable from nonviable spores and can produce positive scores for samples that culture methods would define as negative. As a result, these methods are not useful for evaluating the success of disinfection techniques that do not remove nonviable spores.

Public health officials are urged to understand the limitations of onsite, rapid technologies for *B. anthracis* before using them for public health decision making. Until validation testing is complete and guidelines for effective use are developed, PCR- or immune-based assay results for *B. anthracis* should not be used alone, but should be confirmed with samples analyzed by culture methods to make public health decisions.

## 6.14 Vaccinia (Smallpox) Vaccine Recommendations of the Advisory Committee on Immunization Practices (ACIP), 2001

Brief Summary

SOURCE(S):
MMWR 2001 Jun 22; 50(RR-10):1-25, CE1-7

ADAPTATION:
Not applicable: Guideline was not adapted from another source.

RELEASE DATE:
2001 June

MAJOR RECOMMENDATIONS:
Vaccinia Vaccine

## Routine Nonemergency Vaccine Use

Vaccinia vaccine is recommended for laboratory workers who directly handle a) cultures or b) animals contaminated or infected with, non-highly attenuated vaccinia virus, recombinant vaccinia viruses derived from nonhighly attenuated vaccinia strains, or other Orthopoxviruses that infect humans (e.g., monkeypox, cowpox, vaccinia, and variola). Other healthcare workers (e.g., physicians and nurses) whose contact with nonhighly attenuated vaccinia viruses is limited to contaminated materials (e.g., dressings) but who adhere to appropriate infection control measures are at lower risk for inadvertent infection than laboratory workers. However, because a theoretical risk for infection exists, vaccination can be offered to this group. Vaccination is not recommended for persons who do not directly handle nonhighly attenuated virus cultures or materials or who do not work with animals contaminated or infected with these viruses.

Vaccination with vaccinia vaccine results in high seroconversion rates and only infrequent adverse events (see the NGC Guideline Summary field labeled "Potential Harms"). Recipients of standard potency vaccinia vaccine (Dryvax) receive controlled percutaneous doses (approximately $2.5 \times 10^5$ PFU) of relatively low pathogenicity vaccinia virus. The resulting immunity should provide protection to recipients against infections resulting from uncontrolled, inadvertent inoculation by unusual routes (e.g., the eye) with a substantial dose of virus of higher or unknown pathogenicity. In addition, persons with preexisting immunity to vaccinia might be protected against seroconversion to the foreign antigen expressed by a recombinant virus if inadvertently exposed. However, persons with preexisting immunity to vaccinia might not receive the full benefit of recombinant vaccinia vaccines developed for immunization against other infections.

## ROUTINE NONEMERGENCY REVACCINATION

According to data regarding the persistence of neutralizing antibody after vaccination, persons working with nonhighly attenuated vaccinia viruses, recombinant viruses developed from nonhighly attenuated vaccinia viruses, or other nonvariola Orthopoxviruses should be revaccinated at least every 10 years. To ensure an increased level of protection against more virulent nonvariola Orthopoxviruses (e.g., monkeypox), empiric revaccination every 3 years can be considered.

## SIDE EFFECTS AND ADVERSE REACTIONS

See the NGC Guideline Summary field labeled "Potential Harms."

## TREATMENT FOR VACCINIA VACCINE COMPLICATIONS

*Using vaccinia immunoglobulin*

The only product currently available for treatment of complications of vaccinia vaccination is vaccinia immunoglobulin, which is an isotonic sterile solution of the immunoglobulin fraction of plasma from persons vaccinated with vaccinia vaccine. It is effective for treatment of eczema vaccinatum and certain cases of progressive vaccinia; it might be useful also in the treatment of ocular vaccinia resulting from inadvertent implantation. However, vaccinia immunoglobulin is contraindicated for the treatment of vaccinial keratitis. Vaccinia immunoglobulin is recommended for severe generalized vaccinia if the patient is extremely ill or has a serious underlying disease. Vaccinia immunoglobulin provides no benefit in the treatment of postvaccinial encephalitis and has no role in the treatment of smallpox. Current supplies of vaccinia immunoglobulin are limited, and its use should be reserved for treatment of vaccine complications with serious clinical manifestations (e.g., eczema vaccinatum, progressive vaccinia, severe generalized vaccinia, and severe ocular viral implantation).

The recommended dosage of the currently available vaccinia immunoglobulin for treatment of complications is 0.6 ml/kg of body weight. Vaccinia immunoglobulin must be administered intramuscularly and should be administered as early as possible after the onset of symptoms. Because therapeutic doses of vaccinia immunoglobulin might be substantial (e.g., 42 ml for a person weighing 70 kg), the product should be administered in divided doses over a 24- to 36-hour period. Doses can be repeated, usually at intervals of 2–3 days, until recovery begins (e.g., no new lesions appear). Future reformulations of vaccinia immunoglobulin might require intravenous administration, and healthcare providers should refer to the manufacturer's package insert for correct dosages and route of administration. Centers for Disease Control and Prevention is currently the only source of vaccinia immunoglobulin for civilians (see the section titled "Vaccinia Vaccine Availability").

## OTHER TREATMENT OPTIONS
## FOR VACCINIA VACCINE COMPLICATIONS

The Food and Drug Administration has not approved the use of any antiviral compound for the treatment of vaccinia virus infections or other Orthopoxvirus infections, including smallpox. Certain antiviral compounds have been reported to be active against vaccinia virus or other Orthopoxviruses in vitro and among test animals. However, the safety and effectiveness of these compounds for treating vaccinia vaccination complications or other Orthopoxvirus infections among humans is unknown. Questions also remain regarding the effective dose and the timing and length of administration of these antiviral compounds. Insufficient information exists on which to base recommendations for any antiviral compound to treat postvaccination complications or Orthopoxvirus infections, including smallpox. However, additional information could become available, and healthcare providers should consult Centers for Disease Control and Prevention to obtain updated information regarding treatment options for smallpox vaccination complications (see the section titled "Consultation Regarding Complications of Vaccinia Vaccine").

## CONSULTATION REGARDING
## COMPLICATIONS OF VACCINIA VACCINE

Centers for Disease Control and Prevention can assist physicians in the diagnosis and management of patients with suspected complications of vaccinia vaccination. Vaccinia immunoglobulin is available when indicated. Physicians should telephone Centers for Disease Control and Prevention at (404) 639-3670 during Mondays–Fridays, except holidays, or (404) 639-3311 during evenings, weekends, and holidays. Healthcare workers are requested to report complications of vaccinia vaccination to the Vaccine Adverse Event Reporting System at (800) 822-7967, or to their state or local health department.

## Preventing Contact Transmission of Vaccinia Virus

Vaccinia virus can be cultured from the site of primary vaccination beginning at the time of development of a papule (i.e., 2–5 days after vaccination) until the scab separates from the skin lesion (i.e., 14–21 days after vaccination). During that time, care must be taken to prevent spread of the virus to another area of the body or to another person by inadvertent contact. Thorough hand-hygiene with soap and water or disinfecting agents should be performed after direct contact with the site or materials that have come into contact with the site to remove virus from the hands and prevent accidental inoculation to other areas of the body. In addition, care should be taken to prevent contact of the site or contaminated materials from the site by unvaccinated persons. The vaccination site can be left uncovered, or it can be loosely covered with a porous bandage (e.g., gauze) until the scab has separated on its own to provide additional barrier protection against inadvertent inoculation. An occlusive bandage should not be routinely used because maceration of the site might occur. Bandages used to cover the vaccination site should be changed frequently (i.e., every 1–2 days) to prevent maceration of the vaccination site secondary to fluid buildup. Hypoallergenic tape should be used for persons who experience tape hypersensitivity. The vaccination site should be kept dry, although normal bathing can continue. No salves or ointments should be placed on the vaccination site. Contaminated bandages and, if possible, the vaccination site scab, after it has fallen off, should be placed in sealed plastic bags before disposal in the trash to further decrease the potential for inadvertent transmission of the live virus contained in the materials. Clothing or other cloth materials that have had contact with the site can be decontaminated with routine laundering in hot water with bleach.

Recently vaccinated healthcare workers should avoid contact with unvaccinated patients, particularly those with immunodeficiencies, until the scab has separated from the skin at the vaccination site. However, if continued contact with unvaccinated patients is unavoidable, healthcare workers can continue to have contact with patients, including those with immunodeficiencies, as long as the vaccination site is well-covered and thorough hand-hygiene is maintained. In this setting, a more occlusive dressing might be required. Semipermeable polyurethane dressings (e.g., Opsite®) are effective barriers to vaccinia and recombinant vaccinia viruses. However, exudates can accumulate beneath the dressing, and care must be taken to prevent viral contamination when the dressing is removed. In addition, accumulation of fluid beneath the dressing can increase the maceration of the vaccination site. Accumulation of exudates can be decreased by first covering the vaccination site with dry gauze, then applying the dressing over the gauze. The dressing should also be changed at least once a day. To date, experience with this type of containment dressing has been limited to research protocols. The most critical measure in preventing inadvertent implantation and contact transmission from vaccinia vaccination is thorough hand-hygiene after changing the bandage or after any other contact with the vaccination site.

## Vaccination Method

The skin over the insertion of the deltoid muscle or the posterior aspect of the arm over the triceps muscle is the preferred site for smallpox vaccination. Alcohol or other chemical agents are not required for skin preparation for vaccination unless the area is grossly contaminated. If alcohol is used, the skin must be allowed to dry thoroughly to prevent inactivation of the vaccine by the alcohol. The multiple-puncture technique uses a presterilized bifurcated needle that is inserted vertically into the vaccine vial, causing a droplet of vaccine to adhere between the prongs of the needle. The droplet contains the recommended dosage of vaccine, and its presence within the prongs of the bifurcated needle should be confirmed visually. Holding the bifurcated needle perpendicular to the skin, 15 punctures are rapidly made with strokes vigorous enough to allow a trace of blood to appear after 15–20 seconds. Any remaining vaccine should be wiped off with dry sterile gauze and the gauze disposed of in a biohazard waste container.

## Evidence of Immunity and Vaccination-Response Interpretation

Appearance of neutralizing antibodies after vaccination with live vaccinia virus indicates an active immune response that includes the development of antibodies to all viral antigens and increased vaccinia-specific cell-mediated immunity. In a person with normal immune function, neutralizing antibodies appear approximately 10 days after primary vaccination and 7 days after revaccination. Clinically, persons are considered fully protected after a successful response is demonstrated at the site of vaccination. The vaccination site should be inspected 6–8 days after vaccination and the response interpreted at that time. Two types of responses have been defined by the World Health Organization (WHO) Expert Committee on Smallpox. The responses include a) major reaction, which indicates that virus replication has taken place and vaccination was successful; or b) equivocal reaction, which indicates a possible consequence of immunity adequate to suppress viral multiplication or allergic reactions to an inactive vaccine without production of immunity.

### MAJOR REACTION

Major (i.e., primary) reaction is defined as a vesicular or pustular lesion or an area of definite palpable induration or congestion surrounding a central lesion that might be a crust or an ulcer. The usual progression of the vaccination site after primary vaccination is as follows:

- The inoculation site becomes reddened and pruritic 3–4 days after vaccination.

- A vesicle surrounded by a red areola then forms, which becomes umbilicated and then pustular by days 7–11 after vaccination.

- The pustule begins to dry; the redness subsides; and the lesion becomes crusted between the second and third week. By the end of approximately the third week, the scab falls off, leaving a permanent scar that at first is pink in color but eventually becomes flesh-colored.

Skin reactions after revaccination might be less pronounced with more rapid progression and healing than those after primary vaccinations. Revaccination is considered successful if a pustular lesion is present or an area of definite induration or congestion surrounding a central lesion (i.e., scab or ulcer) is visible upon examination 6–8 days after revaccination.

## Equivocal Reaction

Equivocal reaction, including accelerated, modified, vaccinoid, immediate, early, or immune reactions, is defined as all responses other than major reactions. If an equivocal reaction is observed, vaccination procedures should be checked and the vaccination repeated by using vaccine from another vial or vaccine lot, if available. Difficulty in determining if the reaction was blunted could be caused by immunity, insufficiently potent vaccine, or vaccination technique failure. If the repeat vaccination by using vaccine from another vial or vaccine lot fails to elicit a major reaction, healthcare providers should consult Centers for Disease Control and Prevention or their state or local health department before attempting another vaccination.

### Misuse of Vaccinia Vaccine

Vaccinia vaccine should not be used therapeutically for any reason. No evidence exists that vaccinia vaccine has any value in treating or preventing recurrent herpes simplex infection, warts, or any disease other than those caused by human Orthopoxviruses. Misuse of vaccinia vaccine to treat herpes infections has been associated with severe complications, including death.

## Vaccinia Vaccine Availability

Centers for Disease Control and Prevention is the only source of vaccinia vaccine and vaccinia immunoglobulin for civilians. Centers for Disease Control and Prevention will provide vaccinia vaccine to protect laboratory and other healthcare personnel whose occupations place them at risk for exposure to vaccinia and other closely related Orthopoxviruses, including vaccinia recombinants. Vaccine should be administered under the supervision of a physician selected by the institution. Vaccine will be shipped to the responsible physician. Requests for vaccine and vaccinia immunoglobulin, including the reason for the request, should be referred to:

Centers for Disease Control and Prevention
Drug Services, National Center for Infectious Diseases
Mailstop D-09
Atlanta, GA 30333
Telephone: (404) 639-3670
Facsimile: (404) 639-3717
www.cdc.gov

## Smallpox Vaccine for Bioterrorism Preparedness

Although use of biological agents is an increasing threat, use of conventional weapons (e.g., explosives) is still considered more likely in terrorism scenarios. Moreover, use of smallpox virus as a biological weapon might be less likely than other biological agents because of its restricted availability; however, its use would have substantial public health consequences. Therefore, in support of current public health bioterrorism preparedness efforts, the Advisory Committee on Immunization Practices has developed the following recommendations if this unlikely event occurs.

## SURVEILLANCE

A suspected case of smallpox is a public health emergency. Smallpox surveillance in the United States includes detecting a suspected case or cases, making a definitive diagnosis with rapid laboratory confirmation at CDC, and preventing further smallpox transmission. A suspected smallpox case should be reported immediately by telephone to state or local health officials and advice obtained regarding isolation and laboratory specimen collection. State or local health officials should notify CDC immediately if a suspected case of smallpox is reported. Because of the problems encountered previously in Europe with healthcare–associated smallpox transmission from imported cases present in a hospital setting, health officials should be diligent regarding use of adequate isolation facilities and precautions (see the section titled

"Infection Control Measures"). Currently, specific therapies with proven treatment effectiveness for clinical smallpox are unavailable. Medical care of more seriously ill smallpox patients would include supportive measures only. If the patient's condition allows, medical and public health authorities should consider isolation and observation outside a hospital setting to prevent healthcare–associated smallpox transmission and overtaxing of medical resources. Clinical consultation and a preliminary laboratory diagnosis can be completed within 8–24 hours. Surveillance activities, including notification procedures and laboratory confirmation of cases, might change if smallpox is confirmed.

## PRERELEASE VACCINATION

The risk for smallpox occurring as a result of a deliberate release by terrorists is considered low, and the population at risk for such an exposure cannot be determined. Therefore, preexposure vaccination is not recommended for any group other than laboratory or medical personnel working with nonhighly attenuated Orthopoxviruses (see the section titled "Routine Nonemergency Vaccine Use").

Recommendations regarding preexposure vaccination should be on the basis of a calculable risk assessment that considers the risk for disease and the benefits and risks regarding vaccination. Because the current risk for exposure is considered low, benefits of vaccination do not outweigh the risk regarding vaccine complications. If the potential for an intentional release of smallpox virus increases later, preexposure vaccination might become indicated for selected groups (e.g., medical and public health personnel or laboratorians) who would have an identified higher risk for exposure because of work-related contact with smallpox patients or infectious materials.

## POSTRELEASE VACCINATION

If an intentional release of smallpox (variola) virus does occur, vaccinia vaccine will be recommended for certain groups. Groups for whom vaccination would be indicated include:

- persons who were exposed to the initial release of the virus

- persons who had face-to-face, household, or close-proximity contact (<6.5 feet or 2 meters) with a confirmed or suspected smallpox patient at any time from the onset of the patient's fever until all scabs have separated

- personnel involved in the direct medical or public health evaluation, care, or transportation of confirmed or suspected smallpox patients

- laboratory personnel involved in the collection or processing of clinical specimens from confirmed or suspected smallpox patients

- other persons who have an increased likelihood of contact with infectious materials from a smallpox patient (e.g., personnel responsible for medical waste disposal, linen disposal or disinfection, and room disinfection in a facility where smallpox patients are present)

Using recently vaccinated personnel (i.e., <3 years) for patient care activities would be the best practice. However, because recommendations for routine smallpox vaccination in the United States were rescinded in 1971 and smallpox vaccination is currently recommended only for specific groups (see the section titled "Routine Nonemergency Vaccine Use"), having recently vaccinated personnel available in the early stages of a smallpox emergency would be unlikely. Smallpox vaccine can prevent or decrease the severity of clinical disease, even when administered 3–4 days after exposure to the smallpox virus. Preferably, healthy persons with no contraindications to vaccination, who can be vaccinated immediately before patient contact or very soon after patient contact (i.e., ≤3 days), should be selected for patient care activities or activities involving potentially infectious materials. Persons who have received a previous vaccination (i.e., childhood vaccination or vaccination >3 years before) against smallpox might demonstrate a more accelerated immune response after revaccination than those receiving a primary vaccination. If possible, these persons should be revaccinated and assigned to patient care activities in the early stages of a smallpox outbreak until additional personnel can be successfully vaccinated.

Personnel involved with direct smallpox patient care activities should observe strict contact and airborne precautions (i.e., gowns, gloves, eye shields, and correctly fitted N-95 masks) for additional protection until postvaccination immunity has been demonstrated (i.e., 6–8 days after vaccination). Shoe covers should be used in addition to standard contact isolation protective clothing to prevent transportation of the virus outside the isolation area. After postvaccination immunity has occurred, contact precautions with shoe covers should still be observed to prevent the spread of infectious agents (see the section titled "Infection Control Measures"). If possible, the number of personnel selected for direct contact with confirmed or suspected smallpox patients or infectious materials should be limited to reduce the number of vaccinations and to prevent unnecessary vaccination complications.

Children who have had a definite risk regarding exposure to smallpox (i.e., face-to-face, household, or close-proximity contact with a smallpox patient) should be vaccinated regardless of age. Pregnant women who have had a definite exposure to smallpox virus (i.e., face-to-face, household, or close-proximity contact with a smallpox patient) and are, therefore, at high risk for contracting the disease, should also be vaccinated. Smallpox infection among pregnant women has been reported to result in a more severe infection than among nonpregnant women. Therefore, the risks to the mother and fetus from experiencing clinical smallpox substantially outweigh any potential risks regarding vaccination. In addition, vaccinia virus has not been documented to be teratogenic, and the incidence of fetal vaccinia is low. When the level of exposure risk is undetermined, the decision to vaccinate should be made after assessment by the clinician and patient of the potential risks versus the benefits of smallpox vaccination.

In a postrelease setting, vaccination might be initiated also for other groups whose unhindered function is deemed essential to the support of response activities (e.g., selected law enforcement, emergency response, or military personnel) and who are not otherwise engaged in patient care activities but who have a reasonable probability of contact with smallpox patients or infectious materials. If vaccination of these groups is initiated by public health authorities, only personnel with no contraindications to vaccination should be vaccinated before initiating activities that could lead to contact with suspected smallpox patients or infectious materials. Steps should be taken (e.g., reassignment of duties) to prevent contact of any unvaccinated personnel with infectious smallpox patients or materials.

Because of increased transmission rates that have been described in previous outbreaks of smallpox involving aerosol transmission in hospital settings, potential vaccination of nondirect hospital contacts should be evaluated by public health officials. Because hospitalized patients might have other contraindications to vaccination (e.g., immunosuppression), vaccination of these nondirect hospital contacts should occur after prudent evaluation of the hospital setting with determination of the exposure potential through the less-common aerosol transmission route.

## INFECTION CONTROL MEASURES

Isolation of confirmed or suspected smallpox patients will be necessary to limit the potential exposure of nonvaccinated and, therefore, nonimmune persons. Although droplet spread is the major mode of person-to-person smallpox transmission, airborne transmission through fine-particle aerosol can occur. Therefore, airborne precautions using correct ventilation (e.g., negative air-pressure rooms with high-efficiency particulate air filtration) should be initiated for hospitalized confirmed or suspected smallpox patients, unless the entire facility has been restricted to smallpox patients and recently vaccinated persons. Although personnel who have been vaccinated recently and who have a demonstrated immune response should be fully protected against infection with variola virus (see the section titled "Evidence of Immunity and Vaccination-Response Interpretation"), they should continue to observe standard and contact precautions (i.e., using protective clothing and shoe covers) when in contact with smallpox patients or contaminated materials to prevent inadvertent spread of variola virus to susceptible persons and potential self-contact with other infectious agents. Personnel should remove and correctly dispose of all protective clothing before contact with nonvaccinated persons. Reusable bedding and clothing can be autoclaved or laundered in hot water with bleach to inactivate the virus. Laundry handlers should be vaccinated before handling contaminated materials.

Nonhospital isolation of confirmed or suspected smallpox patients should be of a sufficient degree to prevent the spread of disease to nonimmune persons during the time the patient is considered potentially infectious (i.e., from the onset of symptoms until all scabs have separated). Private residences or other nonhospital facilities that are used to isolate confirmed or suspected smallpox patients should have nonshared ventilation, heating, and air-conditioning systems. Access to those facilities should be limited to recently vaccinated persons with a demonstrated immune response. If suspected smallpox patients are placed in the same isolation facility, they should be vaccinated to guard against accidental exposure caused by misclassification as someone with smallpox.

In addition to isolation of infectious smallpox patients, careful surveillance of contacts during their potential incubation period is required. Transmission of smallpox virus rarely occurs before the appearance of the rash that develops 2–4 days after the prodromal fever. If a vaccinated or unvaccinated contact experiences a fever >101 degrees F (38 degrees C) during the 17-day period after his or her last exposure to a smallpox patient, the contact should be isolated immediately to prevent contact with nonvaccinated or nonimmune persons until smallpox can be ruled out by clinical or laboratory examination.

# Vaccinia Immunoglobulin for Prophylaxis and Treatment of Adverse Reactions during a Smallpox Emergency

If vaccination of persons with contraindications is required because of exposure to smallpox virus after an intentional release as a bioterrorism agent, current stores of vaccinia immunoglobulin are insufficient to allow its prophylactic use with vaccination. Because of the limited stores of vaccinia immunoglobulin, its use in such a scenario should be reserved for severe, life-threatening complications (e.g., progressive vaccinia, eczema vaccinatum, or severe, toxic generalized vaccinia). If additional vaccinia immunoglobulin becomes available in sufficient quantities to allow its prophylactic use, vaccinia immunoglobulin should be administered intramuscularly as a dose of 0.3 mg/kg along with vaccinia vaccine to persons with contraindications who require vaccination.

## CLINICAL ALGORITHM(S):
None provided

## DEVELOPER(S):
Centers for Disease Control and Prevention (CDC)—Federal Government Agency [U.S.]

## COMMITTEE:
Advisory Committee on Immunization Practices

## GROUP COMPOSITION:
*Names of Committee Members*: John F. Modlin, M.D. (Chairman); Dixie E. Snider, Jr., M.D., M.P.H. (Executive Secretary); Dennis A. Brooks, M.D., M.P.H.; Richard D. Clover, M.D.; Jaime Deseda-Tous, M.D.; Charles M. Helms, M.D., Ph.D.; David R. Johnson, M.D., M.P.H.; Myron J. Levin, M.D.; Paul A. Offit, M.D.; Margaret B. Rennels, M.D.; Natalie J. Smith, M.D., M.P.H.; Lucy S. Tompkins, M.D., Ph.D.; Bonnie M. Word, M.D.

## ENDORSER(S):
Not stated

## GUIDELINE STATUS:
This is the current release of the guideline. It updates the previous Advisory Committee on Immunization Practices (ACIP) recommendations (MMWR 1991; 40; No. RR-14:1-10).

An update is not in progress at this time.

## GUIDELINE AVAILABILITY:
Electronic copies: Available from the Centers for Disease Control and Prevention (CDC) Web site in HTML format.

The document is also available in <u>Portable Document Format (PDF)</u>.

Print copies: Available from the Centers for Disease and Control Prevention, MMWR, Atlanta, GA 30333. Additional copies can be purchased from the Superintendent of Documents, U.S. Government Printing Office, Washington, DC 20402-9325; (202) 783-3238.

## COMPANION DOCUMENTS:
None available

## PATIENT RESOURCES:
None available

## NGC STATUS:
This summary was completed by ECRI on August 27, 2001.

## COPYRIGHT STATEMENT:
No copyright restrictions apply.

# NEWS, COMMUNICATIONS, AND INTERNET RESEARCH

## 7.1 NEWS SOURCES AND BULLETINS

**ANSER Institute for Homeland Security Bulletin**
Produced weekly by the ANSER Institute, this newsletter provides information on recent national security issues and activities. Current news, upcoming events, and daily news stories are all made available from this source. Hotlinks are available to related press releases, statements, and hearings. Visitors may also choose to receive this weekly bulletin via e-mail.
http://www.homelandsecurity.org/bulletin/current_bulletin.htm

**Biological and Chemical Weapons from MEDLINEplus Health Information** Visitors to this site will be able to access the latest news and information on biological and chemical weapons. Contents include general information, updates on current research, and resources for coping, prevention and screening, and treatment. Specific conditions and aspects are also covered.
http://www.nlm.nih.gov/
medlineplus/biologicalandchemicalweapons.html

**Bioterrorism and Bioweapons Special Report from NewScientist.com** Up-to-the-minute science-related news is the focus of this media-oriented Web site. In a special section on bioterrorism and bioweapons, users may find recent articles and information related to the topic. All articles are drawn from *New Scientist* magazine.
http://www.newscientist.com/hottopics/bioterrorism/

**Bioterrorism Articles from the Journal of the American Medical Association** Maintained by the *Journal of the American Medical Association (JAMA)*, this site provides full-text articles on all diseases relevant to the bioterrorism threat. Anthrax, smallpox, plague,

and brucella are just a few among the list of diseases covered. All articles are drawn from recent issues of *JAMA*.
http://pubs.ama-assn.org/bioterr.html

**Bioterrorism as a Public Health Threat from Emerging Infectious Diseases**  In a special issue of *Emerging Infectious Diseases* devoted to exploring various perspectives on the threat of bioterrorism, this 1998 article by Dr. Donald Henderson discusses the public health impact of biological warfare. The paper reviews past outbreaks of smallpox and anthrax and considers the implications for healthcare facilities and the population at large.
http://www.cdc.gov/ncidod/EID/vol4no3/hendrsn.htm

**Bioterrorism Information from Medscape Resource Center**  Designed to provide consumers and professionals with timely clinical information, Medscape Resource Center's bioterrorism section is a comprehensive resource for the latest news, information, and findings related to bioterrorism. Coverage includes news, print articles, conference summaries, commentaries, and important information regarding diseases that could potentially be spread by bioterrorist actions.
http://www.medscape.com/Medscape/features/
ResourceCenter/BioTerr/public/RC-index-BioTerr.html

**Bioterrorism News from the Association for Professionals in Infection Control and Epidemiology**  The Association for Professionals in Infection Control and Epidemiology makes available recent news coverage of bioterrorism events. Articles are drawn from such sources as the CDC and major media publications. Topics covered include news and information on anthrax and safe handling of mail and packages.
http://www.apic.org/bioterror/news/

**CDC Updates from Public Health Emergency Preparedness and Response**  Public Health Emergency Preparedness and Response is devoted to providing detailed information about CDC and state activities. This document provides information about ongoing CDC activities and investigation into anthrax cases across the United States.
http://www.bt.cdc.gov/DocumentsApp/
Anthrax/10162001PM/Update10162001PM.asp

*Don't type in long URLs*—use eMedguides site number (www.eMedguides.com/**2T-1234**).

**Chemical and Biological Defense Information Analysis Center Newsletter** Published quarterly, the Chemical and Biological Defense Information Analysis Center (CBIAC) newsletter contains information on chemical and biological agents, preparedness, prevention, awareness, and current news. Past issues of the news dating back to 1995 are available in the site archives. Adobe Acrobat is required to view these documents.
http://www.cbiac.apgea.army.mil/
awareness/newsletter/intro.html

**Counter-Terrorism Operations News and Archive from Emergency.com** The "Counter-Terrorism Archive," sponsored by the Emergency Response and Research Institute (ERRI), is a summary of global terrorist activities, known terrorist groups, and terrorist tactics and strategies. Information on this site dates back to 1989 and continues through the present. Chronicles of terrorist events are available by geographic location or time period. Additionally, users may access recent updates and news resources from ERRI.
http://www.emergency.com/cntrterr.htm

**Dispatch, Chemical and Biological Arms Control Institute Newsletter** Published bimonthly, the *Dispatch* is faxed to policymakers, legislators, military personnel, academics, and journalists. This newsletter chronicles recent developments in chemical and biological weapons and arms control. Back issues of the *Dispatch* are available in the site archives dating back to March of 1999. The *Dispatch* is published on the first and fifteenth of every month. Visitors may request to be added to the mailing list.
http://www.cbaci.org/dispatch.htm

**Emergency Information Infrastructure Partnership Newsletter** The Emergency Information Infrastructure Partnership (EIIP), publishes its monthly newsletter online, providing updates, announcements, partnership information, and articles on events in emergency management and disaster response. Visitors may also sign up to receive the newsletter and notices of EIIP events by e-mail.
http://www.emforum.org/eiip/news.htm

**Emergency Management Assistance Compact** The Emergency Management Association Compact (EMAC) is a mutual aid agreement allowing states to as-

sist one another in responding to all forms of disaster, both natural and human-induced. This site is a comprehensive resource for news and information on the compact. News updates include information on recent additions of new member states, state assistance in response to the September 11 terrorist attacks, and situation reports. Many areas of the site are password-protected but a discussion forum is available to all visitors.
http://www.nemaweb.org/emac/index.cfm

### Environmental Health News, Association of State and Territorial Health Officials Newsletter

*Environmental Health News*, published by the Association of State and Territorial Health Officials (ASTHO), covers topics ranging from air and water quality to children's health and food safety. Although publication has recently been suspended as the newsletter is being redesigned, archived issues from 2000-2001 are still available in PDF format. Updates are gathered from government agencies, including the Environmental Protection Agency and the Centers for Disease Control and Prevention. A calendar of ASTHO events is also included.
http://www.astho.org/environmental/newsletters.html

### Federal Emergency Management Agency News Releases

The Federal Emergency Management Agency (FEMA) Newsroom catalogs full-text versions of recent news releases related to emergency and disaster management. Updates are indexed by month of release and date from early 2000 to the present. Topics covered include terrorist attacks and severe weather conditions. The site also lists weather warnings, flood summaries, and U.S. forecast maps.
http://www.fema.gov/fema/news.htm

### Hazardous Substances and Public Health Newsletter from the Agency for Toxic Substances and Disease Registry

The Agency for Toxic Substances and Disease Registry (ATSDR) produces its quarterly newsletter, *Hazardous Substances and Public Health*, as a public resource designed to increase awareness of environmental safety hazards. Each issue of the newsletter is devoted to an in-depth exploration of a single topic. For example, the summer 2001 edition features detailed information on polychlorinated biphenyls (PCBs) including a toxicological profile, case studies, fish advisories, health effects, and children and PCBs. In addition, read-

ers will find information on educational courses relating to ATSDR concerns, online resources, discussion groups, and a virtual library. The archive contains contents dating back to first publication in the winter of 1995.
http://www.atsdr.cdc.gov/HEC/hsphhome.html

**Hazardous Technical Information Services Bulletin** With contributing staff members from such fields as chemistry, industrial hygiene, chemical engineering, and environmental science, the bimonthly *Hazardous Technical Information Services (HTIS) Bulletin* serves the defense community by promoting the proper management of hazardous materials and wastes. Each issue contains a section devoted to online resources, HTIS updates, and a calendar of events. Featured articles are offered on topics relating to hazardous materials, from commentary on Environmental Protection Agency policy to Department of Transit regulations on chemical transport.
http://www.dscr.dla.mil/htis/

**Impact, Newsletter for Employees of the Federal Emergency Management Agency** Produced by the Federal Emergency Management Agency (FEMA), the *Impact* newsletter addresses the specific concerns of FEMA employees relating to disaster management, relief, and preparedness efforts. Features in *Impact* include FEMA news briefs, dangerous-weather predictions, and updates on FEMA activity. Although intended specifically for FEMA employees, this document contains information for those interested in the agency and its efforts. Archived documents date back to 1998 and require Adobe Acrobat for viewing.
http://www.fema.gov/about/hqnltr/

**Interoperations Newsletter from Consequence Management Interoperability Services** Published by Consequence Management Interoperability (CMI) Services, *Interoperations* is a monthly newsletter reporting on the development of CMI-Services to meet presidential decision directives on countering terrorism and offering military support for domestic preparedness efforts. The newsletter provides updates on recent developments and upcoming events.
http://www.cmi-services.org/Documents/CMIS_Newsltr_Oct01.htm

**Medical NBC Online Information Server** Designed primarily for army medical personnel and health-

care practitioners, Medical Nuclear, Biological and Chemical (NBC) aims to coordinate national medical initiatives and to distribute relevant information to the appropriate recipients. This Web site provides news coverage, updates of progress on bioterrorism research, and a wealth of important scientific information.
http://www.nbc-med.org/ie40/Default.html

**News Articles from the Center for the Study of Bioterrorism and Emerging Infections**   A component of the St. Louis University School of Public Health, the Center for the Study of Bioterrorism and Emerging Infections posts headlines and links to articles on events related to all aspects of bioterrorism and disease.
http://www.slu.edu/colleges/sph/bioterrorism/news.htm

**News by Health Topic from MEDLINEplus**   A service of the National Library of Medicine, MEDLINEplus compiles press articles on health-related issues from the previous 30 days. Articles are sorted alphabetically by subject matter.
http://www.nlm.nih.gov/medlineplus/alphanews.html

**Office for Domestic Preparedness and Support Bulletins**   Bulletins from the Office of Domestic Preparedness (ODP) are not published on a regular basis but are created as the need arises and are delivered to the heads of all state agencies. ODP bulletins contain updates on government procedure, changes in ODP activities, legislation, and policy; any major ODP issues or concerns are publicized via the bulletin. Visitors may read all bulletins dating back to February of 2000.
http://www.ojp.usdoj.gov/odp/docs/bulletins.htm

**Public Health Messages from ACP-ASIM Bioterrorism Resource Center**   Jointly sponsored by the American College of Physicians and the American Society of Internal Medicine, ACP-ASIM Online provides information, news, safety guidelines, medical aspects, and commentary regarding bioterrorism activities.
http://www.acponline.org/bioterro/florida_anthrax.htm

**Testimony, Speeches, and Public Information**   Presented by the U.S. Department of Health and Human Services, this Web site provides online resources addressing anthrax and biological incidents, preparedness, and response activities. Resources devoted to anthrax include clinical information, potential for bioterrorism, and precautionary measures. Similar information is available for smallpox. In addition, an index of current news, media coverage, and important government updates is provided. The most extensive section of the site is devoted to testimony and speeches related to terrorism preparedness and response. This section provides transcripts of speeches from sources including the CDC and the Food and Drug Administration on topics ranging from bioterrorism response and decontamination of federal buildings to smallpox vaccination and increased homeland security. Transcripts are indexed in chronological order dating back to early October 2001.

http://www.os.dhhs.gov/hottopics/healing/biological.html

**The Beacon: Newsletter from the National Domestic Preparedness Office** The National Domestic Preparedness Office (NDPO) seeks to coordinate federal efforts in assisting state and local emergency personnel with all phases of response to a weapon of mass destruction incident. *The Beacon*, the monthly newsletter of the NDPO, is authored entirely by emergency professionals. Recent editions address the topic of a potential national bioterrorism disaster.

http://www.ndpo.gov/beacon.htm

**U.S. Army Center for Health Promotion and Preventative Medicine News and Publications** This extensive index, maintained by the U.S. Army Center for Health Promotion and Preventative Medicine (CHPPM), archives recent and back issues of several CHPPM publications. Under the news section, readers will find links to issues of *CHPPM Today*, a quarterly news publication, *The Sentinel,* and other CHPPM news bulletins. The publications section, located directly below the news archive, includes a fact sheet library, a listing of technical medical bulletins, technical guides, and other medical planning synopsis documents. Users will find information on a wide variety of topics ranging from control of infectious diseases to developing medical directives for occupational health.

http://chppm-www.apgea.army.mil/news.asp

**U.S. Medicine** Founded in 1964 and headquartered in Washington, D.C., *U.S. Medicine* is both an organization and a news resource. News articles and columns authored by *U.S. Medicine* staff and outside contributors are compiled and published on a monthly basis. The newspaper publishes articles on topics such as vaccine

safety, government-sponsored medic training, homeland defense, military mental health, and posttraumatic stress disorder. Previous issues dating back to January of 2000 are available in the site archives. The site also provides information on anthrax drawn from the CDC and news highlights of antiterrorist activities.
http://www.usmedicine.com/

## Weapons of Mass Destruction from Infowar.com

Infowar.com is a comprehensive resource for materials relating to weapons of mass destruction, including chemical, biological, and nuclear warfare. Site contents are drawn mainly from outside sources such as the CDC, the Senate Committee on Governmental Affairs, the Center for Nonproliferation Studies, and major media sources. This site contains direct links to each article of interest.
http://www.infowar.com/wmd/wmd.shtml

## 7.2 CONFERENCES AND SYMPOSIA

## Conference Calendar from the Oklahoma City National Memorial Institute for the Prevention of Terrorism
Information on upcoming terrorism-related conferences is made available through the Oklahoma City National Memorial Institute for the Prevention of Terrorism Web site. Conference details are accompanied by a brief description of the theme and scheduled events as well as information about the sponsoring organization. Links are also available to conference home pages.
http://www.mipt.org/eventscalendar.asp

## International Society of Exposure Analysis Conference 2001: Exposure Analysis: An Integral Part of Disease Prevention
For those interested in the medical science of exposure analysis, the International Society for Exposure Analysis (ISEA) meets for its annual conference in November 2001. Information regarding scheduling and programming as well as background information on the ISEA is accessible via this site.
http://www2.edserv.musc.edu/isea/isea.htm

## National Disaster Medical System
A cooperative effort between all levels of government and divisions of the private sector, the National Disaster Medical System (NDMS) is an asset-sharing program established to pro-

vide necessary medical services in the wake of local disaster. Site contents include the NDMS conference and counterterrorism programs as well as resource links. Access to some of the resources is restricted to members of NDMS response teams.

http://ndms.dhhs.gov/NDMS/ndms.html

### National Disaster Medical System Conference

Sponsored by the Office of Emergency Preparedness, the National Defense Management System Conference is designed to promote interaction between healthcare practitioners and policymakers. Although the theme of each conference differs from year to year, the aim is toward education, awareness, more effective response, prevention, and cooperation. Information is available on submissions and registration for the 2002 conference in Atlanta, Georgia. Visitors may also view programs and multimedia copies of presentations from previous conferences. Topics covered include bioterrorism, preparedness, and vulnerability assessments.

http://192.73.61.152/oepndms/NDMS%20
Conference/2002_Conference/2002_conference.html

### National Environmental Health Association 2002 Chemical and Bioterrorism Preparedness Conference

Founded in 1937 for environmental health practitioners, the National Environmental Health Association sponsors a variety of programs promoting a healthy global environment. The 2002 conference focuses on the topic of chemical and bioterrorism preparedness. It is this year's goal to teach attendees valuable skills for preparing for, coping with, and countering bioterrorist activities. Information about the conference and a registration form are available in PDF format from this Web site.

http://www.neha.org/
pdf%20files/1%20Page%20-%20Bio%202002.pdf

### National Symposium on Bioterrorism

Presented as a joint effort between university, federal, and medical association sponsorship, the 1999 National Symposium on Medical and Public Health Response to Bioterrorism brought together experts from a variety of diverse fields. The goal of this gathering was to understand the threat and address the questions associated with biological warfare. Visitors to this site are able to view webcasts of all of the conference proceedings.

http://www.hopkins-id.edu/bioterror/agenda.html

---

## Preventing Biological Warfare: Strengthening the Biological and Toxin Weapons Convention

Centered in Washington, D.C., the Brookings Institution is a research organization that makes available its scholarly analysis and findings regarding public policy. Research is conducted in the fields of economics, government, foreign policy, and policy centers. The institute publishes books and journals and also maintains video clips, policy briefs, and news releases. The institution has also undertaken a special project, "America's Response to Terrorism," with its own archive of analytical articles, working papers, policy briefs, and commentary. This section of the site also features Internet chats and an e-mail newsletter. http://www.brad.ac.uk/acad/sbtwc/

## Second National Symposium on Medical and Public Health Response to Bioterrorism

Organized by the Johns Hopkins Center for Civilian Biodefense Strategies, this conference took place at the end of November 2001. Intended as an educational forum, the conference was designed to increase the understanding of a bioterrorist threat among national policy, medical, and public health leaders. Users may access written transcripts of all conference proceedings as well as multimedia presentations of conference speakers. The entire conference agenda can also be downloaded and listened to in audio format or browsed via the written transcripts. Topics covered include bioterrorism preparedness, reducing the threat, detecting epidemics, treating sickness, challenges to public health agencies, and containing epidemics. Over 30 presentations, discussions, and speaker panels from this conference are accessible via this site. http://www.hopkins-biodefense.org/sympcast/info.html

## Threat-Related Conferences, Symposia, Workshops, and Seminars from the Defense Threat Reduction Agency

The Defense Threat Reduction Agency provides this listing of upcoming conferences, symposia, and seminars dealing with reducing threats to national safety. All relevant information on future events is available including contact information for event sponsors. http://www.dtra.mil/news/conference/nw_other.html

## 7.3 LITERATURE SEARCHES
## AND ONLINE LIBRARIES

**Article Searches on MEDLINE from Entrez-PubMed** Entrez-PubMed is designed to integrate all information collected by various divisions of the National Center for Biotechnology Information (NCBI). Users can search all NCBI databases for any topic via the Entrez-PubMed search tool. The search engine will retrieve any articles relevant to a given search.
http://www.ncbi.nlm.nih.gov/entrez/query.fcgi

**Medical/Health Sciences Libraries on the Web** Created by the Hardin Library for Health Sciences at the University of Iowa, this site indexes medical and health sciences libraries with online access. The listings are categorized geographically. A link to free electronic journals is also available.
http://www.lib.uiowa.edu/hardin-www/hslibs.html

**National Agricultural Library** This Web site provides a portal to the National Agricultural Library (NAL), a division of the U.S. Department of Agriculture. NAL houses an extensive collection of agricultural information resources and supports research, education, and applied agriculture. Features of the site include AGRICOLA, a bibliographic database of the agricultural literature, and AgNIC, a guide to quality agricultural information on the Internet. The library also sponsors information services and programs and posts a calendar of agricultural conferences.
http://www.nal.usda.gov/

**U.S. National Library of Medicine** Links to all major health-related search engines are accessible on this National Library of Medicine Web site. Visitors will also find a section devoted to information categorized by subject covering such topics as chemical substances, public health, and toxicology.
http://www.nlm.nih.gov/

## 7.4 TOPICAL SEARCH TOOLS

**Centers for Disease Control and Prevention Web Search** By utilizing the Web search guidelines provided on this site, users may perform a variety of broad or nar-

row searches of all CDC documents and the CDC home page for any topic of interest.
http://www.cdc.gov/search.htm

**Google Master Internet Search Tool** The Google search engine provides access to over one and a half billion Web pages. This tool allows visitors to search multiple Internet domains for words or phrases. In addition, Google offers an image directory and a section organized by topic into categories including health and science.
http://www.google.com/

**Journals of the American Medical Association Search** The American Medical Association (AMA) archives all past issues of its journals and provides online access to tables of contents and article abstracts. Full-text articles are available online with subscription. Over 15 AMA publications may be searched using the tool provided on this page.
http://pubsearch.ama-assn.org/search?action=FormGen&Template=search.hts

**Medem Medical Search Database** Medem offers an extensive library of healthcare information provided by the nation's leading medical societies. All content is indexed by category and can be easily searched. Other features of interest on this site include a secure communications network for physician practices, a physician locator tool, and news updates.
http://www.medem.com/

**MEDLINEplus Health Information Database** A broad range of health information is available at MEDLINEplus as a service of the National Library of Medicine. Among its numerous resources, this database catalogs health topics, offers access to drug information, and provides a dictionary of medical terminology.
http://www.medlineplus.gov

**National Library of Medicine Health Information** Links to all major health-related search engines are accessible on this National Library of Medicine Web site. Visitors will also find a section devoted to information categorized by subject covering such topics as chemical substances, public health, and toxicology.
http://www.nlm.nih.gov/hinfo.html

# GENERAL RESOURCE SITES

## 8.1 BIOTERRORISM

**ACP-ASIM Bioterrorism Resources** Co-sponsored by the American College of Physicians and the American Society of Internal Medicine, this Web site provides a broad spectrum of bioterrorism information resources. Sections of the ACP-ASIM Web site are devoted to therapeutic recommendations, medical and psychological resources as they pertain to the bioterrorism threat, and news coverage of recent events.
http://www.acponline.org/bioterro/?idx

**Anthrax and Other Bioterrorism Information from Healthfinder** This portion of the Healthfinder library is devoted to anthrax and related bioterrorism information. Answers to frequently asked questions, recent news articles, fact sheets on diseases and therapeutics, public health advisories, and safety guidelines have all been made available. The site also provides links to government agencies, and some resources are available in Spanish.
http://www.healthfinder.gov/anthrax_bioterrorism.htm

**Ataxia, the Chemical and Biological Terrorism Threat and the U.S. Response** *Ataxia,* part of the Chemical and Biological Weapons Nonproliferation Project at the Stimson Center, is a comprehensive research report exploring the historical and present threat, vulnerability, preparedness, and future recommendations for antiterrorism actions. This extensive multichaptered work covers all aspects of terrorism and counterterrorism, from the first chapter entitled "Grounding the Threat in Reality" to the final "Pitfalls in Front-Line Readiness." *Ataxia* is designed as a detailed analysis of the threat facing the United States and major shortcomings in the fight to counter terrorism. Information in this

document has been gathered from hundreds of interviews with government officials and outside experts, emergency response personnel from more than 30 cities, and approximately 400 printed resources.
http://www.stimson.org/?SN=CB20020111235

**Biological Agent Information Papers from the U.S. Army Institute of Infectious Diseases** Sponsored by the U.S. Army Institute of Infectious Diseases, the Biological Agent Information Papers cover 12 different diseases of bioterrorist interest including anthrax, botulism, cholera, plague, and Q fever. Each paper contains a variety of information presented in a concise format. Topics addressed include a description of agent, signs and symptoms, diagnosis, treatment, prophylaxis, decontamination and isolation, and outbreak control. The information presented in these documents is of a clinical and technical nature designed for use by healthcare providers.
http://www.nbc-med.org/SiteContent/
MedRef/OnlineRef/GovDocs/BioAgents.html

**Biological Warfare and Its Cutaneous Manifestations** Prepared by a team of medical and military experts, this extensive document attempts to dispel some of the mystery surrounding bioterrorist activities by examining the history and origins of biological weapons and reviewing agents that may be used in biological attacks. In addition to providing historical resources, the article also supplies a wealth of scientific and clinical information regarding the causes, clinical symptoms, treatments, and threat of specific diseases including plague, smallpox, and anthrax. This site also provides color photographs that illustrate disease symptoms.
http://telemedicine.org/BioWar/biologic.htm

**Bioterrorism Bibliographies and Resources** The Medical Library Association is an organization dedicated to health sciences research, education, and patient care. This compilation of Web resources was created in response to the events of September 11, 2001, and includes dozens of links to online resources for healthcare providers, parents, children, and adolescents. Print resources and survivor listings are also available.
http://www.mlanet.org/resources/caring/resources.html

**Bioterrorism Information from Senator Bill Frist** Hosted by the office of U.S. Senator Bill Frist, M.D., this site provides information and links relevant to the recent bioterrorism threat. The site is designed as a portal to important bioterrorism-related resources, posting fact sheets on biological agents and links to government sites and other organizations, as well as news and Senate committee statements. Visitors may also submit questions about bioterrorism to an expert panel; answers are posted on the site.

http://www.senate.gov/~frist/Issues/Issues-National_
Defense/FightingTerrorism/Bioterrorism/bioterrorism.html

## Bioterrorism Information from the National Animal Health Emergency Management System

The National Animal Health Emergency Management System (NAHEMS) was founded to deal with animal health emergencies ranging from natural disasters to the introduction of foreign diseases. As part of its ongoing efforts, NAHEMS is exploring bioterrorism and its potential impact on U.S. livestock. This Web page outlines NAHEMS activities in terms of prevention, preparedness, response, and recovery.

http://www.usaha.org/NAHEMS/bioterr.html

## Consumer Information on Bioterrorism from the National Science Foundation International

The National Science Foundation (NSF) International is an independent, not-for-profit scientific organization dedicated to high standards of public health and safety. The NSF Web site provides links to general and clinical information on bioterrorism and prevention, foodborne pathogens, and specific infectious diseases. Information on this site is drawn from outside sources such as the CDC and Johns Hopkins University.

http://www.nsf.org/consumer/consumer_biolinks.html#general

## Countering Bioterrorism Frequently Asked Questions from the Center for Biologics Evaluation and Research

The Center for Biologics Evaluation and Research, a division of the U.S. Food and Drug Administration, aims to protect and enhance public health by regulating biological products including blood, drugs, and medical devices. This page provides answers to frequently asked questions about the center's measures to counter bioterrorism.

http://www.fda.gov/cber/faq/cntrbfaq.htm

## Educational Module on Chemical and Biological Weapons Nonproliferation

The Educational Module on Chemical and Biological Weapons (CBW), created with the cooperation of three European institutions, is available to anyone, at no cost, and is designed to increase the user's knowledge and understanding of CBW nonproliferation. This interactive and guided Web site is divided into chapters that provide extensive coverage of the topics of armament, nonproliferation, and disarmament, in addition to two case studies. Links to glossary definitions and images are available throughout the text. http://cbw.sipri.se/

**Epidemiology of Bioterrorism from Emerging Infectious Diseases** Taken from the CDC publication *Emerging Infectious Diseases* this article explores the science behind disease outbreaks. The article details the proper methods for identifying and dealing with threatening outbreaks and makes recommendations for preparedness. http://www.cdc.gov/ncidod/EID/vol5no4/pavlin.htm

**Information Links from the U.S. Army Medical Research Institute of Chemical Defense** The U.S. Army Medical Research Institute of Chemical Defense (USAMRICD) works to create novel methods of countering chemical warfare agents and to school medical personnel in the proper methods of dealing with chemical exposure. The USAMRICD Web site provides dozens of links to information relating to all aspects of chemical and biological warfare. http://chemdef.apgea.army.mil/related/links.asp

**Medical Aspects of Chemical and Biological Warfare** Published by the Office of the Surgeon General in cooperation with medical experts from across the nation, this document contains nearly 700 pages of clinical information on biological and chemical warfare. The report explores the history and threat of chemical and biological warfare, the clinical symptoms of exposure, and proper methods for dealing with all known chemical and biological warfare agents. Biological agents covered range from anthrax to viral hemorrhagic fevers. Adobe Acrobat is necessary to view the documents. http://www.nbc-med.org/SiteContent/ HomePage/WhatsNew/MedAspects/contents.html

**Medical Aspects of Chemical and Biological Warfare from the Textbook of Military Medicine** This comprehensive resource from the U.S. Army Medical Research Institute of Chemical Defense covers all medical aspects of exposure to chemical and biological

agents. In addition to providing extensive information on the history, threat, and effects of chemical weapons, the textbook addresses numerous diseases that pose a threat as potential biological weapons.

http://chemdef.apgea.army.mil/textbook/contents.asp

### Medical Management of Biological Casualties Handbook from the U.S. Army Medical Research Institute of Infectious Diseases
From the U.S. Army Medical Research Institute of Infectious Diseases (USAMRIID), this document was created with the intention of educating medical professionals about available and effective countermeasures to bacteria, toxins, and viral agents that may be used in acts of bioterrorism and biological warfare. Hundreds of pages of facts, technical data, management techniques, and clinical guidelines relating to the most dangerous biological agents are provided, with chapters covering biological warfare agent characteristics, vaccines and therapeutics, sampling techniques and testing, differential diagnosis, comparative lethality between chemical and biological agents, and aerosol toxicity. Readers will find information on topics ranging from specific symptoms of diseases, such as inhalation anthrax, smallpox, and brucellosis, to clinical guidelines for patient isolation, testing, and notification procedures.

http://www.usamriid.army.mil/education/bluebook.html

### NATO Handbook on the Medical Aspects of NBC Defensive Operations: Biological
This second chapter of the NATO handbook focuses on the medical aspects of biological warfare and potential bioterrorist agents. Among the many sections of this chapter, readers will find an in-depth historical examination of the threat of biowarfare, information on recognizing and responding to biological warfare activities, defense strategies, and management techniques. Other sections cover a huge diversity of topics, with information on subjects ranging from environmental sampling to determine the presence of hostile organisms to treatment and immunoprophylaxis techniques. At the end of the chapter, appendices provide additional information on such topics as potential biological agents and patient management.

http://www.fas.org/nuke/
guide/usa/doctrine/dod/fm8-9/2toc.htm

## 8.2 CHEMICAL WARFARE

**Chemical Agent Terrorism** Written by Frederick R. Sidell, M.D., this article addresses the use of chemical warfare agents during terrorist attacks. The author provides concise descriptions of different classes of chemical warfare agents including nerve agents, vesicants, cyanide, pulmonary agents, and incapacitants. Information provided covers a chemical and physical description of the agent, symptoms of exposure, health effects, and potential treatments/antidotes. The final section of this work addresses medical response activities and the need for increased surveillance and intelligence, preparedness, and rapid response capabilities.
http://www.nbc-med.org/SiteContent/
MedRef/OnlineRef/Other/chagter.html

**Chemical and Biological Weapons Site from the Center for Defense Information** The Center for Defense Information (CDI) is a national independent military research organization. The Web site for their division of Chemical and Biological Weapons (CBW) allows visitors access to CBW fact sheets, links to CDI resources, recent articles regarding CBW, and information on both the chemical and biological weapons conventions. CDI is a comprehensive resource for those seeking information on chemical and biological weapons.
http://www.cdi.org/issues/cbw/

**Chemical Warfare Agents from the National Library of Medicine Specialized Information Services** A division of the National Library of Medicine, Specialized Information Services is devoted to cataloging the history and effects of known chemical warfare agents. Chemical agents are divided into categories based on their effects on the human body. Additional resources and links to selected references on chemical warfare agents are provided.
http://sis.nlm.nih.gov/Tox/ChemWar.html

**Chemical Warfare Agents: An Overview of Chemicals Defined as Chemical Weapons** This page from the Organisation for the Prohibition of Chemical Weapons (OPCW) Web site contains information on a variety of chemical substances. Chemical agents are divided into eight main categories based on their known toxic effects. Headings such as nerve agents,

mustard agents, hydrogen cyanide, tear gases, arsines, psychotomimetic agents, toxins, and potential chemical weapons agents provide links to informational articles.
http://www.opcw.nl/chemhaz/cwagents.htm

### NATO Handbook on the Medical Aspects of NBC Defensive Operations: Chemical
This portion of the NATO handbook is devoted to examining the medical aspects of chemical warfare agents. The document is both extensive and comprehensive, providing detailed information on the origins, specific medical effects, and known treatments for exposure to all categories of chemical agents. The range of topics covered by this report includes nerve agents, vesicants, choking agents, cyanogen (blood) agents, incapacitants, and riot control substances.
http://www.fas.org/nuke/
guide/usa/doctrine/dod/fm8-9/3toc.htm

## 8.3  WEAPONS OF MASS DESTRUCTION

### Bombsecurity.com
Bombsecurity.com provides a central resource for information on explosives-related issues for security and law enforcement personnel. Bomb security news, risk assessment resources, types of bomb-related risk, information and training resources, and training products may all be found on this site. In response to the threat posed by alternative weapons, CABO chemical and biological weapons databases have been developed in a number of areas including agents of interest, incidents, country profiles, and weapons. These databases provide detailed information on a given topic. A preview of specific information provided, a program preview, and purchasing information are all available on this site.
http://www.bombsecurity.com/

### Weapons of Mass Destruction Handbook
Created as a resource for staff officers and civilians involved in preparation for and response to weapons of mass destruction (WMD) incidents, this handbook contains detailed policy, procedure, technical, and clinical information. In over 140 pages of content, this document addresses chemical, biological, nuclear, and radiological weapons. These sections include information on weapons characteristics, methods of delivery, known enemy capabilities, and methods of mitigating the threat. Additional

major sections of this work are devoted to response and consequence management including notification, initial response, continued response efforts, recovery, legal issues, and military/civilian support. http://www.homelanddefense.org/J3WMDHandbook.pdf

## 8.4 AGRICULTURAL BIOWARFARE

**Agricultural Biowarfare and Bioterrorism from the Edmonds Institute** Authored by Dr. Mark Wheelis, Ph.D. in bacteriology, this essay examines the many facets of anti-agricultural biowarfare, the motivations and means behind the threat, and suggestions for reducing that threat. Topics addressed in this work include possible attacks on the food supply, handling food shortages caused by terrorist activities, biological controls, and motivating factors. Recommendations for threat reduction and enhanced preparedness are also offered. http://www.edmonds-institute.org/wheelis.html

**Agricultural Biowarfare and Bioterrorism from the Federation of American Scientists Chemical and Biological Arms Control Program** Originating from the University of California Davis Section of Microbiology and made available by the Federation of American Scientists, this document addresses the questions of motivation for a bioterrorist attack and assesses the potential threat and consequences of this type of action. The author also offers recommendations in areas such as increasing awareness, prevention, and preparedness for attacks. http://www.fas.org/bwc/agr/main.htm

**Agricultural Biowarfare: State Programs to Develop Offensive Capabilities** The Center for Nonproliferation Studies (CNS) has compiled an international listing of all states known or suspected of developing anti-agriculture or anti-livestock agents. A chart outlines information on the state, the status of research, known dates when research was undertaken, disease studied, and additional comments. Information on the agroterrorism activities of 15 major nations is included. http://cns.miis.edu/research/cbw/agprogs.htm

**Agro-Terrorism Resources from the Center for Nonproliferation Studies** Articles and papers, hearing proceedings, legislation, and bioweapons control protocols pertaining to agroterrorism are among the many

resources listed on this Web site. Articles cover topics such as the threat of agrowarfare, use of insects as hostile bioagents, and countering the threat of agroterrorism. For cases in which articles are not available online, reference information has been provided. The remainder of the site is dedicated mainly to policy and protocol in regard to research and use of possible anti-agriculture agents. http://cns.miis.edu/research/cbw/aglinks.htm

### Agro-Terrorism: Chronology of Chemical/ Biological Weapons Attacks Targeting Crops and Livestock, 1915-2000
Summarizing events of agroterrorist importance, this list includes allegations, threats, and known cases of the deliberate use of chemical or biological agents against agricultural resources. Information for each listing includes the date of event, the target nation, responsible parties, and the nature of the attack. Brief descriptions of each incident are provided as well as reference information for those interested in pursuing topics further. This is a comprehensive listing, covering incidents across the globe.
http://cns.miis.edu/research/cbw/agchron.htm

### Agroterrorism Prevention Act of 2001
Introduced into the House of Representatives in June 2001, the Agroterrorism Prevention Act is designed to prevent plant enterprise terrorism. This document is a detailed outline of the six sections of the act that cover plant enterprise terrorism, enhancement of penalties, creation of the National Agroterrorism Incident Clearinghouse, and animal and plant research security programs.
http://www.dola.state.co.us/oem/Terrorism/Reference %20Material/Reference%20Material/agroterrorism_act.htm

### Agroterrorism: Silent Threat
Originally published in *Studies in Conflict and Terrorism* in April of 2001, this document is an excerpt from the original text. Author Joseph Foxell, Jr., of the College of Staten Island, explores the present threat of agroterrorism in light of recent terrorist attacks on the United States. He examines U.S. vulnerabilities to attack including livestock, crops, and land resources; motivations behind agroterrorism; and possible retaliatory agroterrorism in response to the destruction of plants that produce illicit drugs. The article offers recommendations for increased surveillance and preparedness for attacks aimed at agricultural resources.
http://www.pwcglobal.com/extweb/newcoweb.nsf/docid/ 054A7C0A9F75442785256ACC005CF2D7?OpenDocument

**Countering Bioterrorism and Other Threats to the Food Supply from FoodSafety.gov** Intended to serve as a gateway to food safety information, Food-Safety.gov offers an extensive index of links to various government education and information resources relating to bioterrorism and the food supply. These links range from guidelines for preventing agroterrorism to facts about anthrax, smallpox, and other biological agents. Links are organized into three categories according to sponsoring organization: federal government, state and local government, and international government Web sites. Sponsoring organizations include the USDA, the CDC, and the Canadian Food Inspection Agency.
http://www.foodsafety.gov/~fsg/bioterr.html

**Keeping America's Food and Agriculture Safe from the U.S. Department of Agriculture** The U.S. Department of Agriculture (USDA) is entrusted with a broad spectrum of responsibilities including administering federal anti-hunger programs, maintaining national forests, ensuring the quality of agricultural products, and promoting health in rural America. This site provides key information on all USDA programs and activities including the recent adoption of measures for combating the threat of bioterrorism.
http://www.usda.gov/special/biosecurity/safeguard.htm

**National Animal Health Emergency Management System** NAHEMS, the National Animal Health Emergency Management System, works to reduce the threat to the nation's food supply from natural and human-induced disasters and maintains the stability of U.S. animal agriculture markets by focusing on prevention, preparedness, response, and recovery. Information on this site includes current diseases of interest, natural disaster forecasts, and agricultural bioterrorism resources. The bioterrorism section provides a brief overview of the threat to agriculture and NAHEMS' dedication to countering that threat. For those interested in NAHEMS activities, access to the organization's five-year strategic plan is also available.
http://www.usaha.org/NAHEMS/

**Responding to the Threat of Agroterrorism: Specific Recommendations for the U.S. Department of Agriculture** Prepared by Anne Kohnen of Harvard University, this extensive report explores the threat of agroterrorism from historical, economic, and policy perspectives. Kohnen covers background information regarding past incidents of crop disease outbreaks, anti-livestock and anti-crop weapons programs, actual use of anti-agricultural agents, and how governments have responded to the threat. The author presents a detailed analysis of the potential for agroterrorism in the United States, as well as ongoing efforts to control potentially dangerous species.

http://ksgnotes1.harvard.edu/BCSIA/Library.nsf/
1f2b66b14ec00f24852564ec006b733e/f7ea80f01
dfdb03d85256992005518da/$FILE/Responding%
20to%20the%20Threat%20of%20Agroterrorism.pdf

## 8.5 WATERBORNE BIOWARFARE

**Biotechnology and Water Security in the 21st Century** Sponsored by the M.S. Swaminathan Research Foundation, an organization devoted to developing new methods of sustainable agriculture and promoting rural development, the World Commission for Water is dedicated to addressing all concerns regarding global water supplies. Materials on this site relate to the current state of global water and emerging challenges, biotechnology and water security, recommendations, and the future of the World Commission. The "Recommendations" section provides information on the Global Biotechnology Partnership for Water Security including research needs, likely impacts, and policies for the future.

http://www.mssrf.org.sg/d99-biotech-water.html

**Terrorism Alert! from NaturalPureWater.com** The water terrorism section of "Terrorism Alert!" is subdivided into 10 topics addressing areas such as water facility vulnerability, cyber attack and the water system, water information drawn from online resources, and anthrax testing. A special section has also been devoted to providing anthrax information regarding the disease, symptoms, spread, and prevention.

http://www.naturalpurewater.com/terrorism_alert.htm

**Water Industry News** Jointly sponsored by Environmental Market Analysis and the National Council for Public-Private Partnerships, *Water Industry News* presents water facts, industry news, meetings, jobs, and site archives. Contents of this site cover areas such as corporate industry leaders, Environmental Protection Agency

(EPA) rules and regulations, and the public health impact of contaminated drinking water. A special section of the site is devoted to resources for dealing with terrorism, containing industry news relating to antiterrorism projects including anti-anthrax filtration, testing for gas and water contaminants, the creation of the EPA Water Protection Task Force, and new security measures enacted by private filtration facilities.
http://www.waterindustry.org/

**Water Terrorism Questions and Answers** This Web site was created to address some of the major concerns surrounding the threat of water terrorism in light of the September 11 terrorist attacks on the United States. Visitors will find detailed answers to questions regarding potential risk, screening for contaminants, vulnerability, water facility security, and threats to the United States. Additionally, information on water treatment procedures and research into more efficient and safer screening methods is available.
http://www.naturalpurewater.com/water_terrorism.htm

**9**

# PUBLIC POLICY,
# PREPAREDNESS, AND
# RESPONSE

## 9.1 PUBLIC POLICY GUIDELINES,
## CONVENTIONS, AND ANALYSIS

**Advisory Panel to Assess Domestic Response Capabilities for Terrorism Involving Weapons of Mass Destruction** Known as the Gilmore Commission, this advisory body assesses U.S. capabilities for responding to terrorist use of weapons of mass destruction. Contents of this site include the commission charter, legislative issues, news releases, annual reports from the commission to Congress, and minutes from advisory board meetings. In addition, details on recent Gilmore Commission activities and upcoming meetings are available. http://www.rand.org/nsrd/terrpanel/

**Chemical and Biological Arms Control Program from the Federation of American Scientists** To increase the awareness of its Chemical and Biological Arms Control Program, the Federation of American Scientists has designed this site to inform the public of program activities and to provide information regarding recent developments surrounding chemical and biological warfare agents. The site provides links to the Chemical and Biological Weapons Conventions, protocol negotiations, agricultural biowarfare and bioterrorism, and reports and papers from the federation's working group on preventing the development and use of biological weapons. http://www.fas.org/bwc/

**Consequence Management Interoperability Services** A collaborative effort between government and responder agencies, Consequence Management Interoperability (CMI) Services is a congressionally funded project designed to provide information to aid in prevention, planning, preparedness, response, and recovery from terrorist incidents. Resources on this site include CMI services and methods and an online library with documents and the CMI-Services newsletter *Interoperations*. The updates and news section contains registration details for those interested in providing network support to CMI's growing information-sharing endeavor. http://www.cmi-services.org/default.asp

**Countering the Changing Threat of International Terrorism from the National Commission on Terrorism**  This report, compiled by the National Commission on Terrorism, was created to evaluate American laws, policies, and domestic antiterrorism practices. This extensive document reviews current government antiterrorism measures and makes recommendations for increased intelligence and more aggressive antiterrorism policies. The report is divided into several sections and requires Adobe Acrobat for viewing. http://w3.access.gpo.gov/nct/

**Johns Hopkins Center for Civilian Biodefense Strategies**  The Johns Hopkins Center for Civilian Biodefense Strategies is dedicated to raising awareness of the issues, promoting the growth of knowledge, and aiding in the development of practical plans for managing epidemics. The center's focus is on promoting the development of policy for the effective prevention and response to acts of biological terrorism. Information on this site includes biological agents fact sheets, a listing of important related events both past and forthcoming, an online library containing an extensive listing of published works and document reproductions, and an index of bioterrorism news sources, including legislation and government reports. Updated anthrax information, important information on biological agents, publications, FAQs, and a variety of additional articles and links add to this site's value as a resource for everyone from the general public to government officials and healthcare practitioners. http://www.hopkins-biodefense.org/

**Past Hints of Bioterrorism from the National Center for Policy Analysis**  Written by the National Center for Policy Analysis, this portion of the *Daily Policy Digest* is dedicated to reporting historical information on past bioterrorism threats. Most of the information provided deals with U.S. and Soviet interactions in the

1970s and early 1980s. The article takes a modern perspective on past events and attempts to assess the current global threat of bioterrorism.
http://www.ncpa.org/iss/ter/pd102301d.html

**Public Opinion and Public Policy from Public Agenda Online**  Public Agenda is a public opinion research and citizen education organization that seeks to communicate the public's views on major policy issues to government leaders in a nonpartisan manner. The organization covers 20 major issues of concern to the public including campaign finance, healthcare, and Social Security. Public Agenda's Web site contains 2,500 pages of public opinion research and issue analysis. Each issue has its own dedicated information page, containing resources such as a fact file and digest of recent news, as well as findings from public opinion polls. The site also has a special edition dedicated to terrorism.
http://www.publicagenda.org/

**Strategy for the 21st Century from the National Center for Infectious Diseases**  In response to emerging challenges in the fight against infectious disease, the Centers for Disease Control and Prevention (CDC) has created its *Strategy for the 21st Century* which outlines CDC plans for combating infectious diseases over the next five years. This extensive document provides background information, strategic information, a summary of CDC goals and objectives, and anticipated outcomes. Goals are broken down into four major areas: surveillance and response, applied research, infrastructure and training, and prevention and control. Each goal area is further subdivided into specific objectives and methods for meeting those objectives. The entire plan is available for download and review.
http://www.cdc.gov/ncidod/emergplan/1toc.htm

## 9.2  PUBLIC PREPAREDNESS AND RESPONSE

**Addressing Bioterrorist Threats: Where Do We Go from Here? from Emerging Infectious Diseases**  Authored by Dr. Margaret Hamburg within the Department of Health and Human Services, this article was featured in a special issue of *Emerging Infectious Diseases* dedicated to bioterrorism. The author addresses the threat of bioterrorism and public preparedness, stressing the need for stronger public health measures, facilitating communication between the public and policymakers, the threat of hoaxes, and the need for better medical management. The full-text version of the article is available for download.

http://www.cdc.gov/ncidod/EID/vol5no4/hamburg.htm

**Addressing Public Concern about Response to Public Health Emergencies from CDC Health Update** Meant predominantly for healthcare professionals, this CDC update addresses the public's concern over response to public health emergencies. In particular, the update makes reference to anthrax and smallpox, including recommendations for treatment of suspicious cases and public fears concerning these diseases. The document is available in PDF format.

http://www.bt.cdc.gov/
DocumentsAPP/CDCHealthUpdateOctober022001.pdf

**Biological and Chemical Terrorism: Strategic Plan for Preparedness and Response** Originally published in the *Morbidity and Mortality Weekly Report*, this article presents an evaluation of U.S. preparedness for biological and chemical terrorism as well as a strategic plan developed by the CDC in partnership with local and state health officials and other government agencies. The article covers a vulnerability assessment, overt versus covert terrorist activities, preparedness activities, key areas to focus on, partnerships and implementation, and recommendations for public health agencies. This report also reviews a course of action for reducing the threat of terrorism including methods for responding to specific biological agents such as anthrax, plague, and smallpox as well as to dangerous chemical agents.

http://www.cdc.gov/mmwr/preview/mmwrhtml/rr4904a1.htm

**Biological Weapons Convention from the U.S. Department of State** Created in the early 1970s, the Biological Weapons Convention is an international venture aimed at prohibiting the production, stockpiling, and use of biological and chemical weapons. This site, hosted by the U.S. Department of State, is a permanent electronic archive and contains a historical narrative, the text of the convention, and a listing of signatories.

http://www.state.gov/www/global/arms/treaties/bwc1.html

**Bioterrorism and Emergency Response Program from the National Association of County and City Health Officials**  Local public health agencies are the first line of defense against a bioterrorist attack. The Bioterrorism and Emergency Response Program, developed by the National Association of County and City Health Officials (NACCHO), is designed to strengthen defense at the local level. This site provides information regarding bioterrorism performance standards, local centers for public health, and preparedness and response to terrorist activities.  http://www.naccho.org/project63.cfm

**Bioterrorism Preparedness Frequently Asked Questions**  Compiled by the Indiana State Department of Health, this site contains detailed answers to the most frequently asked questions on bioterrorism. The site is designed to assuage the growing fears within the public and to provide factual information about the reality of the threat and the best ways in which to cope with it. Questions regarding such issues as vaccinations for smallpox and anthrax, disease symptoms, and precautionary measures are addressed.
http://www.state.in.us/isdh/healthinfo/bioterrorism.htm

**Bioterrorism: Federal Research and Preparedness Activities from the U.S. General Accounting Office**  This extensive report from the U.S. General Accounting Office details federal activities and funding related to public health and bioterrorism and reviews and evaluates the relationships among federal agencies in coordinating these activities. The report collates information from all federal agencies involved in the response to bioterrorism including the Departments of Agriculture, Commerce, and Transportation. Each department presents its research, preparedness, and response activities.
http://www.gao.gov/new.items/d01915.pdf

**Centers for Public Health Preparedness**  Under the supervision of the CDC, the Centers for Public Health Preparedness (CPHP) work to ensure that public health workers have the necessary skills to respond to large-scale health threats. To this end, the CPHP enlists the aid of a network of academic, specialty, and local healthcare centers to promote education, professional competency, and local preparedness. The content of this site includes contact information for participating institutions and updates on program activities.
http://www.phppo.cdc.gov/
owpp/default.asp?pg=centersforPHP

*Don't type in long URLs*—use eMedguides site number (www.eMedguides.com/**2T-1234**).

### Chemical Weapons Convention: Guided Tour of the Convention on the Prohibition of the Development, Production, Stockpiling, and Use of Chemical Weapons and on Their Destruction

The Organisation for the Prohibition of Chemical Weapons (OPCW) details its convention against the development and use of chemical weapons and its aim to destroy these weapons at this Web site. The guided tour covers the history of chemical disarmament, the development of the convention, and the provisions and actions to be implemented. Links to official documents are also available. http://www.opcw.org/guide.htm

### Citywide Pharmaceutical Preparation for Bioterrorism

Published in the *American Journal of Health-System Pharmacists*, this article summarizes one community's efforts to become pharmaceutically prepared in the event of a biological attack. Featured in this report, accessible in PDF format, is a brief narrative on local efforts followed by a broad plan of preparedness that may be adapted to any community.
http://www.ashp.org/public/pubs/ajhpopen/2a-rTerriff.pdf

### Civilian Emergency Response to Chemical or Biological Weapons Incidents from the National Academy of Science

A project of the Institute of Medicine and the Board of Environmental Studies and Toxicology, this 18-month assessment initiated in December of 1997 examined current military, hazardous waste disposal, and vaccination/treatment capabilities related to an attack on the public-at-large by chemical or biological agents. The objective was to determine which areas required further research and development to improve safety and effectiveness of response by civilian health and medical systems. Full-text versions of the committee's two main reports, "Improving Civilian Medical Response to Chemical and Biological Terrorist Incidents: Interim Report on Current Capabilities" and "Chemical and Biological Terrorism: Research and Development to Improve Civilian Medical Response," are available online free of charge.
http://www4.nas.edu/cp.nsf/57b01c7b1b6493c4852565550058
53cf/a3861123d7632dc4852565690079b6f9?OpenDocument

### Counter-Terrorism from the Environmental Protection Agency

Created by the Environmental Protection Agency (EPA), this site outlines the EPA's role in U.S. counterterrorism measures. Information on prevention, preparedness, response, international cooperation, and general counterterrorism measures is accessible. The site also provides resources specific to citizens, businesses, and tribal partnerships as well as a compendium of laws and regulations, databases, and publications. http://www.epa.gov/swercepp/cntr-ter.html

### Counterterrorism and Incident Response from the Lawrence Livermore National Laboratory
Run by the Nonproliferation, Arms Control, and International Security Directorate of the Lawrence Livermore National Laboratory, the program for Counterterrorism and Incident Response is dedicated to developing technologies and capabilities for responding to terrorism emergencies and large-scale destructive weapon incidents. Main areas of concentration involve nuclear threat assessment, nuclear incident response, chemical and biological detection technologies, and forensic science. The Chemical and Biological Detection Technologies section contains information on biodetectors, biological foundations, modeling and prediction, and decontamination.
http://www.llnl.gov/nai/rdiv/rdiv.html

### Disaster and Emergency Preparedness from MEDLINEplus
MEDLINEplus provides information in several categories related to disasters and emergency preparedness including general information, coping, prevention and screening, specific conditions, law and policy, organization, and child-related resources. The site also provides the latest news in this area including recent updates on terrorist attacks, CDC efforts to control bioterrorism, and medical relief efforts. Additional terrorism-related resources can be found on coping with posttraumatic stress disorder, specific conditions relating to chemical emergencies, disaster preparedness, terrorism response, and disaster assistance.
http://www.nlm.nih.gov/medlineplus/
disastersandemergencypreparedness.html

### Disaster Readiness from the American Hospital Association
In light of recent events, the American Hospital Association has issued this Disaster Readiness Advisory. The advisory is meant primarily for hospital officials and healthcare workers and contains guidance on emergency preparedness for potential terrorist acts.
http://www.aha.org/
Emergency/Readiness/MaDisasterB0921.asp

**Disaster Response: Principles of Preparation and Coordination** Authored by Erik Auf der Heide, this widely popular book is no longer in print. However, by special arrangement and the efforts of the Center of Excellence in Disaster Management and Humanitarian Assistance, this work may be viewed online in its entirety. In 10 chapters, the author addresses the problems associated with disaster management, preparedness and the shortcomings of planned response, interagency communication, the Incident Command System, communicating with the public, triage, and the role of the media in disaster management. Each section includes a detailed summary of key points, planning checklists for taking appropriate action, and additional recommended readings.
http://www.coe-dmha.org/dr/flash.htm

**Elements of Effective Bioterrorism Preparedness: A Planning Primer for Local Public Health Agencies** Produced in January of 2001, this planning primer from the National Association of County and City Health Officials addresses the need for increased preparedness and response to bioterrorist activities at the local level of government. This 28-page report, available in PDF format, outlines state and local responsibilities in first response, describes essential public health services, and details the many elements of effective bioterrorism preparedness and response.
http://www.naccho.org/files/
documents/Final_Effective_Bioterrism.pdf

**Environmental Response Team** Founded in 1978 as part of the Clean Water Act, the Environmental Response Team (ERT) provides support in oil spills, hazardous emergencies, potentially hazardous situations, and long-term recovery efforts. ERT Web resources are designed to provide information and guidance to environmental responders around the world. These resources include health and safety information, response and remediation recommendations, sampling and analysis procedures, and training services. Review of all forms of environmental contaminants from oil spills to air pollutants and chemical agents is available on this site. In addition, visitors may access ERT directories and databases of technical information.
http://www.ert.org/

**Family Readiness Kit: Preparing to Handle Disasters from the American Academy of Pediatrics**   The Family Readiness Kit, available online courtesy of the American Academy of Pediatrics, is designed to help families prepare for many kinds of disasters, outlining survival plans in situations such as floods, hurricanes, and tornadoes. In addition to providing tips on preparing disaster plans, the kit also provides fact sheets on natural disasters. The most recent addition to the kit includes a section dedicated to dealing with the threat of terrorism. http://www.aap.org/family/frk/frkit.htm

**Federal Response Plan from the Federal Emergency Management Agency**   The Federal Emergency Management Agency (FEMA), has developed detailed plans for response to and recovery from national disasters. The Federal Response Plan provides coordinated federal assistance to state and local governments in the event of a biological emergency. Resources available include teams of specialized personnel, equipment and supplies, and on-site facilities. Text of the entire plan is available online.
http://www.fema.gov/r-n-r/frp/frpesf8.htm

**Field Operations Guide from the U.S. Agency for International Development**   Intended as a resource for individuals sent to perform initial assessments of disaster sites and for members of Disaster Assistance Response Teams, this document contains information on general responsibilities, reference materials for assessing populations at risk, field recommendations, and policy guidelines. The multiple chapters of this handbook are devoted to general information and responsibilities, assessments, information on populations at risk, disaster assistance response teams, forms and instructions, and an introduction to commonly used terminology. Readers will also find policy guidelines from the U.S. Agency for International Development relating to disaster management. http://www.usaid.gov/ofda/fog/

**Foreign Quarantine Information from the U.S. Department of Health and Human Services**   Provided as a service of the National Archives and Records Administration, this document has been prepared by the Department of Health and Human Services. Within the department index, visitors will find outlines of rules, regulations, and general provisions regarding the spread of diseases from foreign nations to the United States.

These guidelines cover everything from the quarantine of live animals to the transport of food and waste products and may be read as text files or downloaded in PDF format. http://www.access.gpo.gov/ nara/cfr/waisidx_00/42cfr71_00.html

## Guide to the Disaster Declaration Process from the Federal Emergency Management Agency

The Disaster Relief and Emergency Assistance Act is designed to aid state and local governments in the event of community disaster beyond the response capabilities at the local level. This paper outlines the procedures for obtaining the necessary presidential declaration of disaster and explains the types of assistance available under the program. Content includes individual assistance, public assistance, and hazard mitigation. In addition to an overview of the declaration process, readers will find details on procuring individual and family grants, small business disaster loans, disaster unemployment, and Federal Emergency Management Agency assistance for recovery efforts. http://www.fema.gov/r-n-r/dec_guid.htm

**Health Alert Network** The Health Alert Network (HAN) is a national initiative to build a stronger public health communications infrastructure and to increase the level of defense against large-scale health threats, including bioterrorism. A brief outline of HAN's purpose and role in the public health system is provided in this document. http://www.bt.cdc.gov/ DocumentsAPP/the_health_altert_network.pdf

## How We're Making the Public and Employees Safe from the U.S. Postal Service

In response to recent events, the U.S. Postal Service has devised this site to keep the public up-to-date on its activities to ensure the safety of its employees and of the public as a whole. Details on new safety measures that have been adopted in postal institutions are made available. In addition, users may aid the ongoing investigation by providing any information they might have on anthrax activities. http://www.usps.com/news/2001/press/pr01_1029steps.htm

## Interim Recommended Notification Procedures for Local and State Public Health Department Leaders in the Event of a Bioterrorist Incident from the Centers for Disease Control and Prevention

The purpose of this site is to outline the rec-

ommended protocol for local and state health officials in the event of a bioterrorist incident. The site details a notification procedure including officials and agencies to be notified and their priority. Necessary contact information is provided.
http://www.bt.cdc.gov/EmContact/Protocols.asp

**Interstate Quarantine Information from the U.S. Department of Health and Human Services** Information on the guidelines governing interstate quarantine procedures from the Department of Health and Human Services can be found at the National Archives and Records Administration. Although this document is shorter than the one issued on the topic of foreign quarantine, it contains useful information on communicable diseases, reporting of outbreaks, and measures in cases of inadequate local control.
http://www.access.gpo.gov/
nara/cfr/waisidx_00/42cfr70_00.html

**Local Emergency Planning Committees and Deliberate Releases: Addressing Terrorist Activities in the Local Emergency Plan** Sponsored by the Environmental Protection Agency (EPA) in response to growing terrorist threats, this document addresses the means by which local emergency planning committees can incorporate counterterrorism and preparedness efforts when updating local emergency management plans. The report discusses emergency contact information, response functions, hazard analysis, public health and safety concerns, equipment and training recommendations, and the need for ongoing assessment. The EPA also provides a listing of resources for local emergency planning committees in need of assistance with counterterrorism measures and a table containing information on important explosive chemical, biological, and nuclear devices. http://www.epa.gov/ceppo/factsheets/lepcct.pdf

**Mitigation Practitioner's Handbook** A cooperative effort between several government agencies, including the U.S. Agency for International Developments and the Bureau for Humanitarian Response, this report has been designed as a reference to assist in planning appropriate and effective disaster intervention activities. Major sections of this work are devoted to inventions, seeds and tools, livestock concerns, water, cash reserves, and food. Each section provides an assessment of the option, intervention recommendations, references, and at least one case study. This guide is designed for use by local emergency planning committees in preparation for, and response to, local disasters.

http://www.usaid.gov/hum_response/ofda/files/hbkoct18.pdf

**National Domestic Preparedness Office**   Assisting state and local emergency personnel with all aspects of preparedness, the National Domestic Preparedness Office (NDPO) provides support in strategic planning, training, equipment, and exercises to promote the most effective response in the event of a large-scale terrorist attack. The NDPO Web site provides information about services and publications, as well as resources designed specifically for emergency responders.

http://www.ndpo.gov/

**National Pharmaceutical Stockpile**   Administered under the authority of the CDC, the National Pharmaceutical Stockpile was created to ensure the availability of life-saving substances, including antibiotics and supplies, in the event of a national health emergency. This document, available in PDF format, provides a brief summary of the history, administration, contents, and components of the National Pharmaceutical Stockpile.

http://www.bt.cdc.gov/
DocumentsAPP/national_pharmaceutical_stockpile.pdf

**National Response System, Environmental Protection Agency**   Composed of local, state, and federal agencies in association with industry and independent organizations, the National Response System is designed to share resources and expertise in response to oil spills and the release of other hazardous substances. This Web site offers an in-depth look at the Environmental Protection Agency's emergency response programs and at the many ways in which these programs work together. Visitors will find detailed information on the five headquarters: the Offices of Emergency and Remedial Response; Chemical Emergency Prevention and Preparedness; Prevention, Pesticides, and Toxic Substances; Radiation and Indoor Air; and Underground Storage Tanks. Links to each office's resources and information are provided.

http://www.epa.gov/superfund/programs/er/nrs/index.htm

**Noble Training Center, U.S. Public Health Service**
Sponsored by the Office of Emergency Preparedness, the

---

Noble Training Center is the only U.S. hospital facility devoted to training medical personnel for response to incidents involving weapons of mass destruction. The center is in the process of being converted into a mock hospital environment in which training, drills, and experimentation can be undertaken. Online information includes a summary of the center's Hospital Provider Course and Emergency Medical Services Course. A complete listing of center courses and a course schedule can be obtained through this site.
http://ndms.dhhs.gov/CT_Program/
Noble_Training_Center/noble_training_center.html

**Office for Domestic Preparedness, U.S. Department of Justice**  Improvement of the nation's capacity for crime prevention and control falls under the jurisdiction of the Office of Justice Programs. The Office for Domestic Preparedness (ODP), under the Office of Justice Programs, is entrusted with developing and administering a plan for national domestic preparedness. Updates on ODP activities, training and technical assistance, equipment requisition grants, and additional related resources are available to visitors of this site.
http://www.ojp.usdoj.gov/odp/

**Office of Emergency Preparedness, U.S. Department of Health and Human Services**  The official site for the Office of Emergency Preparedness (OEP) is designed to provide resources for emergency responders, public health officials and practitioners, emergency managers, and the general public. Visitors will find recent news coverage, OEP updates and activities, and links to other OEP programs.
http://ndms.dhhs.gov/

**Public Health Emergency Preparedness and Response from the Centers for Disease Control and Prevention**  Public Health Emergency Preparedness and Response provides information about all CDC and state activities. Features such as an index of CDC health alerts, advisories and updates, anthrax information, surveillance data, planning guides, and health communication networks comprise this expansive site. Emergency contact information has also been provided as a public resource.
http://www.bt.cdc.gov/

**Public Health Emergency Response: The CDC Role**  The CDC plays a key role in ensuring national public health, and the purpose of this site is to illuminate that function in the public health system. This PDF document covers the CDC's training of "disease detectives," covering laboratory capacities, early detection systems, and communications. The National Pharmaceutical Stockpile is also briefly discussed.
http://www.bt.cdc.gov/
DocumentsAPP/Improving_biodefense.pdf

**Quarantine and Inspection from the U.S. Code: Public Health and Welfare**  A concise description of U.S. regulations to control communicable diseases is made available by the CDC. Important legal and ethical guidelines regarding the apprehension, detention, and quarantine of individuals, both foreign and domestic, are contained in this document, available in PDF format at this site.
http://www.bt.cdc.gov/legal/42USC264.pdf

**Response Planning from the Office of Emergency Preparedness Counterterrorism Program**  Hosted by the Office of Emergency Preparedness, this Web site discusses response planning for terrorist incidents involving weapons of mass destruction. To assist local public health systems in developing their response programs, this Web site posts documents from the U.S. Department of Health and Human Services and other federal agencies that provide resources and suggestions for implementing a response plan.
http://ndms.dhhs.gov/CT_Program/
Response_Planning/response_planning.html

**State Emergency Management Agencies, National Domestic Preparedness Office**  Maintained by the National Domestic Preparedness Office (NDPO), this site serves as a portal to the 50 individual State Emergency Management Agencies. Each state maintains its own emergency management Web site with a unique set of resources. Additional NDPO site content includes press information, bulletins and a newsletter, services, and information for emergency responders.
http://www.ndpo.gov/stateema.htm

**Talking About Disaster Guide from the American Red Cross**  The National Educational Disaster Coali-

tion has designed this guide as a reference tool for anyone providing disaster safety information to the public. This comprehensive guide discusses the coalition's recommendations for a family disaster plan and disaster supplies kit. In addition, readers will find information on proper safety precautions in the event of fire, earthquake, chemical emergency, flood, hurricane, tornado, and other disasters. The entire document is maintained by and available through the American Red Cross.
http://www.redcross.org/disaster/safety/guide.html

## 9.3  LEGISLATION AND LEGAL ISSUES

**Biological Weapons, U.S. Code**  The Legal Information Institute (LII) of Cornell Law School maintains Web-linked legal resources designed to aid in the dissemination of legal information, delivery of legal education, and legal practice. This section of LII provides information on the U.S. Code, which can be searched by title, section, or any of 50 preselected topics. Under Title 18, Chapter 10, "Crimes and Criminal Procedure—Biological Weapons," visitors will find information regarding prohibitions of biological weapons, procedures for requesting military enforcement of regulations, seizure and destruction, injunction, and definitions. Each subsection provides a detailed outline of what can be found in a particular chapter of the U.S. Code. Additional titles may also be searched for terrorism-related information.
http://www4.law.cornell.edu/uscode/18/plch10.html

**Center for Law and the Public's Health**  A collaborative effort between Johns Hopkins and Georgetown universities, the center focuses on providing public health law, ethics, and policy resources for public health officials, practitioners, lawyers, and others. Among the recent achievements of the center is the Model State Emergency Powers Act, a policy document that would allow for the development of a plan for the coordination of appropriate response activities in the event of a public health emergency. Provisions of the plan, which is accessible at the site, include granting a variety of emergency powers to state governors and public health authorities. Additional resources on this site include the public health law reader, research information, training materials for public health officials, and conference information.
http://www.publichealthlaw.net

## Counter Terrorism Legislation and Executive Orders Links from the National Security Institute

Sponsored by the National Security Institute (NSI), this Web page provides access to an extensive listing of resources on terrorism including information on legislation and executive orders, facts, commentary on terrorism and terrorism legislation, precautions, and links to other government antiterrorism resources. Under the legislation section, the NSI has indexed complete transcripts of all major acts and congressional hearings on the subjects of terrorism and counterterrorism. "Terrorism Facts" contains information ranging from fact sheets on terrorist profiles to patterns of global terrorism and government counterterrorism measures. Precautions discussed include letter and package bombs, bomb threats, and upgrading federal building security.
http://nsi.org/terrorism.html

## Countering the Changing Threat of International Terrorism, Report of the National Commission on Terrorism

By order of Congress, the National Commission on Terrorism performed an analysis and evaluation of U.S. laws, policies, and preventive and punitive practices in response to terrorist activities aimed at American citizens. This report is the result of that effort containing the commission's analyses and recommendations for future policy. Contents include the international threat of terrorism, recommendations for increased surveillance and intelligence, pursuing a more aggressive antiterrorism strategy, and more effective preparation and response to terrorist-induced catastrophes. The full text of the document, including original graphics, is available from this Web site.
http://www.terrorism.com/
documents/bremercommission/index.shtml

## State of Colorado Rules and Regulations Pertaining to Preparations for a Bioterrorist Event, Pandemic Influenza, or an Outbreak by a Novel and Highly Fatal Infectious Agent or Biological Toxin

This 12-page draft outlines six rules and regulations for increasing preparedness in the event of bioterrorist attacks. The regulations involve preparations by local health agencies, general and critical access hospitals, managed care organizations, regional emergency medical and trauma services advisory councils, and methods for assessing compliance with these regulations. Although they have been drafted by the state of Colorado, these guidelines may be used by any government or organization for increasing preparation in regard to biological attacks. http://www.cdphe.state.co.us/bioterrorismruls.pdf

**Terrorism and Bioterrorism Resources from the National Center for Biotechnology Law**  Presented by the University of Missouri Kansas City School of Law, this site is dedicated to examining the legal issues surrounding bioterrorist activities. Issues including the legal implications of vaccine testing are discussed, as well as antiterrorism laws, recent developments, case studies, and articles on bioterrorism and police authority. An introduction to public health law is also available.
http://plague.law.umkc.edu/blaw/Bioterror.htm

**Terrorism Law and Policy from Jurist Legal Education Network**  The Terrorism Law and Policy section of *Jurist* provides the latest information and coverage on legal and government proceedings on terrorist activities. Visitors to this site will find a wealth of resources and information on terrorism, counterterrorism policy, civil liberties, U.S. antiterrorism laws, and international antiterrorism laws. Users may also conduct searches of terrorism laws, reports, hearings, briefings, and papers.
http://jurist.law.pitt.edu/terrorism.htm

**U.S. Preparations for Biological Terrorism: Legal Limitations and the Need for Planning**  Authored by Juliette N. Kayyem, the Executive Director of the Executive Session on Domestic Preparedness at Harvard University, this report takes a legal perspective on counterterrorism measures, examining their lawfulness and legitimacy. Aside from a brief discussion of conventional terrorism and existing laws, much of this document is devoted to what the author refers to as "the special case of biological terrorism." In over 20 pages of text dedicated to the topic, Kayyem introduces 14 legal issues that arise when dealing with counterterrorism activities. These include legal implications behind restricting the movement of people and the flow of information. The remainder of the document presents feasible legal solutions for overcoming these obstacles.
http://ksgnotes1.harvard.edu/BCSIA/Library.nsf/1f2b66b14ec00
f24852564ec006b733e/389cc3837fdab0cf85256a1c00707bd2/$
FILE/U.S.+Preparations+for+Biological+Terrorism.pdf

# 10

# CLINICAL RESOURCES
# ON BIOTERRORISM

## 10.1 GUIDELINES AND CONSENSUS STATEMENTS

**2T-0145**

**American Medical Association Policy on Terrorism** As part of the American Medical Association (AMA) section on public health and preparedness, the AMA provides access to information regarding policies and resources. Information on this site includes recent press releases, AMA updates on medical preparedness, practical information for physicians, transcripts of speeches by AMA officials, and guidelines for medical personnel for dealing with potential victims of bioterrorism. http://www.ama-assn.org/ama/pub/category/6229.html

**2T-0146**

**Anthrax Information for Clinicians from the Johns Hopkins Center for Civilian Biodefense Strategies and the Infectious Diseases Society of America** Sponsored by Johns Hopkins University, this site deals strictly with the clinical issues surrounding anthrax infection. It provides information on the potential for anthrax as a biological weapon, as well as the medical symptoms and treatments of the disease. In addition, the center supplies answers to a list of commonly asked questions regarding anthrax infection. Links are available to articles and related sites of interest.
http://www.hopkins-biodefense.org/anthrax102201.htm

**2T-0147**

**Investigation of Anthrax Associated with Intentional Exposure and Interim Public Health Guidelines from Morbidity and Mortality Weekly Report** Originally published in an October 2001 issue of the *Morbidity and Mortality Weekly Report,* this update provides a discussion regarding the clinical investigation into recent anthrax cases in Florida and New York. The article reports background information on the patients in question and details the progression of the disease. General description and clinical symptoms of anthrax infection have also been included.
http://www.acponline.org/bioterro/intent_expose.htm

**Medical Aspects of Biological Terrorism from the ACP-ASIM Bioterrorism Resource Center** Taken from the Johns Hopkins Schools of Medicine and Public Health, this site is particularly useful for medical and healthcare professionals. The issues addressed include clinical cases, clinical questions regarding biological weapons and relevant diseases, and key points in reacting quickly to potential bioterrorism events.
http://www.acponline.org/bioterro/medicalaspects.htm

**Medical Management Guidelines for Acute Chemical Exposures from the Agency for Toxic Substances and Disease Registry** Designed to aid emergency healthcare professionals in protecting and de-contaminating themselves and their patients in acute chemical exposures, medical management guidelines (MMGs) are available for a variety of chemical agents including nerve agents and blister agents. More than 40 MMGs are available, providing basic chemical and exposure information, a summary of potential human effects, information on prehospitalization management, emergency management guidelines, and important information for patients who have been exposed. Each MMG is accompanied by a detailed report in PDF format.
http://www.atsdr.cdc.gov/mmg.html

**Medical Management of Biological Casualties Handbook from the U.S. Army Medical Research Institute of Infectious Diseases** Created by the U.S. Army Medical Research Institute of Infectious Diseases, this handbook is designed to provide education on effective countermeasures for bacteria, viruses, and toxins that may be used as biological weapons. In addition to providing historical information on biological warfare, this document presents guidelines for distinguishing between natural and intentional disease outbreaks, 10 steps for managing medical casualties in the field, and specific clinical information on each infectious vehicle. Under the heading for bacteria, users will find information on anthrax, brucellosis, glanders and meliodosis, and plague. Information provided includes a summary of the disease, history, clinical features, diagnosis, medical management, and prophylaxis.
http://www.nbc-med.org/SiteContent/HomePage/
WhatsNew/MedManual/Feb01/handbook.htm

**Medical Management of Chemical Casualties Handbook from the U.S. Army Medical Research Institute of Chemical Defense** This handbook was created as a concise field resource for medical personnel to aid in the rapid treatment of chemical casualties. The text covers a variety of chemical substances including pulmonary agents, cyanide, vesicants, nerve agents, incapacitating agents, riot-control agents, decontamination, casualty management, and defense. Clinical information is provided on the physicochemical characteristics, toxicokinetics, toxicity, toxicodynamics, clinical effects, laboratory findings, detection, and protection for each of the various chemical agents covered. Designed as a quick reference source, this handbook is not intended to be a definitive text on medical management of chemical casualties.

http://ccc.apgea.army.mil/reference_
materials/handbooks/RedHandbook/001TitlePage.htm

**Medical Management of Radiological Casualties from the Armed Forces Radiobiology Research Institute** Authored by Colonel David G. Jarrett of the Medical Corps of the U.S. Army and originally designed as an army educational tool, this handbook was cleared for release to the general public to be utilized mainly by healthcare professionals in the management of patients with uncontrolled exposure to ionizing radiation. Among the major topics covered in this 152-page PDF document are nuclear detonation and other high-dose radiation situations including acute high-dose radiation, management protocols for acute radiation syndrome, and blast and thermal biological effects. The section on radiation dispersal devices and industrial contamination situations includes information on low dose-rate radiation, psychological effects, external and internal contamination, depleted uranium, and biological dosimetry. This is a comprehensive educational resource for those interested in medical management of radiation exposure victims.

http://www.afrri.usuhs.mil/www/
outreach/pdf/radiologicalhandbooksp99-2.pdf

**National Guideline Clearinghouse** Sponsored by the Agency for Healthcare Research and Quality, the National Guideline Clearinghouse is a public resource providing information on clinical practice guidelines. Using the search engine provided, visitors to this site may search for content on any medical topic. The engine returns links to articles sponsored by medical associations,

universities, and government agencies containing information on recommendations, clinical algorithms, and guideline developers.
http://www.guideline.gov/index.asp

**Quick Primer for Clinicians on Detecting Public Health Emergencies from the Medical Society of the State of New York** A collaborative effort between health agencies in New York State and other government offices, this work is designed to educate physicians in dealing with public health emergencies, recognizing potential threats, reporting threats, and seeking information when the need arises. Features of this primer include general symptoms of disease that should arouse suspicions, specific syndromes and disorders that should be reported to the State Department of Health such as anthrax, plague, and viral hemorrhagic fever, and a listing of emergency contact information for reporting outbreaks or gathering more information. Additional bioterrorism resources provided include links to characteristics charts of biological agents, the Strategic Plan for Preparedness and Response, CDC health alerts on terrorism response, recent articles on bioterrorism, and medical fact sheets.
http://www.mssny.org/pub_health/Emergency_Primer.htm

**Recognition of Illness Associated with the Intentional Release of a Biologic Agent from Morbidity and Mortality Weekly Report** Heightened surveillance for the appearance of unusual and life-threatening diseases is the topic of this CDC update. In keeping with the CDC's efforts to encourage all medical professionals to be on alert for anything out of the ordinary, this document is a guide for healthcare professionals on recognizing the patterns of illness that may result from the release of biological agents. The guide provides clinical information on the symptoms of a number of diseases of potential interest to bioterrorists including anthrax, plague, smallpox, inhalational tularemia, and hemorrhagic fever.
http://www.cdc.gov/mmwr/preview/mmwrhtml/mm5041a2.htm

**TB Respiratory Protection Program in Health Care Facilities from the U.S. Department of Health and Human Services** Sponsored in part by the National Institute for Occupational Safety and Health Respiratory Protection Program, this document

presents guidelines for preventing the airborne spread of tuberculosis (TB) in healthcare facilities. Designed for hospital and healthcare facility administration, the plan outlines the controlled use of facial respirators and protective clothing and suits to prevent contamination of healthcare workers. The steps toward implementing such a program are described, including conducting a TB risk assessment, selecting respirators, writing standard operating procedures, and providing training.
http://www.cdc.gov/niosh/99-143.html

**Treatment of Biological Warfare Agent Casualties from the Virtual Naval Hospital** Designed as a guide for army and medical personnel in the diagnosis and treatment of exposure to hostile biological agents, this document offers a description of potential biological weapons; outlines procedures for collection and identification of potential biological agents; describes proper procedures for diagnosis, treatment, and management of exposure victims, and details medical management and treatment in biological weapons operations. Information is provided on agents such as anthrax and brucellosis, viral agents, and toxins, with over 15 biological agents covered in detail, including general information on the disease, potential means of delivery as a biological weapon, environmental detection, prevention, clinical presentation, diagnosis, treatment, control of patients, and medical evaluation. http://www.vnh.org/FM8284/

## 10.2 DIAGNOSTICS

**Anthrax Testing from ABC News** Designed to address public interest in clinical methods of anthrax detection, this site has been made available from ABC News. Answers to frequently asked questions about anthrax infections are posted in combination with a listing of definitions of clinical terminology often used in discussing the disease.
http://abcnews.go.com/sections/
living/DrJohnson/drt_anthraxqna011018.html

**Assay Techniques for Detection of Exposure to Sulfur Mustard, Cholinesterase Inhibitors, Sarin, Soman, GF, and Cyanide from the U.S. Army Medical Research Institute of Chemical Defense** A technical bulletin of the U.S. Army Medical Research Institute of Chemical Defense, this text is designed

mainly for medical practitioners and clinical laboratory specialists. It provides analytical techniques for the identification of toxic chemical agents in urine and blood samples. As the title implies, chemical analyses covered by this document include sulfur mustard, cholinesterase inhibitors, sarin, soman, and cyanide. Each section contains detailed instructions for carrying out clinical laboratory testing for exposure to these chemicals.
http://chemdef.apgea.army.mil/TBMed296/TBMED296.asp

**Basic Laboratory Protocols for the Presumptive Identification of Brucella Species from the Centers for Disease Control and Prevention** These guidelines developed by the CDC provide laboratories with the appropriate techniques for identifying *Brucella* species. This protocol is tailored specifically for laboratory and medical personnel and contains clinical and technical information on processing specimens, collection and transport, culturing conditions, identification, and actions to be taken if *Brucella* is suspected as a bioterrorist threat agent.
http://www.bt.cdc.gov/Agent/Brucellosis/Brucella20010417.pdf

**Serologic Test for B. anthracis from MEDLINEplus** MEDLINEplus offers a concise patient resource for information on the anthrax serologic test. This Web site provides an easy-to-understand overview of the test including information on how and why the test is performed, how it feels, risks, normal values, and abnormal results. In addition, the site provides a listing of important definitions that the patient may wish to review prior to undergoing the procedure.
http://www.nlm.nih.gov/medlineplus/ency/article/003534.htm

**Uncovering Bioterrorism** A featured article in the May 2000 edition of *Science and Technology Review,* this article stresses the necessity of utilizing DNA-based signatures to rapidly and accurately identify biological warfare agents and their makers. In addition to general and background information on the production of biological weapons, the article introduces DNA signatures and their relevance to testing for biological agents. Focusing mainly on the research and continuing efforts of the Lawrence Livermore National Laboratory, the site offers brief descriptions of assay techniques, evaluations of accuracy, and information about ongoing research programs. http://www.llnl.gov/str/Weinstein.html

# 10.3 THERAPEUTICS

**2T-0163**

**Cipro from Bayer Healthvillage** Bayer Healthvillage is a Web-based resource providing information on bacteria and the immune system, infectious disease, prevention, and treatment. A wide variety of information is available on this site, including guidelines for antibiotic usage, recommended drug treatments for both common and rare diseases, and the chemical structures and mechanisms of action of recently developed drugs.
http://infections.bayer.com/
treatment/ciprofloxacin_ciprobay_en.html

**2T-0164**

**Cipro Use by Pregnant and Lactating Women from the Center for Drug Evaluation and Research** Sponsored by the U.S. Food and Drug Administration, this site provides clinical information relating to safety concerns in prescribing Cipro to pregnant and lactating women. The article consists of an expert review and interpretations of published clinical data since no controlled studies have been performed.
http://www.fda.gov/cder/drug/infopage/cipro/cipropreg.htm

**2T-0165**

**CiproUSA** All aspects of the Cipro antibiotic, both general and clinical, are examined on this Web site. In consideration of the wide use of Cipro in combating bacterial infection, the Bayer Corporation has provided prescribing information, indications, dosing charts, and access to recent press releases. The current concern over bioterrorism has prompted the addition of a section devoted specifically to anthrax.
http://www.ciprousa.com/

**2T-0166**

**Doxycycline from RxList** Dedicated to providing detailed information about pharmaceutical products, this site contains extensive technical and clinical information about a wide variety of drugs. In the description of doxycycline, visitors will find its chemical makeup, molecular formula, and general effects in the human body. Also available are sections devoted to clinical pharmacology, indications and dosage, routes of administration, side effects and drug interactions, warnings, overdosage, contraindications, and patient information.
http://www.rxlist.com/cgi/generic/doxycyc.htm

**Doxycycline Use by Pregnant and Lactating Women from the Center for Drug Evaluation and Research** Doxycycline is an antibiotic that has been approved by the FDA for use in treating anthrax infections. This Web page consists of an expert review of published clinical data on the use of doxycycline in pregnant and lactating women. Since no controlled studies have been done, the article considers the potential effects of doxycycline on fetal growth and development based on the information available.
http://www.fda.gov/cder/drug/infopage/penG_doxy/doxypreg.htm

**Post-Exposure Anthrax Prophylaxis from the Medical Letter on Drugs and Therapeutics** *The Medical Letter on Drugs and Therapeutics* is a nonprofit peer-reviewed publication created to promote better understanding of drugs and therapeutics. In response to the threat of bioterrorism, this article is dedicated to the understanding of postexposure prophylaxis of inhalation anthrax. A recommended treatment regime, including dosage and duration, has been formulated and made available to healthcare practitioners.
http://www.acponline.org/bioterro/medical_letter.pdf

**Questions and Answers for Consumers on Cipro from the Center for Drug Evaluation and Research** Consumers interested in learning more about the antibiotic Cipro will find this site a useful resource. The FDA provides answers to frequently asked consumer questions aimed at informing the public about the drug, its effects, government policy on its use, and the role it plays in combating bioterrorism. The site is designed to address the concerns over the medical treatment of anthrax cases.
http://www.fda.gov/cder/drug/infopage/cipro/cipro_faq.htm

**Questions and Answers for Consumers on Doxycycline from the Center for Drug Evaluation and Research** As part of keeping the public up-to-date about the recent risks of exposure to dangerous biological agents, the FDA has established a number of sites to pass along important information about drug treatment to the public. Doxycycline, an approved treatment for all forms of anthrax, is the subject of this particular site at which the FDA issues answers to frequently asked consumer questions regarding the drug and its use.
http://www.fda.gov/cder/drug/infopage/penG_doxy/QA_doxy.htm

**Questions and Answers for Consumers on Penicillin G Procaine from the Center for Drug Evaluation and Research** The FDA provides information at this Web site about the use of the drug Penicillin G Procaine for the treatment of anthrax. Designed mainly to answer consumer questions, this site contains general information about treatment with this drug and recommendations for usage.
http://www.fda.gov/cder/drug/
infopage/penG_doxy/QA_penG.htm

**The Doxycycline Information Line from Hovione** Doxycycline is sometimes offered as an alternative antibiotic in the treatment of anthrax infection. This site provides an overview on how antibiotics work as well as information on when it is advisable to take doxycycline. The report, tailored to physician and patient audiences, also addresses the advantages and disadvantages of the drug and provides a cost comparison chart.
http://www.hovione.com/h_doxy/

**Update on the Use of Doxycycline for Anthrax Exposure from the Food and Drug Administration Public Health Advisory** This public health advisory was issued from the FDA to all healthcare providers. On this site, practitioners will find information on the drug doxycycline and its use in the treatment of all forms of anthrax. Proper dosage and treatment regimens are recommended by the FDA.
http://www.fda.gov/cder/drug/
infopage/doxycycline/advisory.htm

## 10.4 IMMUNIZATION AND VACCINES

**Anthrax Vaccine Immunization Program from the U.S. Coast Guard** The U.S. Coast Guard–sponsored Anthrax Vaccine Immunization Program (AVIP) is discussed at this site. Details about the specifics of the program and information about the disease are included. The site is designed to be a resource for answering questions and providing access to certain briefings and documents pertaining to AVIP. Links to related sites of interest are also provided.
http://www.uscg.mil/hq/g-w/g-wk/g-wkh/
g-wkh-1/uscg_anthrax_vaccine_program.htm

**Anthrax Vaccine Immunization Program from the U.S. Department of Defense** Recently redesigned, this is the official Department of Defense Web site for the Anthrax Vaccine Immunization Program (AVIP). Among the many resources available to visitors, the site includes information regarding the threat, the disease, the vaccine, safety recommendations, and effectiveness. The site also provides information on adverse event reporting and posts answers to questions submitted by site users. http://www.anthrax.osd.mil/

**Anthrax Vaccine Immunization Program from the U.S. Marine Corps** A brief description of U.S. Marine Corps involvement in the Anthrax Vaccine Immunization Program (AVIP) is the focus of this site. Additionally, visitors will find Marine Corps news relating to AVIP, information on the disease, and links to other government resources related to disease control.
http://www.usmc.mil/anthrax.nsf

**Vaccinia (Smallpox) Vaccine Recommendations from Morbidity and Mortality Weekly Report** Dating back to June of 2001, this document reports the recommendations of the Advisory Committee on Immunization Practices in regard to smallpox vaccination. Complete clinical information on the disease progression and its causative agents is contained on this site. Presented in PDF format, the report also examines the range of options for vaccination against the disease and recommendations for future practices.
http://www.cdc.gov/mmwr/pdf/rr/rr5010.pdf

**Vaccinia (Smallpox) Vaccine Recommendations of the Advisory Committee on Immunization Practices** Published in the CDC's *Morbidity and Mortality Weekly Report,* these recommendations cover the use of smallpox vaccination in nonemergency exposure situations as well as cases in which the virus was used as an agent of biological terrorism. In addition to background information on the disease and the vaccine, the committee includes information on routine use of the vaccine; side effects and adverse reactions; precautions and contraindications, including pregnancy, HIV infection, and infants; and treatments for complications. The section devoted to smallpox vaccination for bioterrorism stresses surveillance and provides information on prerelease vaccination, postrelease vaccination, contraindication to vaccination during a smallpox emergency, infection control measures, prophylaxis, and recommendations for research priorities.
http://www.cdc.gov/mmwr/preview/mmwrhtml/rr5010a1.htm

# 11

# HEALTH AND SAFETY GUIDELINES

## 11.1 GENERAL RESOURCES

**Environmental Health Policy Committee, Subcommittee on Risk Communication and Education** Sponsored by the Agency for Toxic Substances and Disease Registry, this primer is designed mainly to reach out to the public health sector. Recommendations covered in this guide provide risk communication practitioners and administrators with the techniques for evaluating the effectiveness of health risk communication messages, campaigns, and materials. The primer covers principles and techniques for evaluating health risk communications activities, the role of formative evaluation and research, and tips for evaluating communication outcomes and impacts.
http://www.atsdr.cdc.gov/HEC/evalprmr.html

**Guideline for Infection Control in Health Care Personnel from the Centers for Disease Control and Prevention** This 66-page article compiled by the CDC contains detailed information on disease, epidemiology, prevention, and control of infections in healthcare personnel. Materials in this article relate to the spread of bloodborne pathogens such as diphtheria, hepatitis A, measles, rabies, and smallpox. The complete list includes over 20 separate infections. Each section contains a concise overview of the disease including the causative agent, symptoms, diagnosis, and progression of the illness. Recommendations for prevention of spreading infections among healthcare personnel are included.
http://www.cdc.gov/ncidod/hip/GUIDE/InfectControl98.pdf

**Guideline for Isolation Precautions in Hospitals from the Centers for Disease Control and Prevention** Compiled by the Hospital Infection Control and Practices Advisory Committee, these guidelines are

designed to assist hospital staff in maintaining effective isolation procedures. The first section of this document, entitled "Evolution of Isolation Practices," is a review of the history of isolation practices in U.S. hospitals as well as an analysis of their advantages, disadvantages, and some of the controversies that surround them. The remainder of the document contains the actual recommendations for isolation precautions in hospitals. These materials cover topics ranging from fundamentals of isolation precautions such as handwashing and use of gloves, to more stringent measures for use of airborne, droplet, and contact precautions. A synopsis of both sections is available in tabular format.
http://www.cdc.gov/ncidod/hip/isolat/isolat.htm

**Guidelines for Protecting the Health and Safety of Health Care Workers from the National Institute of Occupational Safety and Health** Authored from within the Department of Health and Human Services, these guidelines are designed to reduce the risk of injury and infection in healthcare personnel. In addition to an overview of hospital hazards, readers will find information on developing hospital health and safety programs, discussions of safety hazards and disease, proper methods of hazardous waste disposal, and a listing of related agencies and resources. This extensive document contains detailed information on a variety of health-related topics including controlling hazards, surveillance, precaution with hazardous substances, and infections control. http://www.cdc.gov/niosh/88-119.html

**Hospital Emergency Incident Command System Update Project** Originally drafted in 1992, the Hospital Emergency Incident Command System Update Project was designed as a generic disaster response plan involving flexible management responsibilities to avoid panic and maintain function during times of crisis. This update provides information about the project, organizational charts, answers to frequently asked questions, and contact information for project coordinators. The entire plan is available for download and contains nearly 100 pages of information and exercises designed to maximize efficiency with minimal staff in an emergency situation.
http://www.emsa.cahwnet.gov/Dms2/heics3.htm

**How to Handle Anthrax and Other Biological Agent Threats, CDC Health Advisory** The CDC

provides the public with a list of guidelines for the proper handling of a biological threat. This health advisory contains instructions for the safe handling of mail and suspicious packages and presents CDC recommendations covering what to do in the event of contact with questionable powder, aerosol-contaminated rooms, and ways of identifying dangerous packages.

http://www.bt.cdc.gov/Documents
App/Anthrax/10122001Handle/10122001Handle.asp

### Implementation Procedures for Handling Suspicious Letters and Packages
The New Jersey Department of Law and Public Safety hosts this site to publish safety guidelines for preventing exposure to threatening biological agents. The site provides information on preventing anthrax exposure via mail or suspicious packages as well as what to do in the event that dangerous contents are released from a mail item.

http://www.state.nj.us/lps/attack/employnotice_pkgs.htm

### Interim Recommendations for the Selection and Use of Protective Clothing and Respirators against Biological Agents
Published in response to the recent anthrax threat, the CDC has issued its recommendations for protective measures against exposure to biological agents. This Web site provides information regarding approved materials and breathing apparati when dealing with a biological hazard. These interim recommendations promote the use of proper protective gear in order to minimize the risk of exposure to hazardous biological agents.

http://www.bt.cdc.gov/Documents
App/Anthrax/Protective/10242001Protect.asp

### Primer on Health Risk Communication Principles and Practices from the Agency for Toxic Substances and Disease Registry
Intended for government and private organizations, this document from the Agency for Toxic Substances and Disease Registry (ATSDR) was created to provide public health personnel with the principles and approaches necessary for effectively communicating health risk information to a variety of audiences. Although the primer discusses the importance of local community involvement in the health risk communications process, the majority of this document is devoted to the issues and guidelines for communicating health risks. In addition, ATSDR provides suggestions

for effectively presenting information to the public and for interaction with the media.

http://www.atsdr.cdc.gov/HEC/primer.html

**Travel Warnings and Consular Information Sheets from the U.S. Department of State** Maintained by the U.S. Department of State, this site indexes all travel warnings that have been issued by the U.S. government. These warnings are designed to discourage Americans from traveling to nations where they may face danger or hostility and are based on all relevant information. Warnings can be accessed based on destination country and date of issue.

http://travel.state.gov/travel_warnings.html

## 12

# DISEASES

## 12.1 GENERAL RESOURCES

**Agent Fact Sheet Info from the Johns Hopkins Center for Civilian Biodefense Strategies** This Web page provides a portal to fact sheets on a number of biological agents prepared by the Johns Hopkins Center for Civilian Biodefense Strategies including anthrax, botulism, plague, smallpox, and tularemia. The fact sheets cover public health and medical consequences of large-scale release of these agents and provide recommendations on responsive actions following such an attack.
http://www.hopkins-biodefense.org/pages/agents/agent.html

**National Center for Infectious Diseases** Information and resources relating to communicable diseases are available from the National Center for Infectious Diseases (NCID). Features of this site include an infectious disease index, an alphabetical listing of topic pages, and news and event coverage regarding disease control. In response to recent events, the NCID has created a number of resources devoted to education and the prevention of bioterrorism. http://www.cdc.gov/ncidod/

## 12.2 ANTHRAX

**Anthrax and Bioterrorism** Created by the Patient Education Institute, "Anthrax and Bioterrorism" is a free Web-based multimedia program that reviews the causes and types of anthrax. Program content includes symptoms of the disease, diagnosis, treatment, prevention, vaccination, and education/awareness initiatives. Although it is designed as a patient resource, this interactive, downloadable, program covers a variety of technical and clinical information related to the disease. An additional section, added following recent terrorist events, addresses anthrax as a potential bioterrorist weapon, instructions for safe handling of mail, and directions for appropriate actions in case of contact with an anthrax-contaminated package.

http://patient-education.com/anthrax/

**Anthrax as a Biological Weapon: Medical and Public Health Management from the Journal of the American Medical Association Consensus Statement** Originally published in the *Journal of the American Medical Association* in May of 1999, this consensus statement details recommendations for measures to be taken by medical and public health professionals in the wake of a bioterrorist action involving anthrax. The report provides a historical overview of anthrax threats, a review of epidemiology and microbiology, and detailed clinical information on pathogenesis, manifestations, diagnosis and therapy, vaccination, infection control, and decontamination. The text also makes reference to the need for further research to combat the disease.

http://jama.ama-assn.org/issues/v281n18/ffull/jst80027.html

**Anthrax Disease Information from the Division of Bacterial and Mycotic Diseases, Centers for Disease Control and Prevention** The CDC has created this site to provide background information on anthrax. This Web site compiles an extensive list of frequently asked questions about anthrax and provides detailed answers. Visitors will find answers to questions regarding the origin, clinical symptoms, prevention, and treatment of the disease.

http://www.cdc.gov/ncidod/dbmd/diseaseinfo/anthrax_g.htm

**Anthrax Extensive Information from the University of Alabama, Birmingham** The creators of this Web site from the University of Alabama intended it to be a resource for information and continuing education for healthcare providers. The site provides information on the history of anthrax development as a weapon, as well as on the epidemiology and etiology of the disease. Clinical resources include diagnosis, vaccination, prophylaxis, and treatments. A section on protection, isolation, and notification measures is also included.

http://www.bioterrorism.uab.edu/
EmergingInfections/Anthrax/anthrax.htm

**Anthrax from Bacteriology Lecture Topics** A brief history and description of the anthrax bacillus are available on this site sponsored by the University of Wisconsin to accompany a course in microbiology. Visitors will find information on the natural history of the bacterium as well as images of the original micrographs taken of the bacteria in 1977. The site also discusses pathogenicity, specific toxins, immunity and vaccines, and treatments. http://www.bact.wisc.edu/Bact330/lectureanthrax

## Anthrax from MEDLINEplus Health Information

MEDLINEplus provides an anthrax supersite at this location, with information drawn from government, medical, and media sources. Anthrax news, general overviews, therapy, prevention, and research are just a few of the topics that are explored in extensive detail on this site. Some resources are also available in Spanish.
http://www.nlm.nih.gov/medlineplus/anthrax.html

## Anthrax Infection from eMedicine
The eMedicine online textbook presents this article containing clinical information on anthrax, including pathophysiology, disease frequency, and mortality and morbidity. Clinical information is offered on the cutaneous, inhalational, gastrointestinal, oropharyngeal, and meningeal forms of anthrax, and differential diagnoses are available for comparison. Work-up and treatments are covered, including a table of drug information, and the article is accompanied by color photographs.
http://www.emedicine.com/emerg/topic864.htm

## Anthrax Information from the Centers for Disease Control and Prevention
Designed to help public healthcare providers prepare for the threat of bioterrorism, this CDC Web site contains numerous documents and resources on the anthrax disease. In addition to frequently asked questions, the CDC provides links to advisories, updates, general and clinical information, and media coverage.
http://www.bt.cdc.gov/Agent/Anthrax/Anthrax.asp

## Anthrax Information from the Navy Environmental Health Center
The Navy Environmental Health Center provides visitors with access to updates on anthrax events and investigations as well as information from the Department of Defense and the U.S. Navy. Much of the information provided is collected from outside sources, particularly the CDC.
http://www-nehc.med.navy.mil/prevmed/epi/anthrax.htm

**Anthrax Summary from the University of Alabama, Birmingham** Provided as a quick reference guide, this Web site from the University of Alabama condenses the key points from the accompanying Extensive Information Page into a more easily digestible form. The one-page summary covers symptoms for clinical recognition, diagnosis, and treatment.
http://www.bioterrorism.uab.edu/EmergingInfections/Anthrax-SummayInfo/anthrax-summayinfo.htm

**Anthrax, Bioterrorism Agent Fact Sheet** Information on general aspects of anthrax and its associated diseases is presented on this fact sheet. The sheet discusses the three forms of anthrax and provides a sidebar on clinical features of inhalation anthrax. Diagnosis, treatment, infection control, and decontamination are covered, as well as postexposure prophylaxis and vaccination. http://bioterrorism.slu.edu/quick/anthrax01.pdf

**Bacillus** This University of Texas Medical School Web site provides a brief description of the laboratory aspects of the anthrax bacterium and related organisms. The institution has created a summary description of the bacteria's appearance, laboratory behavior, disease manifestations, and clinical treatment.
http://medic.med.uth.tmc.edu/path/00001437.htm

**Cutaneous Anthrax and Its Mimics** Compiled by the American College of Physicians, this Web page presents a brief overview of the physical symptoms of cutaneous anthrax and provides information on a number of similar clinical syndromes. The section on anthrax provides a description of the physical manifestations of the disease, as well as full-color photographs of anthrax skin leisons and a prognosis if the illness goes untreated. In addition, visitors to this site will find information on a number of diseases with similar clinical symptoms, including brief descriptions of these afflictions and photographs of the accompanying physical manifestations of infection, as well as a number of guidelines for distinguishing these diseases from cutaneous anthrax cases.
http://www.acponline.org/bioterro/anthrax_mimics.htm?hp

**Inhalational Anthrax** Sponsored by the Armed Forces Institute of Pathology, this Web site offers information on the pathogenesis and medical imaging of inhalation anthrax. Intended to aid medical practitioners in the

rapid detection, diagnosis, and treatment of the infection, this resource provides clinical information on anthrax infection, prognosis of the disease, symptomology, and treatment. Four detailed case studies are provided that include medical X-rays of disease progression in the pulmonary lymphoid system. This site is supported by medical images and other visual media to illustrate the clinical content. In addition, a concise summary of site materials is available as a quick reference guide.
http://anthrax.radpath.org/

**Inhalational Anthrax**    Excerpted from a number of reference sources, this American College of Radiology Web page provides a concise overview of inhalation anthrax and its progression. Materials in this brief summary include information on initial stages and frequent causes of death. In-text links to images and other resources are included to illustrate clinical content or provide additional information from outside sources.
http://www.acr.org/cgi-bin/fr?mast:masthead-about,text:/announce/102501.html

**Learning about Anthrax from Educational Resources Information Center**    Teachers, students, and parents will find a wide variety of educational resources on this site. Devoted in part to educating the public on the dangers of anthrax, the Educational Resources Information Center provides information about all aspects of anthrax from the origin and behavior of the bacillus to its threat as a biological weapon. Additionally, the creators of this site have included background information on bacteria and other microorganisms.
http://www.ericse.org/anthrax.html

**Medical Treatment and Response to Suspected Anthrax: Information for Health Care Providers during Biologic Emergencies**    Sponsored by the New York City Department of Health Bureau of Communicable Disease, this extensive document contains important information for healthcare providers. In addition to listing the clinical aspects and manifestations of the disease, the report makes recommendations for the best ways in which to respond to potential cases in order to minimize the risks to human life. The report also details handling and disposal of infectious waste.
http://nyc.gov/html/doh/html/cd/antmd.html

**Summary of Confirmed Cases of Anthrax and Background Information from the Centers for Disease Control and Prevention** Released in October 2001, this CDC update reports findings on confirmed cases of anthrax and relevant background information. The document contains a summary of the conditions surrounding each CDC-confirmed case and provides general information on anthrax.
http://www.bt.cdc.gov/Documents
App/Anthrax/10232001PM/10232001PM.asp

**World Anthrax Data Site** A cooperative effort between the World Health Organization Collaborating Center for Remote Sensing and Geographic Information Systems for Public Health, the World Anthrax Data Site is dedicated to compiling anthrax occurrence statistics from across the globe. The site opens with a map of the globe in which each region is color coded according to the severity of anthrax prevalence. By clicking on any shaded region the user is transferred to a listing of countries in that region. The links in the list will direct the user to a detailed table of anthrax data for that country, including species, number of confirmed cases, vaccination programs, and population size. This is a comprehensive site for global anthrax occurrence information.
http://www.vetmed.lsu.edu/whocc/mp_world.htm

**Zoonosis (Anthrax) from AccessScience** A concise description of anthrax and its attributes is available from AccessScience. Topics covered on this site include a brief history, microbiology and pathogenesis, clinical manifestations, epidemiology, diagnosis, and prevention.
http://www.mheducation.com/
news_room/zoonosis_update1.htm

## 12.3 BOTULISM

**Botulinum Toxin as a Biological Weapon from the Journal of the American Medical Association** Published in the *Journal of the American Medical Association* this consensus statement serves as a concise and comprehensive resource for botulism information. The history of the threat, microbiology and virulence factors, pathogenesis and clinical manifestations, epidemiology, therapy, prophylaxis, and decontamination are all explored in extensive technical detail. This site is designed healthcare practitioners and as an educational

healthcare practitioners and as an educational resource for the public.
http://jama.ama-assn.org/issues/v285n8/ffull/jst00017.html

**Botulinum Toxin Information from the Johns Hopkins Center for Civilian Biodefense Strategies**    A summary of the clinical aspects of botulinum toxin has been prepared by the Johns Hopkins Center for Civilian Biodefense Strategies. This informative resource includes an examination of the organism's potential as a biological agent and details its laboratory behavior, toxicity in the body, symptoms of botulism poisoning, and what to do in the event of suspected cases. Links are also available to fact sheets on other bioterrorist agents including anthrax and plague.
http://www.hopkins-biodefense.org/
pages/agents/agentbotox.html

**Botulism Infection from eMedicine**    Technical and clinical information on botulism has been compiled and made available through eMedicine as part of its online textbook of medicine. Content includes background information, classification, pathophysiology, epidemiology, pathogenesis, morbidity and mortality, and clinical and laboratory information such as workup, medications, and follow-up treatments. This resource is designed to provide healthcare professionals with the information necessary to study, diagnose, and treat the illness.
http://www.emedicine.com/emerg/topic64.htm

**Botulism Information from the Centers for Disease Control and Prevention**    As part of the CDC's ongoing efforts to help healthcare providers develop plans to prepare for and respond to acts of bioterrorism, the agency has created a number of Web sites dedicated to specific diseases of potential bioterrorist focus. The resources for botulism provided at this site include a fact sheet, general information, medical information, surveillance case definitions, and important laboratory protocols for identifying the microorganism.
http://www.bt.cdc.gov/Agent/Botulism/Botulism.asp

**Botulism Information from the Washington University Neuromuscular Disease Center**    Formatted as a detailed outline, this site provides technical, scientific, and clinical information on *Clostridium botulinum,* the causative agent of botulism. In addition to the clinical features, protein structure, and behavior of the organism, the outline also includes disease diagnosis, clinical syndromes, prognosis, and prevention. Links are available throughout the text to additional scientific information.

http://www.neuro.wustl.edu/neuromuscular/nother/bot.htm

**Botulism Toxin Seen as Potential Bio-Weapon from FreeRepublic.com** The threat of botulinum toxin as a biological agent is examined in this article from WorldNetDaily.com. The article reports on the history and toxicity of the disease, its potential as a biological weapon, clinical symptoms, and domestic vulnerability. Links are provided to related stories, and a discussion forum on the article is available.

http://www.freerepublic.com/forum/a3a9e06922039.htm

**Botulism, Bioterrorism Agent Fact Sheet** Botulism, its diagnosis and treatment, postexposure prophylaxis, vaccination, and decontamination procedures are among the many topics addressed on this fact sheet. These documents were created to provide information to healthcare professionals regarding potential biological weapons, including important clinical information on symptomatology and treatment.

http://bioterrorism.slu.edu/quick/botulism01.PDF

**Medical Treatment and Response to Suspected Botulism: Information for Health Care Providers during Biologic Emergencies** The New York City Department of Health Bureau of Communicable Disease has responded to the threat of biological warfare by making key information and resources available to healthcare providers and the public. This site contains clinical information for the diagnosis and treatment of botulism, as well as proper protocols to be enacted in the event of a large-scale botulism threat.

http://nyc.gov/html/doh/html/cd/botmd.html

**Pathogenic Clostridia: Tetanus and Botulism from Bacteriology Lecture Topics** This educational resource from the University of Wisconsin is designed to support the study of bacteriology, focusing on the pathogens that cause tetanus and botulism. Visitors will find information regarding the life cycle of the organism, toxicity mechanisms, immunity, and prevention.

http://www.bact.wisc.edu/Bact330/lecturetetbot

## 12.4 BRUCELLOSIS

**Brucellosis Disease Information from the Centers for Disease Control and Prevention: Division of Bacterial and Mycotic Diseases**  A brief summary of information relating to brucellosis has been posted on this CDC Web site. Basic facts are presented on topics such as transmission, incidence, and risks. This site serves as a good resource for those seeking a concise overview of the disease.
http://www.cdc.gov/ncidod/dbmd/diseaseinfo/brucellosis_t.htm

**Brucellosis Information from the Centers for Disease Control and Prevention**  Made available as part of CDC efforts to combat the threat of bioterrorism, this Web site contains general information and surveillance data on brucellosis. Details about the disease, recognition, treatment, and related special issues are provided and intended for use by healthcare practitioners. Laboratory protocols for identifying the microorganism are also available in PDF format from this Web site.
http://www.bt.cdc.gov/Agent/Brucellosis/Brucellosis.asp

**Brucellosis, Bioterrorism Agent Fact Sheet**  Drafted as an educational resource, this PDF document provides information regarding the threat of brucellosis as a biological agent. Aspects of the disease covered include diagnosis, treatment, and vaccination. Clinical features of the disease and information about infection control are also supplied on this fact sheet.
http://bioterrorism.slu.edu/quick/brucellae01.PDF

**Facts about Brucellosis from the Animal and Plant Health Inspection Service**  Sponsored by the National Animal Health Programs of the U.S. Department of Agriculture, this site provides factual information about the disease brucellosis. Information is presented in a question and answer format covering topics such as causative agents, symptoms, epidemiology, and prevention. http://www.aphis.usda.gov/oa/brufacts.html

## 12.5 PLAGUE

**Medical Treatment and Response to Suspected Plague: Information for Health Care Providers during Biologic Emergencies**  Sponsored by the

New York City Department of Health, this resource is designed to provide vital information to prevent and respond to the threat of bioterrorism, with a focus on plague. The document covers clinical manifestations, handling of laboratory specimens, treatment, and patient management. Important protocols to be enacted in the event of plague outbreak are available for healthcare practitioners. http://nyc.gov/html/doh/html/cd/plaguemd.html

**Plague as a Biological Weapon, Journal of the American Medical Association Consensus Statement** This Web site from the *Journal of the American Medical Association* presents *JAMA's* consensus statement on managing a plague epidemic. In addition to examining plague as a potential biological weapon, the site provides clinical information on the epidemiology, microbiology, pathogenesis, diagnosis, and treatment of the disease. All relevant aspects of infection and control are reviewed.
http://jama.ama-assn.org/issues/v283n17/ffull/jst90013.html

**Plague from eMedicine** This article from the eMedicine online textbook compiles historical and clinical information on plague. Clinical symptoms, diagnosis, laboratory studies, and treatment regimes are covered in detail. In addition, the site provides color photographs of physical characteristics of the disease and of the plague bacillus itself.
http://www.emedicine.com/emerg/topic428.htm

**Plague Information from the Centers for Disease Control and Prevention** In order to provide appropriate information for bolstering preparedness and response efforts to disease outbreaks, the CDC has prepared this Web site dedicated to plague. The resources available include fact sheets, general information, medical and clinical information, recommendations from biodefense organizations, and surveillance data. This Web site is designed as an educational resource to increase the rapidity of response to plague cases and, subsequently, to reduce human mortality.
http://www.bt.cdc.gov/Agent/Plague/Plague.asp

**Plague Information from the Division of Vector-Borne Infectious Diseases Centers for Disease Control and Prevention** This CDC Web site is a comprehensive resource for information on all aspects of

plague. Topics covered include the natural history, diagnosis, epidemiology, prevention and control, and current surveillance data of the disease. Information presented on this site ranges from general facts to detailed medical and scientific information on the plague bacterium.
http://www.cdc.gov/ncidod/dvbid/plague/index.htm

**Plague, Bioterrorism Agent Fact Sheet**  Clinical features and manifestations, diagnosis, treatment, post-exposure prophylaxis, and infection control are among the many topics contained on this fact sheet about plague. This PDF document discusses the three forms of plague and covers aspects of diagnosis, treatment, and postexposure prophylaxis. Sidebars also provide information on clinical presentation and infection control.
http://bioterrorism.slu.edu/quick/plague01.pdf

**Plague, WHO Report on Global Surveillance of Epidemic-Prone Infectious Diseases**  The World Health Organization (WHO) maintains surveillance data on all important communicable diseases. This section of the WHO report is an in-depth study of plague and related subjects. Topics addressed include background information, transmission, history, prevention and control, surveillance data, and trends. Graphical representations of plague incidence and mortality over approximately the last 50 years are available. This site is part of a larger document on a global surveillance report of epidemic-prone infectious diseases.
http://www.who.int/emc-documents/surveillance/
docs/whocdscsrisr2001.html/plague/plague.htm

## 12.6  Q Fever

**Medical Treatment and Response to Suspected Q Fever: Information for Health Care Providers during Biologic Emergencies**  The concern over communicable diseases being used as biological weapons has prompted the launch of this New York City Department of Health Web site devoted to Q fever. The site is designed mainly to aid healthcare professionals in the quick recognition and response to outbreaks of the disease, providing information on epidemiology, clinical manifestations, treatment, and proper protocols for dealing with infection, prevention, and control of Q fever.
http://nyc.gov/html/doh/html/cd/qfmd.html

**Q Fever from eMedicine** A collaborative effort among a number of medical experts has produced this extensive resource on Q fever as part of eMedicine's online resource. Detailed clinical, laboratory, and medical information is provided primarily for healthcare professionals. Recommendations for diagnosis and treatment, including effective drug therapy regimes, are presented. http://www.emedicine.com/EMERG/topic492.htm

**Q Fever from the Merck Manual of Diagnosis and Therapy** This section of the *Merck Manual* provides a brief introduction and outline of important aspects of Q fever. History, epidemiology, symptoms, diagnosis, and treatment are all described, with access available to information on other rickettsial diseases and infectious diseases.
http://www.merck.com/pubs/
mmanual/section13/chapter159/159i.htm

**Q Fever Information from the Centers for Disease Control and Prevention** This section of the Centers for Disease Control and Prevention Web site on viral and rickettsial zoonoses provides a brief overview of Q fever. A description of the disease, including its symptoms in humans, diagnosis, and treatment methods, is contained in this document. The site presents a concise introduction to Q fever. Prevention measures are provided, as are links to a list of articles and a glossary of related terms.
http://www.cdc.gov/ncidod/dvrd/qfever/

## 12.7 SMALLPOX

**Interim Smallpox Response Plan and Guidelines** With recent growing concern over the threat of bioterrorist activities targeted at American citizens, the CDC has been designated as the lead organization for updating public health capabilities for preparedness and response to bioterrorist events. This extensive and highly detailed document outlines the CDC plan for response to the use of the smallpox virus in a bioterrorist attack. In addition to presenting the criteria for calling the CDC plan into action, this report provides information on every step to be undertaken thereafter. Preliminary response activities include case investigation, laboratory testing, contact identification, site visits, sources of exposure, surveillance, daily case tracking, hospital surveillance, and vaccination referrals. Subsequent activities cover vaccination guidelines, quarantine and isolation, specimen collection, health communications, and decontamination. This CDC document is a comprehensive resource for preparedness, response, and safety guidelines in the event of a smallpox outbreak.

http://www.bt.cdc.gov/
DocumentsApp/Smallpox/RPG/index.asp

**Medical Treatment and Response to Suspected Smallpox: Information for Health Care Providers during Biologic Emergencies** This Web site, part of a New York City Department of Health series on biological weapons, provides information on the potential for smallpox as a biological weapon. In addition to clinical information on symptomatology, diagnosis, treatment, and prevention, this document alerts healthcare practitioners to government-issued protocols to be followed in the event of a smallpox outbreak.

http://nyc.gov/html/doh/html/cd/smallmd.html

**Smallpox and Its Eradication** Published in 1988 by the World Health Organization, *Smallpox and Its Eradication* is a comprehensive work containing clinical and historical information on the variola virus. Chapter topics include clinical features of smallpox; pathogenesis, pathology, and immunology information; the epidemiology of smallpox; historical data on its spread around the world; vaccine development; and eradication efforts according to year and area. The document also examines potential animal reservoirs for the disease and means by which the virus may return to man. This report is both a clinical resource and a historical document for those interested in variola and related viruses.

http://www.who.int/emc/
diseases/smallpox/Smallpoxeradication.html

**Smallpox as a Biological Weapon from the Journal of the American Medical Association** This consensus statement from the *Journal of the American Medical Association* provides *JAMA's* recommendations for public health management of a smallpox outbreak. Geared toward healthcare professionals, the document presents an account of the disease's history, epidemiology, microbiology, and diagnosis. Aspects of vaccine administration, hospital epidemiology, and decontamination are also covered.

http://jama.ama-assn.org/issues/v281n22/ffull/jst90000.html

**Smallpox Extensive Information from the University of Alabama, Birmingham** This Web site maintained by the University of Alabama provides access to extensive information on smallpox. All aspects, from history to threat as a biological agent to vaccination information, are covered in full detail through a hotlinked table of contents.
http://www.bioterrorism.uab.edu/
EmergingInfections/SmallPox/smallpox.htm

 **Smallpox from eMedicine** eMedicine has prepared this comprehensive resource on the study, diagnosis, and prevention of smallpox as part of its online textbook. This site contains clinical and technical information regarding the disease, diagnosis, symptoms, treatment, and epidemiology. Color photographs of infection and physical symptoms of the disease are also available.
http://www.emedicine.com/emerg/topic885.htm

 **Smallpox from Emerging Infectious Diseases** Drawn from the CDC publication *Emerging Infectious Diseases,* this article examines the clinical features of smallpox and provides data on vaccination efforts to combat the disease. In addition to providing detailed clinical information, the author devotes a large portion of the document to exploring the potential for smallpox as a biological agent. The article examines the threat in light of a historical and scientific perspective.
http://www.cdc.gov/ncidod/EID/vol5no4/henderson.htm

 **Smallpox Information from MEDLINEplus Health Information** The latest news, general overviews, clinical trials, pictures and diagrams, and research information are among the many resources accessible on this MEDLINE Web site from the National Library of Medicine. Resources are drawn from government agencies such as the CDC, the National Institutes of Health, and the World Health Organization. Some resources may also be viewed in Spanish.
http://www.nlm.nih.gov/medlineplus/smallpox.html

 **Smallpox Summary from the University of Alabama, Birmingham** This smallpox summary collects key points from the accompanying "Extensive Information" page and compiles them into a quick reference guide. For easy access to vital information, this page

outlines clinical features of the disease in a clear and concise manner.
http://www.bioterrorism.uab.edu/Emerging
Infections/SmallPox-SummaryInfo/smallpox-summaryinfo.htm

**Smallpox, Bioterrorism Agent Fact Sheet**
Created to improve preparedness and response efforts in the event of large-scale release of smallpox by bioterrorists, this fact sheet contains information on the disease, its diagnosis, treatment, prevention, and infection control. Presented in PDF format, the document covers vaccination and postexposure prophylaxis, as well as clinical features and decontamination procedures.
http://bioterrorism.slu.edu/quick/smallpox01.pdf

## 12.8  TULAREMIA

**Medical Treatment and Response to Suspected Tularemia: Information for Health Care Providers during Biologic Emergencies**  Maintained under the continuing efforts of the New York City Department of Health to educate both the public and healthcare professionals on potential biological agents, this Web site provides general and clinical information on tularemia. Topics covered include clinical manifestations, laboratory confirmation of the pathogen, treatments, and patient management. In addition, the Department of Health protocol in the event of an outbreak has been provided for use by healthcare practitioners.
http://nyc.gov/html/doh/html/cd/tulmd.html

**Tularemia as a Biological Weapon from the Journal of the American Medical Association**
This consensus statement from the *Journal of the American Medical Association* provides vital information for medical and public health management of tularemia. Aspects of the disease explored include history and potential as a biological weapon, epidemiology, microbiology, virulence, diagnosis, vaccination, and prevention. Postexposure antibiotic therapy is also considered, as well as infection control and environmental decontamination.
http://jama.ama-assn.org/issues/v285n21/ffull/jst10001.html

**Tularemia from MEDLINEplus Medical Encyclopedia**  This National Library of Medicine Web site provides a concise resource for materials relating to tularemia. On this site, visitors will find illustrations, definitions, causes and prevention information, descriptions of

symptoms, and treatment and prognosis details. Intended mainly as an overview, the site also provides color images and links to related topics of interest.
http://www.nlm.nih.gov/medlineplus/ency/article/000856.htm

**Tularemia Information from the Johns Hopkins Center for Civilian Biodefense Strategies** The Johns Hopkins Center for Civilian Biodefense Strategies has prepared this fact sheet that reviews the history of tularemia as a biological weapon, as well as the natural history of the disease. Also included in the text are some previously published surveillance data, and clinical information on the disease.
http://www.hopkins-biodefense.org/
pages/agents/agenttularemia.html

**Tularemia Information from the Centers for Disease Control and Prevention** Sponsored by the CDC, this Web site devoted to tularemia contains key medical information and surveillance and case data on the disease. Designed to improve preparedness and response to biological agents, it also provides laboratory protocols for identifying the tularemia microbe.
http://www.bt.cdc.gov/Agent/Tularemia/Tularemia.asp

**Tularemia, Bioterrorism Agent Fact Sheet** Part of an effort to educate healthcare professionals on the dangers of biological weapons, this fact sheet on tularemia provides a detailed introduction to important features of the disease. In addition to background information on the types of tularemia, this PDF document contains overviews of clinical manifestations, diagnosis, treatment, vaccination, and decontamination.
http://bioterrorism.slu.edu/quick/tularemia01.PDF

## 12.9 VIRAL HEMORRHAGIC FEVER

**Management of Patients with Suspected Viral Hemorrhagic Fever** Originally published by the CDC in 1988, this document presents detailed historical surveillance data on viral hemorrhagic fever outbreaks. Although some clinical information has been incorporated, the article is mainly dedicated to tracking the progression of the disease in each case of outbreak. The CDC warns that this site is maintained for strictly historical purposes and new content will not be added.
http://wonder.cdc.gov/wonder/
prevguid/m0037085/m0037085.asp

**Viral Hemorrhagic Fevers from eMedicine** The viral hemorrhagic fevers are divided among four viral families. This site provides brief information on each of the four classes in combination with historical, clinical, and medical information. Topics covered include morbidity and mortality, symptoms, diagnosis, and treatment. Photographs of physical symptoms resulting from a variety of viral infections are presented at the end of the document. http://www.emedicine.com/emerg/topic887.htm

 **Viral Hemorrhagic Fevers from the Centers for Disease Control and Prevention Special Pathogens Branch** Sponsored by the CDC Special Pathogens Branch, this Web site contains a compendium of fact sheets on a number of the viral hemorrhagic fevers. These documents cover such topics as how the disease is spread, symptoms, and typical progression of infection. Information on four categories of viruses is available in addition to links to teaching and prevention materials, a glossary of terms, and other resources. http://www.cdc.gov/ncidod/dvrd/spb/mnpages/factmenu.htm

 **Viral Infections from MEDLINEplus Health Information** Hosted by the National Library of Medicine, this Web site of health information from MEDLINEplus covers general aspects of viral infections. Links are provided to resources categorized as latest news, overviews, anatomy and physiology, specific conditions, statistics, and children. Portions of the site are also available in Spanish. http://www.nlm.nih.gov/medlineplus/viralinfections.html

**Chemical Hazard Response Information System (CHRIS) from the U.S. Coast Guard** The CHRIS manual, sponsored by the U.S. Coast Guard, contains regulatory and scientific information related to chemical safety. The Chemical Hazards Response Information System is composed of two parts, hazardous chemical data and the hazardous assessment computer system. Additional information in this text includes an explanation of relevant terms, other information systems, conversion factors, selected properties of fresh and sea water, ice and air, and a guide to chemical compatibility. The manual is intended mainly for Coast Guard personnel to aid in decision-making during emergencies involving water transport of hazardous chemicals.
http://www.chrismanual.com/

**CHEMTREC, the 24-Hour HazMat Emergency Communications Center** CHEMTREC is an organization affiliated with the American Chemistry Council which aids transporters of hazardous materials in complying with federal regulations, reducing overall risk, and promoting responsible care. CHEMTREC runs a 24-hour emergency call center that provides technical information and links chemical experts with emergency responders in the event of a chemical disaster. Shippers may register with CHEMTREC for around-the-clock coverage on the emergency response network.
http://memberexchange.cmahq.com/chemtrec.nsf

**Developing a Hazardous Materials Exercise Program: A Handbook for State and Local Officials from the National Transportation Library** Composed of 14 federal agencies, the National Response Team (NRT) is entrusted with major responsibilities affecting the environment, transportation, emergency management, worker safety, and public health. This handbook was created by the NRT as an educational resource emphasizing the value of emergency preparedness exercises and providing guidelines for selecting the appropriate exercises on the basis of actual risk, resources, capabilities, and governmental support. The major sections of this document are devoted to selection of the appropriate exercise, an overview of exercise activities, learning from the experience of others, and an index of federal agency resources. http://ntl.bts.gov/DOCS/254.html

**Hazardous Materials Information System** The Hazardous Materials Information System (HMIS) is an automated database of the Department of Defense serving as a central repository for Material Safety Data Sheets and other important information on hazardous substances used by government and civilian organizations. Intended for federal government personnel involved in the purchase, use, storage, transportation, and disposal of hazardous materials, use of this resource is restricted to authorized personnel. Resources available to the public include the HMIS user's guide, contact information, news and updates, and registration forms. http://www.dlis.dla.mil/hmis/

**Hazardous Waste Operations and Emergency Response from the Occupational Safety and Health Administration** Owing to the dangers presented by misuse and uncontrolled disposal of hazardous wastes, the Occupational Safety and Health Administration (OSHA) has put together this information booklet containing guidelines for establishing safety and health programs. This OSHA resource contains information on site evaluation and control, training programs, protective equipment, monitoring, medical surveillance, decontamination, and emergency response. Readers will also find OSHA standards and guidelines, provisions for record keeping, labeling of hazardous substances, sanitation, and risk communication. http://www.osha-slc.gov/ Publications/OSHA3114/osha3114.html

**HazMat for Healthcare** Intended for use by hospitals and healthcare organizations, this program was designed to improve existing hazardous materials emergency response programs. Site resources include information on handling of contaminated patients, training modules, safety equipment recommendations, guidelines from the Occupational Safety and Health Administration, and a calendar of events. HazMat for Healthcare provides four downloadable training modules addressing awareness, operations, personal protective equipment, and decontamination. http://www.hazmatforhealthcare.org/

**HazMat on the Web**  Maintained for authorized use by U.S. Air Force personnel and affiliates, HazMat on the Web is a Department of Defense resource containing information on material safety, environmental safety, and regulations from the Environmental Protection Agency. Accessible information includes the top 10 Material Safety Data Sheets on substances such as hydrochloric acid, ammonia, and "Simple Green," along with links to CDC anthrax information. Other resources are restricted to authorized users only. http://www.hazmat48.wpafb.af.mil/

**Material Safety Data Sheets Index from Vermont Safety Information Resources**  The Material Safety Data Sheets (MSDS) index serves as a database for information on a variety of chemical substances. Users may search for data sheets based on substance registration numbers, product name, or production company. The information indexed on this site is a matter of public domain and is available to all users. The material provided in the data sheets differs by product as the contents of data sheets are the responsibility of the submitting organization. Other site resources include a database of toxicology reports for various substances. http://hazard.com/msds/

**Occupational Safety and Health Guidance Manual for Hazardous Waste Site Activities**  Composed by the Department of Health and Human Services, this document contains over 100 pages of safety information and safety program recommendations for use by a variety of organizations. Topics addressed include an introduction to waste-related hazards, site characterization, air monitoring, personal protective equipment, site control, decontamination, and handling of waste containers. Appendices contain information on generic safety plans, samples of hazardous substance information and decontamination procedures, and federal government regulations for waste management from the Occupational Safety and Health Administration and the Environmental Protection Agency. The entire document is available for download in PDF format. http://www.cdc.gov/niosh/85-115.html

**Office of Hazardous Materials Safety, Department of Transportation** Housed under the U.S. Department of Transportation, the Office of Hazardous Materials Safety is dedicated to regulating and enforcing standards designed to maintain national safety in the commercial transportation of hazardous materials. This site serves as a portal to all of the office's resources, including listings of standards and regulations, answers to frequently asked questions, and an emergency response guidebook. http://hazmat.dot.gov/

**ToxFAQs, Frequently Asked Questions about Contaminants Found at Hazardous Waste Sites from the Agency for Toxic Substances and Disease Registry** Developed by the Agency for Toxic Substances and Disease Registry Division of Toxicology, ToxFAQs is a collection of summaries on various chemical substances. These concise and easy-to-understand fact sheets provide answers to frequently asked questions about exposure and health effects related to chemical exposure. The ToxFAQs index contains an alphabetical catalog of over 100 common chemical substances such as ammonia, arsenic, chromium, lead, and zinc. http://www.atsdr.cdc.gov/toxfaq.html

**TOXNET, Toxicology Data Network** Sponsored by the National Library of Medicine's Department of Specialized Information Services, TOXNET is a collection of databases on toxicity, hazardous chemicals, and other related topics. Databases indexed on this site cover toxicology data; toxicology literature including scientific studies, reports, and bibliographical material; toxic release information; and chemical information such as nomenclature, identification, and structure. The site also maintains fact sheets, links, and TOXNET NEWS, which provides toxicity and environmental health news. http://toxnet.nlm.nih.gov/

**U.S. National Response Team** Hazardous material preparedness and response is the focus of the U.S. National Response Team (NRT). Aside from providing information on the NRT and member agencies, this Web site offers access to NRT publications, upcoming events lists, and news updates. The NRT also provides contact information to be used in the event of a hazardous material spill. http://www.nrt.org/

# 14

# DETECTION

**2T-0268**

**Biological Integrated Detection System** The Biological Integrated Detection System (BIDS) is a military device designed to protect soldiers against a biological attack. BIDS is intended to mitigate the effects of large-scale biological offensives and provide a safe vantage point from which to collect surveillance information during a biological attack. Information about the BIDS program, its status, and specifications is available on this Web site.
http://in1.apgea.army.mil/products/bids.htm

**2T-0269**

**Chemical Biological Mass Spectrometer** The Chemical Biological Mass Spectrometer (CBMS) is an ion trap mass spectrometer designed to detect the presence of harmful chemical agents on the battlefield. Created by the Oak Ridge National Laboratory, this device can be used both on the battlefield and in the laboratory. Device specifications, technical information, and functions are listed on this Web site. A complete and detailed overview of the CBMS and its capabilities is available for download. http://ntser3.cad.ornl.gov/webica/cbms_dnc.htm

**2T-0270**

**Hand-Held Immunoassays for Detection of Bacillus anthracis Spores** Released in October of 2001, this CDC Health Advisory addresses the use of hand-held assays for the rapid detection of anthrax spores. These assays are sold commercially and are used for the screening of environmental samples. This advisory contains cautionary information on the use of these assays and updates on the ongoing CDC evaluation of these devices to measure sensitivity and specificity.
http://www.bt.cdc.gov/DocumentsApp/Anthrax/
10182001HealthAlertPM/10182001HealthAlertPM.asp

**2T-0271**

**U.S. Army Soldier and Biological Chemical Command: Nuclear, Biological, and Chemical Defense** The U.S. Army Soldier and Biological Chemical Command (SBCCOM) is dedicated to enhancing defense capabilities by promoting research, development and acquisition, and emergency preparedness and response. This site from SBCCOM offers an extensive listing of biological and chemical weapons defense technologies and provides information on the agency's major projects and recently developed defense technologies. These products fall into three main categories: contamination avoidance, modeling and simulation, and individual/group protection devices. For each device, a photograph is provided, along with specification information, capabilities, advantages, and field uses.

http://www.sbccom.army.mil/products/nbc.htm

# 15

# DECONTAMINATION

## Decontamination of Chemical Warfare Agents

Created by the Organisation for the Prohibition of Chemical Weapons (OPCW), this Web site serves as an introduction to the methods and chemicals used for the decontamination aspect of chemical warfare. In addition to information on personal decontamination, methods for cleaning surfaces and equipment are presented.

http://www.opcw.org/chemhaz/decon.htm

## First Responders' Environmental Liability due to Mass Decontamination Runoff, Environmental Protection Agency

In July 2000, the Environmental Protection Agency released this alert to address the question, "Can emergency responders undertake necessary actions in order to save lives in dire situations without fear of environmental liability even when such emergency actions have unavoidable adverse environmental impacts?" Information provided addresses Good Samaritan provisions, liability issues and state tort laws, federal support during a weapons of mass destruction incident, and the necessity of pre-planning. To illustrate the issues that arise in such a situation, the alert details a case study of the "Nerve Agent Drill," which tested the ability of multiple government agencies to respond to a purported nerve agent attack.

http://www.epa.gov/ceppo/pubs/onepage.pdf

## Guidelines for Mass Casualty Decontamination during a Terrorist Chemical Agent Incident

These decontamination guidelines were produced by the U.S. Army Soldier and Biological Chemical Command (SBCCOM) in a study of technical and operational issues for civilian mass casualty decontamination after a chemical terrorist attack. Created for the development of emergency responder mass casualty decontamination policies, this document reports on purposes and methods of decontamination, procedures and approaches, types of chemical victims, prioritizing casualties for decontamination, and processing casualties. A listing of Inter-

net resources, related medical publications, newsletters, and periodicals is also provided.
http://www2.sbccom.army.mil/hld/cwirp/
cwirp_guidelines_mass_casualty_decon_download.htm

## Sandia National Labs Decontamination Foam

This commercial site provides information on Reeves decontamination products and delivery systems. Information provided includes product specifications, toxicity, effectiveness against biological agents, packaging, and delivery. For those seeking to purchase decontamination products or systems, this Web site offers a variety of solutions. http://www.reevesmfg.com/SNL_Technical_Data.htm

# 16

# PSYCHOSOCIAL ISSUES

## 16.1 GUIDELINES AND RESOURCES

**Common Reactions to Trauma from the National Center for Post-Traumatic Stress Disorder** These guidelines, created by the National Center for Post-Traumatic Stress Disorder, address a number of common problems that may arise following a stressful event. The basis of each problem is explored and a simple means of dealing with the problem is offered. Common reactions covered include fear and anxiety, avoidance, guilt and depression, and negative self-image.
http://www.ncptsd.org/facts/disasters/fs_foa_handout.html

**Coping with a National Tragedy from the American Psychiatric Association** This statement from the American Psychiatric Association (APA) addresses the national need for stress and grief management, written in response to recent tragic events. The APA feels that the American public should have the appropriate tools for managing the barrage of emotions associated with such an event. These guidelines present simple methods for dealing with fear and anger and promoting renewed mental health.
http://www.psych.org/public_info/copingwtragedy91301.cfm

**Disaster Mental Health from the U.S. Department of Health and Human Services** The Center for Mental Health Services (CMHS), in cooperation with the Federal Emergency Management Agency, is overseeing national efforts aimed at providing psychiatric services for victims of presidentially declared disasters. Program resources include tips for discussing disasters, bioterrorism information, grant application materials, program guidance, technical assistance, a mental health services locator, information on related mental health topics, and featured publications. The CMHS section on bioterrorism provides links to outside resources including

the CDC, the Occupational Safety and Health Administration, and other federal agencies.
http://www.mentalhealth.org/
cmhs/EmergencyServices/default.asp

**Disaster Psychiatry from the American Psychiatric Association**  Developed by the American Psychiatric Association Committee on Psychiatric Dimensions of Disaster, this Web site is designed to provide psychiatrists with information on preparation and response to disaster and traumatic events. In order to aid psychiatrists in coping with such an event, this Web page provides a number of disaster psychiatry articles, information on coping with a national tragedy, and access to online psychiatric resources. Articles available at this site have all been previously published in *Psychiatric Quarterly*.
http://www.psych.org/pract_of_psych/disaster_psych.cfm

**Field Manual for Mental Health and Human Service Workers in Major Disasters from the Center for Mental Health Services**  Intended for use by mental health and human services workers in major disasters, this field manual from the Center for Mental Health Services is a pocket reference guide to the basics of disaster mental health and provides specific and practical suggestions for field workers. Contents of the manual include key concepts of disaster mental health, addressing survivors' needs and reactions, a disaster counseling tutorial, suggestions for making referrals to emergency mental health services, high-risk groups, and stress prevention and management. Visitors may also request additional copies of the manual at no charge.
http://www.mentalhealth.org/
publications/allpubs/ADM90-537/default.asp

**Guidelines for Psychological Trauma from the American College of Occupational and Environmental Medicine**  As part of the program on emergency preparedness and disaster response, the Mental Health Committee and the Council on Scientific Affairs of the American College of Occupational and Environmental Medicine have prepared an extensive set of guidelines for dealing with the psychological trauma emerging as a result of recent terrorist events. These guidelines are designed to aid physicians in providing the appropriate stress and grief management tools for victims of disaster.

A wide variety of stress-related syndromes are covered on this site.
http://www.acoem.org/member/guidelines.htm

### How Pediatricians Can Respond to the Psychosocial Implications of Disasters from the American Academy of Pediatrics
Produced by the Committee on Psychosocial Aspects of Child and Family Health, these guidelines expand upon the pediatrician's role in providing appropriate care before, during, and following a disaster. These recommendations are designed to illuminate and standardize the pediatrician's responsibility to his or her patients and community in times of disaster. Some of the situations addressed include school and child-care settings, designing public service announcements, and disaster preparedness.
http://www.aap.org/policy/re9813.html

### How to Address Psychosocial Reactions to Catastrophe from the World Health Organization
The way in which traumatic events affect the abilities to cope, understand, and respond is the subject of this brief text from the "Mental Health and Brain Disorders" section of the World Health Organization. The document offers background information on psychosocial responses and makes recommendations to mental health professionals for proper handling of patients during stressful times.
http://www.who.int/mental_health/
Topic_psychosocial_reactions/catastrophe.html

### Psychosocial Resources in the Aftermath of Natural and Human-Caused Disasters from the National Center for Post-Traumatic Stress Disorder
Mental and public health professionals will find a number of useful recommendations and resources provided at this Web site by the National Center for Post-Traumatic Stress Disorder. This document reviews a variety of resources available to health professionals to aid patients in coping with mental trauma. Both psychological and social support networks are examined.
http://www.ncptsd.org/facts/disasters/fs_resources.html

### Response to Terrorist Acts against America from the National Institute of Mental Health
The National Institute of Mental Health has launched this Web site as a resource for all those affected by recent terrorist events. Post-traumatic stress disorder, depression, and

anxiety are emphasized, with links to articles under each topic. Users will also find material dedicated to child-related mental health disorders. Some resources are available in Spanish.
http://www.nimh.nih.gov/outline/responseterrorism.cfm

**Self-Care and Self-Help following Disasters from the National Center for Post-Traumatic Stress Disorder** This fact sheet from the National Center for Post-Traumatic Stress Disorder presents a useful patient guide for dealing with personal stress and grief. Recommendations for self-care include methods of coping, helping children to deal with trauma, and when to seek professional help. A listing of resources from which appropriate help is available is also provided.
http://www.ncptsd.org/facts/disasters/fs_self_care_brief.html

**Terrorism and Children from the National Center for Post-Traumatic Stress Disorder** Published by the National Center for Post-Traumatic Stress Disorder, this article addresses the unique needs of young people in coping with terrorist events. The author divides the discussion into three sections dealing with young children, school-aged children, and adolescents. Topics covered include typical reactions to stress in each age category and methods of coping and talking to a child.
http://www.ncptsd.org/facts/disasters/fs_children_disaster.html

## 16.2 POST-TRAUMATIC STRESS DISORDER

**Helping Survivors in the Wake of Disaster from the National Center for Post-Traumatic Stress Disorder** This document from the National Center for Post-Traumatic Stress Disorder provides information regarding the normal reactions to stress, severe symptoms in disaster response, survivorship issues, and identifying individuals particularly at risk for severe response. The article expands upon the duties and priorities of the mental health professional during times of disaster. The center also offers recommendations regarding situations in which medical intervention may be necessary to help an individual cope with disaster.
http://www.ncptsd.org/facts/disasters/fs_helping_survivors.html

**Post-Traumatic Stress Disorder—What It Is and What It Means to You from American Family Physician** Sponsored by the American Academy of

Family Physicians, this patient handout addresses the topic of post-traumatic stress disorder. Answers to commonly asked questions about the disorder and a link to a related in-depth article are included.
http://www.aafp.org/afp/20000901/1046ph.html

**Primary Care Treatment of Post-Traumatic Stress Disorder from American Family Physician** Practical therapeutic information on the diagnosis and treatment of post-traumatic stress disorder is the focus of this mental health text from *American Family Physician*. The article presents detailed criteria for diagnosing the disorder as well as recommended screening techniques. A number of frequently used drug treatment regimes are explored along with patient management and tips on prevention. http://www.aafp.org/afp/20000901/1035.html

**What Are the Traumatic Stress Effects of Terrorism? from the National Center for Post-Traumatic Stress Disorder** Traumatic stress resulting from terrorist activities is the focus of this article from the National Center for Post-Traumatic Stress Disorder. The article explores the large-scale public traumatic stress effects of disaster events. The authors examine the far-reaching stress effects of terrorist activities such as the attack on the World Trade Center and the Oklahoma City bombing.
http://www.ncptsd.org/facts/disasters/fs_terrorism.html

## 17

# AGENCIES,
# ORGANIZATIONS,
# AND CENTERS

## 17.1 U.S. GOVERNMENT AGENCIES AND PROGRAMS

**Agency for Toxic Substances and Disease Registry** The Agency for Toxic Substances and Disease Registry is responsible for minimizing exposure and preventing harm to human health resulting from exposure to hazardous substances and environmental pollutants. This Web site offers information on hazardous substances, hazardous waste sites, and emergency response as well as education in environmental health and measuring health effects. Each area of the site provides links to articles, reports from expert panels, and related sites. Resources for specific audiences, such as children and parents, healthcare professionals, and communities, are also available. http://www.atsdr.cdc.gov/

**Animal and Plant Health Inspection Service from the U.S. Department of Agriculture** A collection of links is available on this U.S. Department of Agriculture Web site. The "Functions" section provides access to information on major department activities in areas such as agricultural biotechnology, animal health, plant health, and wildlife services. "News and Information" indexes important resources such as the five-year strategic plan and regulations and guidelines, and the "Hot Issues" section covers areas of current interest including anthrax information, West Nile virus, and foot-and-mouth disease. http://www.aphis.usda.gov/

**Armed Forces Institute of Pathology, U.S. Department of Defense** Housed under the Department of Defense, the Armed Forces Institute of Pathology (AFIP) is dedicated to consultation, education, and research. Site resources include department information, consultation overviews, educational courses and infor-

mation, publications, and news updates. Terrorism resources provide comprehensive coverage of the AFIP response to recent terrorist activities. The AFIP inhalation anthrax page includes pathogenesis and imaging, histopathology, and microbiology of the disease.
http://www.afip.org/

**Awareness of National Security Issues and Response Program**  As part of the National Security Awareness Program, the Awareness of National Security Issues and Response (ANSIR) program was created as a means of providing unclassified FBI information on issues of national security to public, corporate, and law enforcement audiences as well as other government bodies. Information pertaining to national security threats is made available to participating institutions via e-mail and fax networks. This site outlines the goals of the program and expands upon the protocol followed under this program. http://www.fbi.gov/hq/nsd/ansir/ansir.htm

**Center for Food Safety and Applied Nutrition, U.S. Food and Drug Administration**  A subsidiary of the Department of Health and Human Services, the Center for Food Safety and Applied Nutrition covers a broad spectrum of topics on its Web site. Sections of this site are devoted to recent news, an overview of the center, program areas, national food safety programs, documents from the Food and Drug Administration, interacting with the center, and special interest areas. Information on topics ranging from biotechnology and the cosmetics industry to foodborne illness and microbiology can be found here.
http://vm.cfsan.fda.gov/list.html

**Centers for Disease Control and Prevention**  The CDC is the definitive source for all material relating to public health. Under the auspices of the U.S. Department of Health and Human Services, the CDC aims to develop and apply increasingly more effective measures for disease control and prevention, environmental health, health promotion, and education. In addition to providing general, clinical, and surveillance data on many diseases, this site provides access to CDC updates and publications. Many CDC resources have also been translated into Spanish.
http://www.cdc.gov/

## Chemical Emergency Preparedness and Prevention Office, U.S. Environmental Protection Agency

The Chemical Emergency Preparedness and Prevention Office (CEPPO) of the U.S. Environmental Protection Agency (EPA) was created to help prepare for and prevent chemical emergencies, to respond to environmental crises, and to keep the public informed about local chemical hazards. CEPPO focuses on preparedness, prevention, rapid response, and counterterrorism to ensure the safety of the environment. Information on CEPPO's role and all its programs is accessible via this Web site. http://www.epa.gov/ceppo/

## Commissioned Corps Readiness Force, U.S. Public Health Service

Created in 1994 by the Office of the Surgeon General, the Commission Corps Readiness Force (CCRF) is intended to enhance the Department of Health and Human Services' ability to respond and aid recovery in cases of public health emergencies. Membership in CCRF is subject to stringent background requirements, education, and skills training. Basic CCRF information, membership information and applications, training materials, news and events coverage, and access to the organization's LISTERV are available via this site. Specialized resources including ready rosters and event information are reserved for access by corps members only. http://oep.osophs.dhhs.gov/ccrf/

## Council of State Governments

The Council of State Governments (CSG) works to build leadership skills and to improve the quality of decision making, promotes interstate cooperation, prepares states for changes in future political environments, and advocates states' sovereignty and rights. Information on CSG regions, daily news, programs and legislation, policy, products and services, and events can be accessed via this Web site. Recently added terrorism resources include anthrax information, daily updates for leaders from government agencies including the CDC and the Federal Emergency Management Agency, articles of interest, suggested legislation, and CSG statements.
http://www.statesnews.org/

## Critical Infrastructure Assurance Office

Created in May of 1998, the Critical Infrastructure Assurance Office (CIAO) was designed to educate and protect the public, to integrate vital infrastructure systems, and to mitigate the risks of dependency on critical government infrastructure. Accordingly, the CIAO directs its efforts toward protecting important government computer networks, recruiting and training federal information technology experts, and identifying critical federal assets. This site provides information on all aspects of the CIAO and related programming, including key initiatives, federal documents, and answers to frequently asked questions. http://www.ciao.gov/

**Emergency and Environmental Health Services, National Center for Environmental Health** The National Center for Environmental Health (NCEH), part of the CDC, has adopted policies for the management and deployment of emergency environmental health services. Visitors to this site will find materials relating to NCEH services and resources, including extensive information on chemical and biological defense. The Web page can also be accessed in Spanish. http://www.cdc.gov/nceh/divisions/eehs.htm

**Emergency Management and Terrorism from the National Governors Association Center for Best Practices** The role of the nation's governors in emergency management is described at this site. The National Governors Association Center for Best Practices was created as an information-sharing network between emergency managers and providers, as well as to provide a forum for discussing issues of emergency management and policy. The latest documents, news, legislative updates, and indexes of content are available to visitors of this site. http://www.nga.org/center/topics/1,1188,D_854,00.html

**Federal Bureau of Investigation** The Federal Bureau of Investigation (FBI) is dedicated to upholding federal law and to protecting the United States and its people from harm. This site provides basic information for all FBI activities and related agencies. Visitors to this site will find comprehensive materials relating to such issues as terrorist investigations, national security, media releases, and fugitives. http://www.fbi.gov/

**Federal Emergency Management Agency** The Federal Emergency Management Agency (FEMA) is responsible for administering aid for disaster relief at both the local and national levels. In response to catastrophic events, FEMA heads efforts for recovery and relief for victims and local government agencies. Content

victims and local government agencies. Content on this site includes current information on terrorist disaster relief efforts, news updates, information on FEMA departments, and a variety of Web-based resources.
http://www.fema.gov/

**Federal Structure for Terrorism Response from the Center for Nonproliferation Studies** Federal structures and organizations dedicated to combating terrorism are described at this address. Presented by the Center for Nonproliferation Studies, this organizational flowchart illustrates the power structure among various federal agencies, officials, programs, and offices that play a role in antiterrorism, counterterrorism, and domestic response. Additional sections of this site are devoted to weapons of mass destruction civil defense teams and information on federal funding to combat terrorism.
http://cns.miis.edu/research/cbw/domestic.htm

**Health and Medical Services Support Plan for the Federal Response to Acts of Chemical/Biological (C/B) Terrorism from the U.S. Department of Health and Human Services** Dating back to June of 1996, this support plan was created to assist in the implementation of a coordinated federal response to situations requiring urgent public health and medical care resulting from terrorist activities. The 27-page document outlines the policies, situations, concepts of operation, responsibilities, and resource requirements of responding parties. Additional subsections are devoted to emergency conditions, organization, notification, response actions, and support agencies. This text is a product of the Department of Health and Human Services and a part of continuing efforts to ensure public health and reduce the threat posed by terrorism by enhancing preparedness and prevention.
http://ndms.dhhs.gov/
CT_Program/Response_Planning/C-BHMPlan.pdf

**Health Information and Surveillance Systems Board** In order to integrate efforts at the local and state levels in disease surveillance, the CDC has implemented the National Electronic Disease Surveillance System (NEDSS). When completed, the NEDSS will electronically link various surveillance efforts in order to rapidly disseminate information to the appropriate authorities and to promote more prompt and accurate reporting.

This site provides updates on NEDSS progress and related information.

http://www.cdc.gov/od/hissb/index.htm

**National Association of Counties** Representing over 3,000 counties of various sizes, locations, and backgrounds, the National Association of Counties covers a variety of interests and works to promote public understanding of local counties. General resources on this site include U.S. county information, demographics, county codes and ordinances, policies, and model county programs. Additional resources are dedicated to legislative affairs, programs and projects, discussion forums, conferences and events, publications, and membership information. Of particular interest are the sections devoted to "Counties and Homeland Security," which provide information on the NAC Homeland Security Task Force, current research, news coverage, and a legislative agenda.

http://www.naco.org/index.cfm

**National Center for Injury Prevention and Control** The National Center for Injury Prevention and Control (NCIPC), works to reduce the costs in terms of suffering, disability, and human life associated with injury. Materials on this site are devoted to injury care, violence, and unintentional injury. Visitors to this Web site may access all of NCIPC's extensive listings of resources, publications, and data.

http://www.cdc.gov/ncipc/

**National Infrastructure Protection Center** Composed of representatives from U.S. government agencies, state and local governments, and the private sector, the National Infrastructure Protection Center (NIPC) is dedicated to the protection of the nation's vital infrastructures including telecommunications, water systems, and emergency services. Serving as the federal government's focal point for threats or attacks against U.S. infrastructures, NIPC seeks to reduce vulnerability to attack and to increase capabilities in responding to threats. Features of this site include information sharing, legal issues, access to publications, press releases, major investigations, and incident reporting.

http://www.nipc.gov/

**National Institute for Occupational Safety and Health** An agency of the CDC, the National Institute

for Occupational Safety and Health (NIOSH) conducts research and makes appropriate recommendations for eliminating work-related injury and disease. Web site contents include access to NIOSH databases and publications, information on funding opportunities, health hazard evaluations, and safety and health topics. A special section of the home page has been devoted to emergency response resources including access to information on respirators and protective clothing.
http://www.cdc.gov/niosh/homepage.html

 **National League of Cities**  The National League of Cities (NLC) is a cooperative organization created with the broad intent of strengthening and promoting cities as centers of opportunity, leadership, and governance. The NLC Web site is an extensive resource for information relating to city governance and activities including sections devoted to leadership activities, policy and legislation, conferences, news and events, and membership information. Sections of particular interest include "American Cities Respond to Terrorism," which indexes a variety of news and information resources on terrorism response. Visitors will find information on charitable donations, state funding for terrorism recovery efforts, preparedness and economic impact surveys, outlines of federal actions, news stories, and world support.
http://www.nlc.org/nlc_org/site/

 **National Response Center**  The National Response Center (NRC) is a national institution dedicated to recording all incidents of oil, chemical, biological, or similar discharges into the environment. As a function of its unique role, the NRC reports to other branches of government, manages information on biological incidents, and makes appropriate recommendations. The NRC has recently started offering surveillance and reporting on biological agents and the threat of bioterrorism.
http://www.nrc.uscg.mil/index.htm

 **National Wildlife Health Center, U.S. Geological Survey**  The National Wildlife Health Center, a biomedical research center of the U.S. Geological Survey, assesses the impact of disease on wildlife and identifies the role of various pathogens in contributing to wildlife losses. Research projects at the center cover mortality and health information, foot-and-mouth disease, emerging diseases, and animal welfare. The center also posts information sheets on diseases of interest and wildlife

health alerts. Recent news and updates on West Nile virus are also available.
http://www.nwhc.usgs.gov/

**Occupational Safety and Health Administration, U.S. Department of Labor**   For over 30 years, the Occupational Safety and Health Administration (OSHA) has been working to ensure safe and healthy work environments throughout the United States. Current events, conferences and hearings, news releases, and a library are among the many resources that may be accessed via the OSHA home page. The site also features a section dedicated to workers, where employees can learn about rights and responsibilities and how to handle complaints. Outreach programs cover training, ergonomics, small businesses, and specific industries such as construction and maritime. Additionally, visitors will find detailed listings of OSHA standards and regulations.
http://www.osha.gov/

**Office of Homeland Security, Executive Branch**   Established by executive order, the Office of Homeland Security is responsible for developing and implementing a national strategy to protect against terrorist threats or attacks in the United States. The office coordinates federal, state, and local counterterrorism efforts in terms of detection, preparedness, prevention, protection, response and recovery, and incident management. This official Web site posts the latest homeland security developments, briefings, actions, and recommendations concerning how citizens can help.
http://www.whitehouse.gov/homeland/

**Office of the Coordinator for Counterterrorism, U.S. Department of State**   Working to improve counterterrorism cooperation with foreign powers, the Office of the Coordinator for Counterterrorism plays an important role in current events. This Web site is a permanent electronic archive of information released prior to January 20, 2001. Resources available include information regarding the fight against terrorism, U.S. policies, annual reports, travel security, statements, and summits.
http://www.state.gov/www/global/terrorism/index.html

**Office of the Surgeon General, U.S. Department of Health and Human Services**   Providing leadership, management, and analysis, the Office of the Surgeon General speaks on all matters relating to public health, seeking to protect and advance public health through education and advocacy for disease prevention. Resources available at this site include a detailed overview of the office and its duties as well as key information intended for public education. Official reports and documents are cataloged under the virtual library, and a section of the site has been designed specifically for children. http://www.surgeongeneral.gov/

**Plum Island Animal Disease Center** Dedicated to protecting U.S. animal industries and exports against economic losses resulting from foreign animal diseases, the Plum Island Animal Disease Center performs research, diagnosis, and analysis relating to problems such as foot-and-mouth disease and intentionally introduced bioterrorist agents. Materials on this site include information about ongoing center research projects, national programs, research locations, news and media coverage, safety regulations, and environmental protection activities. Detailed information on operations and maintenance, laboratory safety, animal room operations, environmental protection, and the transportation of specimens can be found under the safety heading. http://www.ars.usda.gov/plum/

**President's Commission on Critical Infrastructure Protection** Established in July 1996, the President's Commission on Critical Infrastructure Protection (PCCIP) is the first initiative of its kind designed to address national vulnerabilities resulting from the rise of information technologies, including telecommunications, electrical power supplies, water sources, government and emergency services, and transportation services. The majority of the information on this site is intended to educate the user on what types of roles the PCCIP plays and in what capacity it serves to protect national security. Site contents include recent news; information on PCCIP structure, function, and mission; answers to frequently asked questions, and a "quick tour" that provides a brief overview of PCCIP daily activities and past efforts. http://www.info-sec.com/pccip/web/

**Public Health Service, U.S. Department of Health and Human Services** Public Health Services is composed of eight government agencies, with each agency devoted to a different section of public health.

This site provides information on, as well as links to, all
Public Health Service institutions and programs.
http://www.os.dhhs.gov/phs/

**U.S. Department of Justice**  The U.S. Department
of Justice is charged with upholding all aspects of the
law to prevent and control crime, to punish the guilty,
and to see to the fair administration of the legal system.
A complete listing of all Department of Justice components is available at this site, along with organization information and budgets. Other features include publications and documents, press releases, employment information, and descriptions of fugitives and missing persons. http://www.usdoj.gov/

**U.S. Environmental Protection Agency**  Responsible for protecting human health and safeguarding the
natural world, the Environmental Protection Agency
(EPA) addresses all matters of environmental interest including air, water, pollutants, and toxic chemical and
biological agents. In addition to resources on laws and
regulations, media releases, EPA programs and topics,
and educational resources, the EPA provides information
regarding the current threat of terrorism as it relates to
human health and the environment.
http://www.epa.gov/

**U.S. Food and Drug Administration**  A member of
Public Health Services, the U.S. Food and Drug Administration (FDA) regulates the safety of foodstuffs, drugs,
medical devices, biologics, animal feed, cosmetics, and
radiation-emitting products. Features of the FDA home
page include current topics of interest such as bioterrorism; safety alerts; product approvals; FDA activities; information resources for consumers, patients, and practitioners; and FDA regulations. http://www.fda.gov/

**U.S. Postal Service**  Under the recent threat of
anthrax, the U.S. Postal Service has intensified efforts to
provide safe and secure handling of the mail. Online
mailing services, news and events, recommendations for
safe mail handling, and postage information are just a
few of the features that visitors will find. The site takes
on the dual role of addressing the postal needs of the nation and of informing the public about the threat and
safety measures currently under way.
http://www.usps.com/

## 17.2  U.S. MILITARY AGENCIES AND PROGRAMS

**2001 Incident Management Handbook from the U.S. Coast Guard**  Sponsored by the U.S. Coast Guard, this manual is intended to aid Coast Guard responders in the use of the Incident Command System during response operations. In addition to general information on Coast Guard personnel duties and responsibilities, the handbook addresses a number of different operation types including search and rescue, law enforcement, oil spills, hazardous substance releases, terrorism, marine fire, and multi-casualty incidents. The terrorism section covers a variety of topics ranging from responding to a weapon of mass destruction incident and recommendations for action directly after the event to mental health coordination and technical teams support. Other topics covered in this 22-chapter work include planning cycles, unified command, logistics, finance and administration, and organization. This document is also available in Spanish and in Russian.
http://www.uscg.mil/hq/g-m/mor/page2index.htm

**Armed Forces Radiobiology Research Institute**  Since its charter in 1961, the Armed Forces Radiobiology Research Institute (AFRRI) has conducted research in the field of radiobiology and related matters for the operational and medical support of the Department of Defense and military services. Visitors to this site will find information on the institute's organization, its research programs and goals, outreach activities, news, training and seminars. AFRRI provides free access to casualty management information and outlines of recent educational seminars.
http://www.afrri.usuhs.mil/

**Chemical and Biological Defense Information Analysis Center**  Under the contract of the Office of the Secretary of Defense, the Chemical and Biological Defense Information Analysis Center (CBIAC) is responsible for generating, acquiring, processing, analyzing, and distributing information to appropriate destinations. Sections of this site are devoted to CBIAC information services such as bibliographic databases, current awareness such as newsletters and upcoming events, products, and technical area tasks. Authorized users may also access CBIAC databases. Highlighted information includes resources on bioterrorism, anthrax, and mail handling.

*Don't type in long URLs*—use eMedguides site number (www.eMedguides.com/**2T-1234**).

This information is drawn from outside sources, mainly from the CDC and other federal agencies.
http://www.cbiac.apgea.army.mil/

**Chemical Casualty Care Division, U.S. Army Medical Research Institute of Chemical Defense**
This Web site is produced by the Chemical Casualty Care Division of the U.S. Army Medical Research Institute of Chemical Defense. The center seeks to educate medical professionals and first responders in both the military and civilian populations by offering training courses on casualty management in biological and chemical warfare. The center also offers free online access to a variety of educational resources such as textbooks, handbooks, and articles. A schedule of courses offered may also be found in a calendar of events.
http://ccc.apgea.army.mil/

**Chemical School, U.S. Army** The U.S. Army Chemical School is an institute that develops doctrine, equipment, and training for the Army's defense against nuclear, biological, and chemical weapons. The school trains commissioned officers within the Department of Defense in areas such as biological integrated detection systems, radiological safety, and emergency response to weapons of mass destruction. Training development and career management resources are available for Army personnel. The site also offers links to other command centers in the Army.
http://www.wood.army.mil/usacmls/

**Command Center, U.S. Coast Guard** The U.S. Coast Guard Command Center serves as the primary notification and information management body for the Coast Guard Headquarters, the Department of Transportation, and the National Response Team. Visitors to this site will find a brief outline of Command Center duties, news highlights, a briefings archive, case management, and organizational flowcharts. Other sections are devoted to the Commandant's Situation Room, the Incident Management Center, Contingency Preparedness, the Chemical and Biological Hotline, and the National Response Team. The "Highlights" section provides a weekly synopsis of global Coast Guard activities including response to recent terrorist events.
http://www.uscg.mil/hq/commandcenter

**Counterproliferation Center, U.S. Air Force** A division of the Air War College of the U.S. Air Force, the Counterproliferation Center (CPC) is designed to aid Air Force personnel with research and education by functioning as an information repository, organizing conferences, publishing related materials, and carrying out research projects. To this end, the CPC maintains an extensive resource and information index addressing all related topics. Major sections of this site are dedicated to nuclear, biological, and chemical weapons; missiles; conventional weapons; terrorism; treaties; organizations; reference materials; and an online library. Each section of the site contains a separate listing of relevant resources, such as general information, recent news articles, ongoing research projects, government reports, commentary, policy information, historical documents, and related government agencies. http://www.au.af.mil/au/awc/awcgate/awc-cps.htm

**Defense Information Systems Agency** The Defense Information Systems Agency (DISA) was designed to maintain and regulate the flow of information to all Department of Defense members. DISA develops new and better methods for transferring, sharing, and utilizing information. This site contains an abundance of information on DISA topics of interest and activities and related DISA programs.
http://www.disa.mil/

**Defense Threat Reduction Agency** In order to safeguard the United States and allies from the threat of weapons of mass destruction, the Defense Threat Reduction Agency aims at reducing the current threat and enhancing preparedness for the future. Sections of this site are devoted to cooperative threat reduction, technology development, security, combat support, and bio-defense. Additional news and information resources are also available. http://www.dtra.mil/

**DefenseLINK: Official Web Site of the U.S. Department of Defense** DefenseLINK is the U.S. Department of Defense resource for all defense-related news, images, and publications. An extensive listing of news releases, special reports, and related sites are among the detailed contents that visitors will find. Links to other department sites are also available, including a section dedicated to anthrax. DefenseLINK is mainly designed to be an information-sharing network for individuals seeking current information on the U.S. military

and on the policies, operations, and functions of the Department of Defense.
http://www.defenselink.mil/

**Director of Military Support, Department of Defense**  The Director of Military Support (DOMS) is responsible for coordinating Army support activities in cases of presidentially declared disasters and related missions. This site provides a brief overview of DOMS, including its mission, roles, and responsibilities; information exchange requirements; and current capabilities, as well as an assessment of future needs. This document is one section of a larger work entitled the "Emergency Support Function Requirements Analysis Report," which provides information on the 12 Emergency Support Functions (ESFs). ESFs are the mechanisms by which the federal government aids states during times of disaster including transportation, communication, public works, information and planning, and mass casualty care.
http://www.ncs.gov/ncs/html/DOMS.htm

**Field Management of Chemical Casualties Handbook from the U.S. Army Medical Research Institute of Chemical Defense**  Although not an official Army publication, this text has been authored by the Chemical Casualty Care Division of the U.S. Army Medical Research Institute of Chemical Defense and is intended to be a concise guide to field management of victims of chemical exposure. Major sections of this document are devoted to the management of cases relating to nerve agents, vesicants, cyanide, lung-damaging agents, and biological agents. Each of these sections contains a summary of agent properties, information on toxicity, effects of exposure, treatment, self-aid, and potential drug therapies. Additional chapters cover field management, patient decontamination, and chemical defense equipment.
http://ccc.apgea.army.mil/reference_
materials/handbooks/fmcc/ncohandbook2000.htm

**Health Service Support in a Nuclear, Biological, and Chemical Environment**  This field manual is intended to provide techniques, tactics, and procedure recommendations for military personnel working in nuclear, biological, and chemical environments. It contains general, clinical, and technical information relating to weapons of mass destruction. Contents include medical threats; effects of nuclear, biological, and chemical weapons; command and control; medical aspects of exposure; health support services; and hospitalization procedures. Each chapter is subdivided into smaller sections to address more specific topics. The chapter on weapons effects, for example, has sections devoted to general, physical, and physiological effects of radiation, chemical, and biological weapons. The guide's appendices offer guidelines for health service support, protective systems, patient decontamination procedures, and decontamination of food and water.

http://155.217.58.58/cgi-bin/atdl.dll/fm/8-10-7/toc.htm

### Incident Command System, U.S. Coast Guard
The Incident Command System (ICS), a U.S. Coast Guard program, is designed as a standardized response system for crisis management operations, including flood, fire, earthquakes, and oil spills. The complete Field Operations Guide may be downloaded in PDF format. ICS electronic forms, organizational charts and diagrams, and training materials are also accessible via this Web site. ICS training materials include National Wild Fire Coordination and information on the National Response Team.

http://www.uscg.mil/hq/g-m/mor/Articles/ICS.htm

### Installation Preparedness for Weapons of Mass Destruction
Published by the Department of the Army, this document is intended to provide aid to Army installation commanders in the prevention and preparation for attacks involving weapons of mass destruction. The text emphasizes the importance of cooperation with local communities and host nations and highlights ways in which command personnel can increase surveillance and improve intelligence by using human and technological resources to reduce the threat. This document addresses the specific duties and responsibilities of the installation commander, including the need for personal involvement in providing intelligence support, assessing and reducing critical vulnerabilities, evaluating plans of action, and creating civil/military partnerships.

http://www.hqda.army.mil/
acsimweb/fd/policy/fire/docs/handbook0420final.pdf

### Interagency Domestic Terrorism Concept of Operations Plan, U.S. Government
Several federal agencies, under the leadership of the FBI, have launched CONPLAN, the Concept of Operations Plan, which out-

lines the capacity for a rapid coordinated federal response to a terrorist threat or act. This 30-page document provides background information on terrorist activities, outlines U.S. terrorism policies, introduces different terrorist situations such as minimal threat, potential threat, and weapons of mass destruction, outlines the appropriate concept of operations for each threat, and details phasing of the federal response. This document covers every phase of federal involvement from preparedness to threat assessment to response and recovery operations. CONPLAN is designed to provide guidance to all federal, state, and local agencies concerning federal government response to terrorist threat or attacks with weapons of mass destruction.
http://www.fema.gov/r-n-r/conplan/conplan.pdf

**Medical NBC Battlebook from the U.S. Army Center for Health Promotion and Preventive Medicine** The *Medical Nuclear, Biological and Chemical (NBC) Weapons Battlebook* is a technical guide intended to serve as a training and field resource, addressing operational health concerns in areas of NBC threat. The focus of the book is to provide a quick reference to determine whether a potentially hazardous situation requires expert consultation rather than to offer treatment guidelines. Battlebook contents include information on general operational aspects, nuclear weapons, radiological hazards, lasers and radiofrequency, equipment, and points of contact. In addition to policy and procedural guidelines, readers will encounter detailed technical and clinical information regarding the effects of nuclear, biological, and chemical weapons. This document of over 300 pages is available in PDF format.
http://ccc.apgea.army.mil/
reference_materials/handbooks/batbooka.pdf

**Military Infectious Disease Research Program from the U.S. Army Medical Research and Material Command** The U.S. Army Medical Research and Material Command (USAMRMC) is devoted to research, acquisitions, logistics, and technology in the defense of U.S. military forces. This extensive site provides information on USAMRMC functions, goals, and ongoing research programs in medicine, advanced technologies, information technologies, and logistics and acquisitions management. The section on the Military Infectious Disease Research Program (MIDRP) is only accessible by following the links from the main home page. Users will first click on "medical research and development" and then follow the link for "research areas directorates." The MIDRP section provides a brief overview of vaccine research initiatives and research into the discovery of novel treatments, more rapid detection, and prevention and control. http://mrmc-www.army.mil/

**Modeling and Simulation Information Analysis Center**   The Modeling and Simulation (M&S) Information Analysis Center provides scientific, technical, and operational support information and services in an effort to assist in activities of the Department of Defense. Online contents include answers to frequently asked questions, the M&S calendar of events, M&S community news, center publications, and educational resources for authorized users. Special interest areas include sections dedicated to homeland security and weapons of mass destruction, in which users can access M&S related resources, recent news, and important policy documents. http://www.msiac.dmso.mil/

**National Guard**   As the oldest component of the U.S. Armed Forces, the National Guard has been working in defense of the nation for over 365 years. This Web site is a comprehensive guide to National Guard activities and interests including information on its history, accessibilities, international role, and the defense community. The "Hot Topics" section of this site indexes information of current interest and includes sections devoted to anthrax and weapons of mass destruction. These sections consist of answers to frequently asked questions, recent news articles, information resources, and important updates and bulletins. http://www.ngb.dtic.mil/

**Office of Counterproliferation and Chemical and Biological Defense, U.S. Department of Defense**   The Office of Counterproliferation and Chemical and Biological Defense is housed by the U.S. Department of Defense (CP/CBD). As its name implies, this agency is devoted to counterterrorism programming. Features of the site include CP/CBD reports and an extensive online library. http://www.acq.osd.mil/cp/index.html

**Program Director for Biological Defense Systems**   Responsible for the development, production, testing, and logistics support of biological defense systems aimed at enhanced detection, this office was offi-

cially closed September 26, 2000, having accomplished all of its goals. The site remains as an information resource on biological defense systems including the Biological Integrated Detection System (BIDS), the Chemical/Biological Mass Spectrometry Block (CBMS), and the Integrated Biodetection Advanced Technology Demonstration. These systems were developed by the Program Director for Biological Defense Systems during its functioning years and are currently in field use. The page provides brief descriptions of products and color images.
http://www.sbccom.apgea.army.mil/RDA/pdbio/index.htm

## Publications from the Army Medical Department
Although not all Army Medical Department publications are available on the Web, this site maintains an index of links to the official versions of several of the department's documents. Publications are categorized as administrative, doctrinal and training, technical and medical, and supply bulletins. Links include the U.S. Army Publishing Agency, Army Doctrinal and Training Digital Library, and the U.S. Army Center for Health Promotion and Preventive Medicine. Documents are available in a variety of formats; some are restricted to Army Medical Department personnel.
http://www.armymedicine.army.mil/
armymed/publications/publications.htm

## SBCCOM Online: U.S. Army Soldier and Biological Chemical Command
Research, development, and acquisition, along with emergency preparedness and response in situations requiring chemical weapons storage, remediation, and demilitarization, form the focus of the U.S. Army Soldier and Biological Chemical Command (SBCCOM). The command is dedicated to all functions of chemical and biological defense systems. Information on this site includes SBCCOM product lists, programs and technology demonstrations, services and technologies, facilities, and partnership opportunities. Products developed by this organization include clothing and individual protective equipment, field services equipment, rations and field feeding, shelters, and decontamination devices designed to protect soldiers from risk of exposure to chemical and biological agents. Visitors may also access additional information on recent SBCCOM changes, upcoming events, publications, press releases, and site archives. http://www.sbccom.apgea.army.mil/

**Technical Escort Unit, U.S. Army** Provisions of the U.S. Army Technical Escort Unit (TEU) include chemical and biological advice; verification, sampling, detection, decontamination, and remediation of chemical and biological hazards and devices; and crisis management. This site provides access to TEU fact sheets, equipment overview, training information and program overviews, historical information and details of major operations, and organizational charts. The site provides an overview of TEU duties, functions, resources, and programs.
http://www2.sbccom.army.mil/teu/

**U.S. Army Center for Health Promotion and Preventive Medicine** Established over 50 years ago, the U.S. Army Center for Health Promotion and Preventive Medicine (USACHPPM) has grown into a team of nearly 1,100 individuals dedicated to providing scientific expertise in the areas of clinical and preventive medicine, health promotion and wellness, environmental and occupational health, and epidemiology and disease surveillance. Web site resources cover center news and publications, training and conferences, and recent updates from the center commander. Additional resources are dedicated to anthrax information drawn from Army and public health agencies, preventive medicine resources, information on deployment medication, surveillance data, and flu season updates. The majority of these supplemental resources are links to outside organizations or are collected from other sources. USACHPPM professionals represent many areas of expertise including chemistry, engineering, medicine, optometry, epidemiology, industrial hygiene, and entomology.
http://chppm-www.apgea.army.mil/

**U.S. Army Medical Department** The U.S. Army Medical Department (AMEDD) has developed this Web site to provide information to the public, the news media, and to beneficiaries of the Army Medical Department. Visitors will find resources on military treatment facilities, locating medical records, healthcare programs including anthrax vaccination, the TRICARE healthcare system of the Department of Defense, and health education including Department of Defense information on depleted uranium. AMEDD's home page also provides a brief information handout on anthrax in PDF format. *Mercury*, AMEDD's newspaper, can also be accessed from this site under "News and Media.
http://www.armymedicine.army.mil/armymed/default2.htm

---

***Don't type in long URLs***—use eMedguides site number (www.eMedguides.com/**2T-1234**).

**U.S. Department of Defense Global Emerging Infections System** The Global Emerging Infections System (GEIS) was developed by the U.S. Department of Defense to provide surveillance, response, training and capacity building, and systems research and development. Materials on this site range from general information on GEIS and its history to overviews of key programs and surveillance reports. Access is also available to GEIS publications and training programs for healthcare personnel. http://www.geis.ha.osd.mil/

**Weapons of Mass Destruction Civil Support Teams** Weapons of Mass Destruction Civil Support Teams work with civilian agencies and are the military's first responder to incidents involving weapons of mass destruction. Features of this Web site include information on support team activities, press releases, statements, commentary, radio reports (available in audio format), and photographic coverage of support team actions. Featured articles and photo documentations are available from the American Forces Press Service. For more extensive information on terrorism and weapons of mass destruction, this site maintains an extensive listing of related outside resources and organizations. http://www.defenselink.mil/specials/destruction/

## 17.3 ASSOCIATIONS

**American Academy on Veterinary Disaster Medicine** Founded in 1984 and consisting of veterinarians and public and private interest groups, the American Academy of Veterinary Disaster Medicine is one of the oldest organizations dedicated to the care of animals during natural and manmade disasters. The academy's extensive network of professionals works to promote awareness, education, and communications and provides a forum for the distribution of information during crisis situations. Site contents include historical information, membership details, newsletter archives, and an overview of organization activities. The breaking news section contains background information and media coverage on recent areas of interest such as foot-and-mouth disease and bovine spongiform encephalopathy. http://www.cvmbs.colostate.edu/clinsci/wing/aavdm/aavdm.htm

**American College of Emergency Physicians** The American College of Emergency Physicians promotes quality emergency medical care and the interests of emergency physicians. This Web site provides practice resources as well as information on government and advocacy, meetings and continuing medical education, news and publications, and discussion forums. Also available are safety tips for consumers, located in a section on health information. The site also has a special section devoted to bioterrorism, including anthrax diagnosis and CDC updates.
http://www.acep.org/

 **American Industrial Hygiene Association** The American Industrial Hygiene Association (AIHA) is dedicated to preventing occupational disease and injury and promoting a safe and healthy work environment. Resources available at the site include information on AIHA news and events, membership information, publications, and access to AIHA services.
http://www.aiha.org/

 **American Public Health Association** The American Public Health Association (APHA) is composed of more than 50,000 members representing more than 50 areas of public health. At this address, the APHA provides a forum for professional exchange, study, and action. The site is divided into sections encompassing news, meetings, and public health associations. Public health news covered includes journals and newspapers, books, and continuing education opportunities. The meetings section contains APHA initiatives including its annual meeting, special projects and task forces, and legislative issues. Links are also available to domestic and international public health organizations. A section of the site is dedicated to the public health response to the events of September 11, 2001.
http://www.apha.org/

 **American Red Cross** The American Red Cross is a volunteer-based humanitarian organization that provides emergency relief to victims of disaster and helps to prevent, prepare, and respond to crisis situations. In addition to disaster relief, the Red Cross provides a variety of services including biomedical services such as blood and tissue banking and distribution; armed forces emergency services such as communications and financial assistance and aid for veterans; community services for seniors, youth, and the homeless; health and safety services including community health, water safety, and HIV/AIDS education; and international services such as primary healthcare and feeding programs. Additional online features include general information on Red Cross functions, soliciting aid, news coverage, press releases, and publications. Visitors to this site will not only find out how to donate time, money, and blood but will also learn exactly how donations are applied by accessing the "spotlight" section, which provides information on recent Red Cross activities. A variety of news and activities are related to recent terrorist attacks on America, Red Cross involvement, and areas in which additional help is still needed. http://www.redcross.org/

**American Society for Microbiology**  For over 100 years, the American Society for Microbiology (ASM) has promoted the study of the microbiological sciences and their applications. Web site resources include sections on communications, where visitors may access media information and public education initiatives, and public policy, which includes updates, legislative and regulatory alerts, and position papers. Also available are journals published by the society, meetings including audioconferences and exhibits, and books from the ASM press such as reference manuals and textbooks. Selected areas and services require ASM membership for access.
http://www.asmusa.org/

**American Society of Professional Emergency Planners**  The American Society of Professional Emergency Planners (ASPEP) is devoted to the advancement of knowledge about disaster and the enhancement of emergency management practices. This professional association composed of certified emergency managers promotes continuing education, encourages professional development and exchange, and produces a yearly journal as a forum for sharing ideas, research information, and opinions. Site features include membership details, the ASPEP journal overview, a call for papers for the upcoming edition, and the ASPEP newsletter.
http://www.iprimus.ca/~tmheath/INDEX.htm

**American Water Works Association**  Focused on providing safe drinking water, the American Water Works Association (AWWA) is an online resource for water professionals. Topics addressed on this site include

consumer information, conservation, research, management, water quality, engineering, and operations. In addition, AWWA provides security information, technical resources, news, and information on organization publications, events, and exhibits. The resources on this site include sections dedicated to networking, safe water programs, government affairs, and continuing education. Visitors will find overviews and summaries of articles from the most recent issues of the association's journal.
http://www.awwa.org/

### Association for Professionals in Infection Control and Epidemiology
The Association for Professionals in Infection Control and Epidemiology (APIC) is dedicated to the study and prevention of spreading infections. The site features highlights of bioterrorism and infection control news, anthrax updates, and bioterror readiness. APIC also offers bioterrorism resources including information on specific agents, economic impact, conferences, readiness planning, and vaccination. Other features available from the site include continuing education resources, surveillance and consensus reports, position papers, and tips for consumers.
http://www.apic.org/

### Association of Contingency Planners
As an international networking and information exchange organization, the Association of Contingency Planners (ACP) is dedicated to promoting growth, development, and enhancement of efforts to mitigate, respond to, and recover from emergency situations. ACP functions as an information-sharing network and education resource for active members. Information on this site is limited to membership information, ACP affiliate and sponsor information, and locations of ACP chapters. Access to other ACP resources is protected by password and reserved to organization members only.
http://www.acp-international.com/

### Association of Metropolitan Water Agencies
For over 20 years the Association of Metropolitan Water Agencies (AMWA) has been providing information on drinking water–related concerns to providers of urban water supplies. Materials on this site address water policy and legislation, special water projects, AMWA programs, meetings, and services. A large portion of this site is reserved for AMWA members only. Accessible information provides a briefing of water-related activities in the

government, including tracking recently proposed bills and regulations from the Environmental Protection Agency. AMWA also offers workshops and publications on water utility competitiveness and business services as well as summaries and analysis of amendments relating to safe drinking water.

http://www.amwa.net/

### Association of Public Health Laboratories

Dedicated to advancing the quality of laboratory practice, the Association of Public Health Laboratories supports the role of public health laboratories in national and global programs designed to ensure and improve the quality of laboratory methods. In addition to clinical laboratory alerts and updates, visitors to this site may access national conference information, education and training resources, environmental health information, and global activities. The site also offers a section on newborn screening and genetics and links to individual public health laboratories.

http://www.aphl.org/

### Association of Schools of Public Health

Representing the deans, faculty, and students of accredited member schools, the Association of Schools of Public Health focuses on strengthening the public health infrastructure at the academic and national level. Materials on this site include resources directed specifically to students and faculty, distance learning programs, governmental relations, public health reports, and publications from the association. The site also provides background on the public health profession and links to individual schools of public health.

http://www.asph.org/

### Association of State and Territorial Health Officials

Focused on formulating and implementing sound public health policy, the Association of State and Territorial Health Officials (ASTHO) is a national nonprofit organization representing public health agencies at the state and territorial level. Committees acting on behalf of public health exist in the areas of access to care, environmental health, infectious diseases, prevention, and public health information and infrastructure. Each committee posts projects, position statements, newsletters and documents, and other resources on the site. In-

formation on government relations, policy recommendations, and a calendar of events are also available.
http://www.astho.org/

## Business Executives for National Security

Business Executives for National Security (BENS) is a nonpartisan organization composed of senior business executives dedicated to lobbying for enhanced national safety and security. Partnering with the Centers for Disease Control and Prevention, BENS is a joint business/government venture aiming to develop and coordinate concerted efforts for defense against bioterrorist attacks. The bioterrorism section of this site offers recent BENS projects, policy recommendations, and upcoming BENS events.
http://www.bens.org/

## Chemical and Biological Warfare Defense Directorate of the Systems Technology Group

SRS Technologies is a business venture that provides technical and scientific support for the development of defense, aerospace, and commercial systems and products. The Chemical and Biological Warfare Defense Directorate, a subsection of SRS, focuses on biodefense and biotechnology. The group maintains a counterterrorism database of biological agents against crops and livestock and conducts analytical studies on threats from, and vulnerability to, chemical and biological weapons.
http://www.stg.srs.com/cbw.htm

## Council of State and Territorial Epidemiologists

The Council of State and Territorial Epidemiologists (CSTE) is responsible for public health surveillance of disease at the state level, focusing mainly on infectious and chronic diseases and environmental health. The CSTE home page offers materials detailing CSTE policy, conferences, and position statements, as well as information on chronic disease indicators and council reports in its "Resources" section.
http://www.cste.org/default.htm

## Emergency Information Infrastructure Partnership

The Emergency Information Infrastructure Partnership (EIIP) is an association of organizations and individuals whose focus is on enhancing disaster management skills and effectiveness by utilizing electronic technology for the sharing of information and ideas. To this end, EIIP offers a variety of online resources divided into

four sections: the "Virtual Forum" which provides access to online discussions, coverage of recent and ongoing discussions, and information on topics of interest; the "Virtual Library" and the "Virtual Classroom" sections, which contain links to online publications and continuing education resources; and the "Technology Arena," which contains resources for those interested in information technology, data management, and technology discussion. Additional site features include mailing lists, newsletters, coverage of EIIP events and activities, and the group's annual report.
http://www.emforum.org/

**International Association for Counterterrorism and Security Professionals** Founded in 1992, the International Association for Counterterrorism and Security Professionals was created to provide educational services and to promote professional ethics in the counterterrorism field. This Web site contains the "Terror Information Bank," which offers background information on terrorist groups, patterns of global terrorism, and a chronology of past terrorist incidents. A section called "Terrorism Watch" posts current news reports on terrorist actions. Other features from the association include discussion forums, a newsletter, and a calendar of events.
http://www.iacsp.com/

**International Association of Emergency Managers** The International Association of Emergency Managers (IAEM) is a nonprofit organization that promotes education for enhancing efforts to save human lives and protect property during periods of disaster. IAEM provides a large number of information resources on its Web site including the IAEM news room, terrorism information, a conferences and events calendar, membership information, and a newsletter and archives. The terrorism section offers a number of features that include guidelines for addressing the media, preparedness and prevention, emergency management, and historical information on terrorist events. Additional coverage of more recent terrorist activities and U.S. response can be found under the "news" heading.
http://www.iaem.com/

**International Society for Environmental Epidemiology** Dedicated to providing a communication forum for concerns relating to environmental health, the

International Society for Environmental Epidemiology (ISEE) sponsors workshops, newsletters, annual meetings, and interaction with government and business institutions. Information on environmental health ethics, ISEE events, committees, and regional chapters can be found on this Web page.
http://www.iseepi.org/

**International Society of Exposure Analysis** The International Society of Exposure Analysis (ISEA) works toward understanding the science of exposure analysis for both human populations and ecosystems with respect to environmental contaminants. Sections of this site include ISEA announcements, membership, newsletters, and journals. Information on the ISEA annual conference is also available.
http://www.iseaweb.org/

**National Association of County and City Health Officials** Serving public health at the local level, the National Association of County and City Health Officials (NACCHO) provides education, research, information, and technical assistance to local health departments. Visitors to this site will find NACCHO programs and software developed to support local health departments as well as information on the association's public health advocacy activities. NACCHO also logs daily news reports and maintains a special section on its response to bioterrorism with links to legislative testimony and statements, programs, publications, and best practices for healthcare providers.
http://www.naccho.org/

**National Association of Local Boards of Health** The National Association of Local Boards of Health (NALBOH) represents and communicates the interests of local boards across the United States. NALBOH's Web site compiles an extensive listing of news, events, learning resources, lectures, and public health resources including performance standards and links to individual state associations. The site also offers a special section about bioterrorism and links to bioterrorism updates from the CDC.
http://www.nalboh.org/

**National Association of SARA Title III Program Officials** Composed of members of various emergency response organizations at all levels of government and

several federal agencies, the National Association of SARA Title III Program Officials (NASTTPO) takes on a variety of responsibilities. Among these are the protection of human health and well-being, protection of the environment, ensuring the effective use of resources in responding to incidents involving hazardous substances and toxic chemicals, and providing information on hazardous substances to members and to interested parties. Contents of this site cover general information, membership information, laws and regulations, information exchange networks, and annual conference details.
http://www.geocities.com/CapitolHill/6286/index.htm

## National Emergency Management Association

The National Emergency Management Association (NEMA) is a professional association composed of state, Pacific, and Caribbean emergency management directors and is dedicated to providing leadership, expertise, information, and assistance in preparedness and crisis situations. NEMA resources include conferences, an online library, a database of natural disasters sorted by state, state contracts, membership information, and a membership directory. In response to terrorist events of September 11, NEMA has added a number of counterterrorism and information resources to its site including the association's recently published report entitled "Trends in State Terrorism Preparedness." Other features include recent news articles on related events, bioterrorism preparedness information, policy information and recommendations, and additional NEMA publications. All NEMA resources are aimed at enhancing practices and forging strategic partnerships for improvement of emergency management techniques.
http://www.nemaweb.org/index.cfm

## National Security Institute

The National Security Institute (NSI) serves as a comprehensive Internet resource for the security professional. Features of the site include industry and product news, computer alerts, travel advisories, a virtual security library, and an index of products and services. For those interested or employed in the field of security, the NSI Web site offers many resources for security technology, legislation, and implementation.
http://www.nsi.org/

## National Voluntary Organizations Active in Disaster

Involved in coordinating planning efforts for numerous volunteer organizations at the national, state, and territorial levels for disaster response, National Voluntary Organizations Active in Disaster (NVOAD) focuses on cooperation, communications, coordinated efforts, and collaboration between groups. Visitors to this site may access general and historical information on NVOAD covering the organization, its structure, principles, and membership requirements; member organizations each have their own hotlink. The site also features NVOAD updates, information on the group's annual meetings, workshops in Power Point format, and daily disaster news. Copies of NVOAD articles, writings, and official speeches are also available online.
http://www.nvoad.org/

## NBC Industry Group

The NBC Industry Group is a coalition of about 100 companies and organizations that works for the support of nuclear, biological, and chemical (NBC) defense activities. In addition to a listing of member organizations, Web site materials include coming events and current and archived news and information. The group also offers a forum for the exchange of ideas and discussion of current events.
http://www.nbcindustrygroup.com/

## Oklahoma City National Memorial Institute for the Prevention of Terrorism

The Oklahoma City National Memorial Institute for the Prevention of Terrorism was created as a living memorial to the victims of the bombing of the Murrah Federal Building in April of 1995. The institute seeks to prevent and reduce the effects of terrorism primarily by supporting first responders through research and training programs. The first responder audience may access information on bioterrorism detection and response; reports on equipment, public health, and preparedness management; and training materials. The site also maintains a library of articles, fact sheets, journals, images, and reports as well as a special section on preventing terrorism.
http://www.mipt.org/index.html

## The American Civil Defense Association

Composed of a diverse group of individuals, organizations, institutions, and agencies with a common goal, The American Civil Defense Association (TACDA) is a nonprofit, nonpartisan group whose focus is on strategic civil

defense, disaster preparedness, and disaster mitigation. TACDA resources include the *Journal of Civil Defense,* published with the aim of helping individuals and communities to understand all types of disasters; disaster preparedness products and supplies; and an online resource library addressing such topics as natural and manmade disasters and preparing for terrorism in America. Most library resources are linked from outside organizations such as the Federal Emergency Management Agency, and the CDC. TACDA membership information is also available via this site.
http://www.tacda.org/

## 17.4 Research and Policy Centers

**Agency for Healthcare Research and Quality** The Agency for Healthcare Research and Quality (AHRQ) is dedicated to improving the overall quality of healthcare by promoting research initiatives. Information on this Web site has been organized into categories such as clinical information, consumer and patient information, funding opportunities, data and surveys, research findings, and quality assessment. Much of the consumer information can be viewed in Spanish.
http://www.ahcpr.gov/

**ANSER Institute for Homeland Security** In cooperation with nonprofit and academic institutions, the Analytic Services (ANSER) Institute for Homeland Security addresses emerging national security concerns at many levels of response including deterrence, prevention, preemption, crisis management, consequence management, attribution, and retaliation. Web site features include current news, upcoming events, legislative updates, suggested readings, a weekly e-mail newsletter, and a virtual library. The institute also publishes the *Journal of Homeland Security,* which may be accessed from this home page.
http://homelandsecurity.org/

**Carnegie Endowment for International Peace** Since its establishment in 1910, the Carnegie Endowment for International Peace has studied the causes and impacts of war and promoted international cooperation. The organization's Web site details its programs in a section that covers the group's international efforts toward

peace. A special project on nonproliferation focuses on information and analysis of weapons of mass destruction. In the "News & Resources" section, visitors may contact experts on international affairs, subscribe to e-mail newsletters, and visit a library of links. Publications and events are also listed on the site.
http://www.ceip.org/files/nonprolif/
weapons/weapon.asp?ID=2&weapon=chemical

### Center for Biologics Evaluation and Research, U.S. Food and Drug Administration
A subsidiary of the U.S. Food and Drug Administration, the Center for Biologics Evaluation and Research (CBER) was created to regulate the use of biological products, including blood, vaccines, and drugs, as well as the use of medical devices. CBER aims to improve overall public health through the proper regulation of biological agents and related devices. This site contains information regarding the products under CBER authority and updates on recent CBER activity.
http://www.fda.gov/cber/

### Center for Civilian Biodefense Strategies
The Johns Hopkins Center for Civilian Biodefense Strategies seeks to raise public awareness of biological threats, to improve the distribution of knowledge of biological agents to the medical and public health communities, and to foster the development of response systems to bioterrorist actions. The center provides fact sheets on biological agents, archives of expert testimony on bioterrorism, and a library of published materials. The Web site is also home to the *Biodefense Quarterly*, the center's newsletter, and offers news items on legislation and specific diseases.
http://www.hopkins-biodefense.org/index.html

### Center for Defense Information
The Center for Defense Information is an independent organization focused on military and defense research. The center conducts several research projects, highlighting terrorism, military reform, missile defense, nuclear issues, and U.S. military spending on this Web site. Within each project section, visitors may access articles with in-depth analysis of relevant issues. In addition, the site features news updates, media reports, television coverage, and an online library. The center also publishes a weekly newsletter, the *Weekly Defense Monitor*.
http://www.cdi.org/

**Center for International Security and Cooperation**   Part of Stanford University's Institute for International Studies, the Center for International Security and Cooperation (CISAC) brings together specialists from a variety of fields to address security concerns of current interest. CISAC conducts research in areas such as chemical and biological weapons issues, information security and policy, and preventive defense. Project listings are accompanied by descriptions and contact details. In response to recent events, CISAC has also posted the proceedings of its global conference, "International Disease Surveillance, Bioterrorism, and Global Security," which may be viewed online or received by e-mail.
http://cisac.stanford.edu/

**Center for Nonproliferation Studies**   Established in 1989 under the Monterey Institute of International Studies, the Center for Nonproliferation Studies is dedicated to combating the spread of weapons of mass destruction by training specialists, performing analyses, and educating the public. Terrorism is covered under the special subject heading, where users will find information on biological and chemical weapons, agroterrorism, preparedness and response, and treaties, as well as testimony by experts. Additional resources include databases on nuclear trafficking and nuclear and missile developments, programs on monitoring and nonproliferation, publications, and online learning resources.
http://cns.miis.edu

**Center for Strategic and International Studies**   Providing world leaders with strategic insight and policy recommendations on global concerns is the focus of the Center for Strategic and International Studies (CSIS). CSIS handles a broad range of topics including arms control, nuclear affairs, and terrorism issues. Each section presents analytical reports, many of which may be downloaded in PDF format. The center also catalogs congressional testimony from its resident experts, press releases, and media advisories.
http://www.csis.org/

**Center for Terrorism Preparedness**   Sponsored by the University of Findlay, the Center for Terrorism Preparedness is an educational resource offering practical training for the public health and medical communities, corporate safety and security personnel, city and county officials, law enforcement personnel, and first responders. Overviews of training courses for each population are offered and registration information is available. http://gcampus.findlay.edu/Nceem/terrorism.asp

### Center for the Study of Bioterrorism and Emerging Infections
The Center for the Study of Bioterrorism and Emerging Infections (CSB&EI) is sponsored by St. Louis University and is an extensive resource for information relating to bioterrorism and disease. Quick references including fact sheets, slide shows, and data tables are provided, along with current news, congressional testimony, and case study articles on bioterrorism. The site also details ongoing CSB&EI research projects, lists education and training resources, and covers how to report and handle emergencies, including related hotline numbers. http://bioterrorism.slu.edu/

### Chemical and Biological Arms Control Institute
Based in Washington, D.C., the Chemical and Biological Arms Control Institute (CBACI) works to limit the threat posed by weapons of mass destruction. Research ongoing at the CBACI involves health and security, biological weapons, terrorism, and arms control. Current news coverage, recent updates, and information on terrorist activities are also available on the home page. http://www.cbaci.org/

### Chemical and Biological Weapons Nonproliferation Project from the Henry L. Stimson Center
The Stimson Center is composed of a group of analysts working toward developing real-world solutions to concerns of domestic and international security. The Chemical and Biological Weapons Nonproliferation Project was designed to examine issues related to chemical and biological terrorism. This section contains information on chemical and biological weapons, answers to frequently asked questions, congressional testimony, relevant U.S. legislation, and articles. http://www.stimson.org/cbw/?SN=CB2001112951

### Energetic Materials Research and Testing Center
A division of the New Mexico Institute of Mining and Technology, the Energetic Materials Research and Testing Center is focused on fundamental and applied research in the areas of explosives research and testing. Web site features cover program overviews such as workshops and courses; information on specialized test facili-

ties, including large-scale facilities, gun ranges, and the Torres laboratory complex; research and development activities information, and organizational structure. Educational resources encompass a wide variety of areas including National Domestic Preparedness Consortium Training Programs, incident management, and antiterrorism assistance projects. Brief summaries of course information and sponsoring organizations are available on this site.
http://www.emrtc.nmt.edu/

**Harvard Sussex Program on Chemical/Biological Warfare Armament and Arms Limitation** A collaborative effort between Harvard University and the University of Sussex, the Harvard Sussex Program (HSP) undertakes research, communications, and training in support of informed policy-making on chemical and biological weapons (CBW) issues, focusing predominantly on counterproliferation. In addition to historical information on CBW, visitors will find material relating to HSP research, meetings, events, and publications including the *CBW Conventions Bulletin*, invited articles, occasional papers, and publication archives. The group also posts archived CBW conventions and treaties.
http://fas-www.harvard.edu/~hsp/

**Henry L. Stimson Center** In addition to chemical and biological weapons, the Stimson Center deals with numerous issues relating to national and international security such as determining and enhancing global security, regional security, and weapons of mass destruction. The center also maintains archives of past projects, press releases, and publications including a newsletter. Publications may be sorted categorically, chronologically, or geographically and may be ordered online.
http://www.stimson.org/

**International Policy Institute for Counter-Terrorism** Research and innovation in promoting practical public policy solutions for international terrorism is the goal of the International Policy Institute for Counter-Terrorism (ICT). Among the resources on this page are news updates, policy analyses, articles and documents, and conference proceedings. A special section of the site is devoted specifically to the September 11 attacks and their aftermath, while other areas of the site focus on international terrorism, the Arab-Israeli conflict, and coun-

terterrorism. Each section is supported by updates, articles, and documents which may be viewed online.
h.ttp://www.ict.org.il/

**National Institute of Allergy and Infectious Diseases** The National Institute of Allergy and Infectious Diseases (NIAID) supports scientific research aimed at developing more efficient methods for diagnosis, treatment, and prevention of a variety of medical afflictions. General information about NIAID, including its origins, roles, and resources, is available through this Web site. In addition, the site features clinical information on current research topics and diseases of interest.
http://www.niaid.nih.gov/default.htm

**National Institutes of Health** One of the eight agencies that comprise the Public Health Service, the National Institutes of Health (NIH) is one of the world's foremost medical research centers. Health information, grants and funding, news and events, and scientific resources are among the many features of the NIH Web site. Visitors to the site will find a wide variety of health-related materials, including extensive coverage of bioterrorist threats, policy, and prevention.
http://www.nih.gov/

**Nuclear Threat Initiative** Created jointly by Ted Turner and Sam Nunn, the Nuclear Threat Initiative is a charitable organization dedicated to reducing the risk posed by, and preventing the spread of, weapons of mass destruction. To this end, NTI combines the knowledge and efforts of experts in a variety of fields, all working toward reducing threat and enhancing response capabilities. Visitors to the NTI Web site will have access to a wide variety of resources, such as a research library; online databases including one dedicated to biological and chemical terrorism; recent news and media coverage; a terrorism preparedness tutorial; and related publications. http://www.nti.org/

**Project on Terrorism and American Foreign Policy from the Brookings Institution** Centered in Washington, D.C., the Brookings Institution is a think tank that makes available its scholarly analysis and findings regarding public policy. Research is conducted in the fields of economics, government, foreign policy, and policy centers. The institute publishes books and journals and also maintains video clips, policy briefs, and news releases. One section of the site is devoted to a special project, "America's Response to Terrorism," which has its own archive of analysis, working papers, policy briefs, and commentary. This section also features Internet chats and an e-mail newsletter. http://www.brook.edu/

**Public Responsibility and Mass Destruction: The Bioterrorism Threat from the Critical Incident Analysis Group**   The Critical Incident Analysis Group (CIAG) is composed of experts from academia and the private sector dedicated to improving the overall ability to understand, prevent, and cope with critical incidents. Defining a critical incident as any event that may cause trauma and undermine social trust, CIAG directs its efforts toward major newsworthy events of environmental, economic, and national import. The group's Web site details CIAG research projects and services, and its reports and publications may be read online. http://faculty.virginia.edu/ciag/bioterr.html

**RAND Corporation**   RAND, short for research and development, is a nonprofit think tank providing research, analysis, and recommendations for improved policy-making and decision-making related to public interest. RAND research programs cover a wide variety of areas including environment and energy, health, national security, and science and technology. Each research area has been provided with its own site and resources. National security, for example, offers information on hot topics relating to global security, personnel, training and health, logistics and infrastructure, and technology, as well as a listing of recent publications. RAND publications are available in full-text versions free of charge via this site. http://www.rand.org/

**Stockholm International Peace Research Institute**   The Stockholm International Peace Research Institute (SIPRI) was assembled in 1966 to contribute to the understanding and promotion of stable international peace. The institute conducts research in areas such as arms control and disarmament, chemical and biological warfare, and military technology. Resources in each research area include project papers, fact sheets, and publications. The Web site also provides databases on international relations and security trends, military expenditure, export control systems, and chemical and biological weapons nonproliferation. http://www.sipri.se/

**Terrorism Research Center** Founded in 1996, the Terrorism Research Center (TRC) is an independent institute working to educate the public about terrorism and information warfare. This Web site offers media and news coverage of the latest headlines, analysis of terrorist acts, profiles of terrorist groups and of other counterterrorist organizations, and a list of related documents and essays. In addition, TRC provides a discussion forum for visitors interested in counterterrorism. The center also maintains a Web page dedicated to the terrorist attacks of September 11.
http://www.terrorism.com/index.shtml

**U.S. Army Medical Research Institute of Chemical Defense** Dedicated to developing medical countermeasures to chemical attacks, the U.S. Army Medical Research Institute of Chemical Defense has a variety of resources at its disposal. Visitors to this site will find training information on chemical casualties, clinical information on biological weapons, conference information, and related publications.
http://chemdef.apgea.army.mil/

**U.S. Army Medical Research Institute of Infectious Diseases** The U.S. Army Medical Research Institute of Infectious Diseases is the Department of Defense's leading laboratory for the study of medical aspects of biological defense. The institute conducts a broad spectrum of vaccine, drug, and diagnostic research. General information on programming and additional educational resources are available to users of this site. Educational content includes online course information and training programs for military and civilian healthcare providers.
http://www.usamriid.army.mil/

## 17.5 INTERNATIONAL AGENCIES

**Canadian Centre for Emergency Preparedness** The Canadian Centre for Emergency Preparedness (CCEP) works to promote effective disaster management and aims at reducing the risk, impacts, and costs of natural, human-induced, and technological disasters. CCEP site resources include sections dedicated to personal preparedness, research and publications, education, training, and certification, frequently asked questions, the CCEP newsletter, conference information, and a calendar of

events. The "Personal Preparedness" section contains information on creating and practicing an evacuation plan, emergency supplies and equipment, preparing one's automobile, and links to other personal preparedness Web sites.
http://www.ccep.ca/

**Canadian Institute of Strategic Studies** Since 1976, the Canadian Institute of Strategic Studies (CISS) has focused on developing informed opinions on issues of national importance and promoting public awareness of these issues. CISS is dedicated to independent research, discussion, and education. Online resources include events and news, publications and seminars, and press releases.
http://www.ciss.ca/

**CANUTEC, Promote Public Safety in the Transportation of Dangerous Goods** Transport Canada is the department responsible for the design and administration of regulations, policies, and services aimed at a more efficient and effective Canadian transportation system. CANUTEC, the Canadian Transport Emergency Centre, is a division of Transport Canada dedicated to assisting emergency responders in the handling of hazardous materials. CANUTEC services include an extensive database of potentially hazardous commercial products, information services and networking, research and analysis, and consultation services. Site features include news updates on recent CANUTEC developments, yearly activity statistics, news articles, and a HazMat calendar. Additional links are provided to Transport Canada programs and services, publications, public safety information, and related resources.   http://www.tc.gc.ca/canutec/en/menu.htm

**Pan American Health Organization** A subsidiary of the World Health Organization (WHO), the Pan American Health Organization (PAHO) is an international public health agency specializing in improving the health and living standards of the people of the Americas. Working with the WHO and the United Nations, PAHO strives for increased sanitary conditions, better overall health infrastructure, and disease control and prevention. This comprehensive Web site maintains health data including basic health indicators, country health profiles, and trends analysis, as well as a resource list of public health articles categorized into areas such as communicable diseases, mental health, and nutrition and food protection. In addition, PAHO offers educational opportunities and grants in international health. http://www.paho.org/

**Sunshine Project** The Sunshine Project is an international nonprofit organization working in the United States and internationally to counter the hostile use of biotechnology, including chemical and biological weapons. The site provides a detailed introduction to biological warfare, with links throughout the text to related articles and documents. The Sunshine Project runs programs in biotechnology and weapons proliferation, treaty reinforcement, environmental modification, and biodefense monitoring. The group also maintains a list of its publications with specific areas dedicated to environmental modification techniques and to Agent Green, pathogenic fungi used in forced crop eradication programs. This site is also available in Spanish and in German. http://www.sunshine-project.org/

**United Nations Action Against Terrorism** This Web site is dedicated to the United Nations (U.N.) actions against terrorism. The site links to the U.N. News Centre with the latest developments in the fight against terrorism and archives resolutions, presidential statements, and records from the U.N. Security Council. Records from the General Assembly debates on how to eliminate international terrorism are also available, as well as proceedings from the Economic and Social Council and the Secretary-General. The site also links to the U.N. Charter, conventions and declarations, U.N. agencies, multimedia resources, and an online library. All resources are available in several languages. http://www.un.org/terrorism/index.html

**United Nations Peace and Security Council** Headed by the United Nations (U.N.), the Peace and Security Council works toward international stability, cooperation, and safety. This site serves as a portal to all U.N. peace-related activities, providing a news center, daily briefings, multimedia resources, documents and maps, and publications and databases. The council provides resources on peacekeeping, peacemaking and preventive action, and disarmament, as well as specific projects on land mines and peacekeeping in Africa. Other councils of the U.N. accessible from this site include eco-

nomic and social development, human rights, humanitarian affairs, and international law.
http://www.un.org/peace/

**World Health Organization**   The World Health Organization (WHO) is a comprehensive resource for all areas relating to human health, defined as physical, mental, and social well-being. As a multinational organization, the WHO has created many resources to promote proper health including an online A-to-Z library of health topics, data records, a press media center, disease surveillance information, and resources on emergencies and travelers' health. The site also posts recent news stories and analysis as well as upcoming events of interest to the public health community,
http://www.who.int/home-page/

**18**

# PUBLIC HEALTH
# RESOURCES ON THE
# INTERNET

## 18.1 GENERAL RESOURCES

**Public Health Resources from MedBioWorld**
Sponsored by the largest site for medical journals, associations, and databases, the MedBioWorld public health index catalogs over 80 important public health resources including associations, organizations, institutes, databases, and portals. Each listing provides a link directly to the site of interest.
http://www.medbioworld.com/med/assocdb/publichealth.html

**Separatist, Para-Military, Military, Intelligence, and Aid Organizations** A unique Web-based resource, this index catalogs the Internet homes and resources of known terrorist organizations, military groups, nationalists, and other armed conflict groups. The site maintains an alphabetical listing of hundreds of such groups, organized in an index of over 50 countries of origin. In addition to information regarding the parent country, readers will find a brief synopsis of the organization, its mission, and its activities. Links are provided to the official Web sites of each organization, including the Taliban and Osama bin Laden.
http://www.cromwell-intl.com/security/netusers.html

## 18.2 JOURNALS

**Biodefense Quarterly from the Johns Hopkins Center for Civilian Biodefense Strategies** *The Biodefense Quarterly*, sponsored by the Johns Hopkins Center for Civilian Biodefense Strategies, addresses issues of significance to the fight against biological warfare and terrorism. The most recent issue is posted on the site.

The newsletter covers topics such as international security, specific diseases, and government hearings on terrorism. In addition, the site maintains an archive of past issues, specific resources on smallpox, links to legislative issues, and government reports.
http://www.hopkins-biodefense.org/pages/news/quarter.html

**Emerging Infectious Diseases**   Published by the Centers for Disease Control and Prevention, *Emerging Infectious Diseases* is devoted to the epidemiology, surveillance, and clinical research of infectious disease. Recent special issues have been dedicated to the emerging threat of bioterrorism, potential biological weapons, smallpox, and historical trends in disease surveillance. Full-text articles are available for review. Visitors may also access archives and upcoming issues.
http://www.cdc.gov/ncidod/eid/vol5no4/contents.htm

**Hazardous Materials Management**   Full-text articles are available from *Hazardous Materials Management* online, pertaining to all aspects in the handling and disposal of these materials. The publication covers current events of environmental and economic impact as well as legislative issues, industry news, and business developments. A full-text version of the current issue is posted on the Web site, which maintains archives dating back to late 1998. Visitors will also find guidelines for submitting works for publication as well as subscription information. http://www.hazmatmag.com/

**Index to Military Periodicals from Air University Library**   Provided by the Defense Technical Information Center, this index lists significant articles, news items, and editorials from various military periodicals. Users may browse the comprehensive listing of topics, arranged alphabetically by subject heading, review the listing of available periodicals, or search for articles by phrase or keyword. Many of these publications provide full-text versions of articles accessible via the Internet while others require password access. Periodicals covered include *Armed Forces Journal International, Defense & Foreign Affairs Strategic Policy,* and the *Journal of Electronic Defense.* http://www.dtic.mil/search97doc/aulimp/main.htm

**Job Safety and Health Quarterly Magazine**   A publication of the Occupational Safety and Health Administration (OSHA), this journal addresses all job

safety, work environment, and occupational health-related concerns. Complete full-text versions of this publication are available for download from the OSHA Web site. More than 15 issues are currently available online, dating back to the summer of 1997. Hard-copy versions of these publications can be obtained from OSHA for a fee. Online documents require a PDF viewing program.
http://www.osha-slc.gov/html/jshq-index.html

### Journal of Homeland Security
The *Journal of Homeland Security,* published by the ANSER Institute for Homeland Security, provides commentaries, interviews, book reviews, and science and technology articles. All articles are available online in full-text format. Most content has been independently authored by experts in a given field and submitted for publication. Visitors may also subscribe to receive the newsletter by e-mail.
http://homelandsecurity.org/journal/

### Military Medical Technology Online
Published six times per year, *Military Medical Technology* hails itself as the world's only 100% military medical magazine. As such, the publication covers a wide variety of related topics such as medical information technology, pharmacology research, medical and technological advancement, and vaccine development. Resources on this site include journal contents, registration information, a media kit, archives, editorial calendar, and details on upcoming events. Although registration is required to access full-text versions of articles and site archives, subscriptions are offered free of charge to military, industry, and interested individuals. Site archives maintain an index of all issues published in the year 2001.
http://www.mmt-kmi.com/index.cfm

### Morbidity and Mortality Weekly Report
*Morbidity and Mortality Weekly Report,* a publication of the Centers for Disease Control and Prevention (CDC), consists of CDC weekly updates, facts about specific diseases, and feature articles on current topics of interest. This special issue covers information about anthrax and bioterrorism. Full-text articles of the current issue are available on the Web site, as well as archives dating back to 1982. Submission guidelines for publishing consideration and important bioterrorism-related information are also available at this Web site.
http://www.cdc.gov/mmwr/indexbt.html

**National Fire and Rescue** *National Fire and Rescue* is a magazine dedicated to all aspects of fire search and rescue operations including coverage of recent major events, technological advancements in the field, and related topics. Recent issues of the publication feature articles dedicated to the World Trade Center search and rescue operations, photographic coverage of recovery activities, anthrax information, and commemorative materials for New York City firefighters. Other site contents include editorials, letters, news, and a calendar of events. Full-text versions of articles are available online. Additional features, including access to back issues, require a paid subscription.
http://www.nfrmag.com/

**Nonproliferation Review** Sponsored by the Center for Nonproliferation Studies, this periodical focuses on the causes, consequences, and control of the spread of weapons of mass destruction. Materials covered by *Nonproliferation Review* include theoretical analyses, case studies, and policy debates on a number of issues relating to foreign affairs, treaties, export control, individual country's programs, and the environmental effects of these weapons. Site archives provide access to a limited number of full-text articles from each issue. Tables of contents and abstracts may be viewed for all issues dating back to the fall of 1993. The onsite search engine allows users to search all online journal contents for topics of interest. http://cns.miis.edu/pubs/npr/index.htm

**Public Health and Environmental Health Journals from MedBioWorld** MedBioWorld's journal index contains a listing of over 80 links to journal home pages related to all aspects of public and environmental health. Most journals provide access to tables of contents and abstracts of recent articles; some also publish full-text articles. Archives of back issues are usually available, along with subscription and ordering information. Links are also available to journals on medical economics and assessment, occupational and environmental medicine, and hospital and healthcare management.
http://www.medbioworld.com/journals/medicine/public.html

**Terrorism and Political Violence** In an effort to encourage comparative study and to promote the overall academic growth of the field, *Terrorism and Political Violence* publishes scholarly works from a variety of per-

spectives and related fields, including the study of rebellion, protest, terrorism, revolution, and human rights. Journal contents and article abstracts for current and archived issues are available on this Web site. Full-text articles will soon be available to subscribers. Ordering information, including back issues, is provided. Site archives cover issues dating back to early 1995.
http://www.frankcass.com/jnls/tpv.htm

## 18.3 HOTLINES AND ALERTING SERVICES

**Center for the Study of Bioterrorism and Emerging Infections Hotline/Helpline** Due to the dramatic response and concern over recent terrorist activities, several organizations have created information and reporting hotlines as public resources. This Web site from the Center for the Study of Bioterrorism and Emerging Infections includes hotline information for the CDC, guidelines for biological terrorism threats, reporting procedures, and contact information for the Chemical and Biological Emergency Hotline.
http://bioterrorism.slu.edu/hotline.htm

**Emergency Email Network** The Emergency Email Network (EEN) is a free public service designed to rapidly notify citizens of local and international emergency situations by utilizing electronic mail networks. The EEN provides information from government agencies and other organizations regarding severe weather, evacuations, health emergencies, natural disaster, and similar life-threatening situations. Users register for this free service by entering state, county, and zip code information. In addition to disaster and emergency news, visitors may also choose to receive information on electric, gas, and water outages; locations of emergency supplies; organ donation; and blood drives.
http://208.184.24.125/

**Federal Environmental Hotlines** Maintained by the Government Institutes division of ABS Consulting, this site indexes information on over 30 government hotlines and centers for environmental and health-related concerns. This alphabetical listing provides a brief description of each hotline's purpose and sponsoring organization as well as specific contact information. Links are also provided to sponsoring organization Web sites, if available. Visitors to this site may access information hot-

lines ranging from the Acid Rain Hotline to the Emergency Planning and Community Right-to-Know Hotline.
http://www.govinst.com/
resourcecenter/resource/envirohotlines.html

**Health Alert Network, Centers for Disease Control and Prevention** Sponsored by the CDC, the Health Alert Network is intended to facilitate communication among local and state health departments, to promote education and competency, and to ensure an informed public. News and events and educational resources are among the many sections to be explored on this Web site. In addition, a large portion of the site is devoted to cataloging recent public health warnings and CDC advisories.
http://www.phppo.cdc.gov/han/

**National Warnings Area** The Interactive Weather Information Network (IWIN) created by the National Weather Service provides coverage of all weather-related events, broadcasts, and warnings, including access to all National Weather Service home pages by state, live satellite images of weather patterns, and radio broadcasts of forecasting information. This section of IWIN provides immediate access to all available U.S. weather warnings. These warnings cover tornados, hurricanes, flash floods, severe thunderstorms, winter storms, flooding, and non-precipitation alerts such as heat, cold, and wind. This page is designed to update every 60 seconds to provide up-to-the-minute coverage of weather warnings.
http://iwin.nws.noaa.gov/iwin/nationalwarnings.html

**ProMED-mail** Sponsored by the International Society for Infectious Diseases, ProMED-mail is a global electronic reporting system for incidents and outbreaks involving emerging infectious disease and dangerous biological toxins. ProMED-mail provides daily coverage of disease reports and maintains an index of postings from the previous 30 days. Postings provide brief overviews of cases, locations, and ongoing activities surrounding infectious disease outbreaks. The most recent postings involve West Nile virus and viral hemorrhagic fever. In addition, special sections are devoted to daily updates on anthrax, West Nile virus, and foot-and-mouth disease.
http://www.promedmail.org/pls/promed/promed.home

**Rapid Response Information System**  The Rapid Response Information System, a program of the Federal Emergency Management Agency, has established hotline and helpline telephone numbers to aid in the rapid reporting of emergencies and to answer questions related to these events. Additional related information on preparedness, response, and chemical and biological agents can also be found on this page.
http://www.rris.fema.gov/

**Vulnerable Zone Indicator System from the Environmental Protection Agency**  Under the Emergency Planning and Community Right-to-Know Act, private individuals are granted the right to access information on facilities in their localities that produce potentially hazardous chemicals. The Vulnerable Zone Indicator System (VZIS), created by the Environmental Protection Agency (EPA), allows a user to input a street address or longitude/latitude and find out if that location could be affected by a chemical accident. The system will e-mail users information regarding potential hazards in that area, drawn from an index of all facilities that submit a Risk Management Plan to the EPA.
http://www.epa.gov/ceppo/vzis.htm

## 18.4  ONLINE TEXTS AND TUTORIALS

**Bioterrorism and Biological Safety from the American Society for Microbiology**  Historical information and practical procedural safety recommendations in response to bioterrorism are featured in this document from the American Society for Microbiology. The authors of this work have included information on a variety of safety topics including emergency response agencies and resources, occupational health, personnel protection in a laboratory environment, engineering control, personal protective equipment, decontamination procedures, laboratory safety and security measures, and personnel protection during incident response. Tabular information includes an extensive listing of viral, bacterial, and other agents of interest, and a summary of protective equipment and levels of protection is offered.
http://www.asmusa.org/pcsrc/biosafetyChap37.pdf

**Bioterrorism from the Association for Professionals in Infection Control and Epidemiology**  Authored by Kelly J. Henning and Marcie Leyton of the

Association for Professionals in Infection Control and Epidemiology, this chapter examines the threat of bioterrorism from a clinical and epidemiological perspective. Sections of this text provide a definition and background information, etiological effects, clinical manifestations, treatment, management of exposure, and infection control. Specific bioterrorist agents covered in this work include anthrax, plague, tularemia, Q fever, brucella, smallpox, viral encephalitides, botulism, Staphylococcal enterotoxin B, and ricin. The disease summary provides information on the causative agent, scientific name, incubation period, clinical syndromes, and diagnostic assays. Additional information in this document includes a summary of treatments, available vaccines, and prophylaxis for the agents discussed. This text is designed as an overview of potential bioterrorism agents and provides concise information for rapid diagnosis, treatment, and prevention. http://www.apic.org/bioterror/chapter124.pdf

**Bioterrorism: A Real Modern Threat from the American Society for Microbiology** Written by Michael T. Osterholm of the University of Minnesota and published by the American Society for Microbiology, this text provides an analysis of a theoretical bioterrorist event. The author provides historical background information and examines the present threat of bioterrorism. He addresses such topics as critical elements necessary for a bioterrorist event, potential perpetrators and agents, characteristics of an ideal bioterrorist agent, and methods of delivery. Osterholm devotes the final section of this chapter to an overview of preparedness activities that should be undertaken to mitigate the threat. http://www.asmusa.org/pcsrc/13.213_222.pdf

**Chemical and Biological Terrorism: Research and Development to Improve Civilian Medical Response from National Academy Press** This document is the result of a collaborative effort between the Institute of Medicine and the Commission on Life Sciences and is designed to assess existing U.S. research, development, and technology information on prevention, detection, and response to chemical and biological attacks. Contents of this report cover a variety of topics including pre-incident communications and intelligence, personal protective equipment, detection procedures, patient decontamination and mass triage, available treatments and therapies, and prevention capabilities. The in-

formation in each category provides an in-depth examination of existing technologies, research, and resources as well as a critique of current capabilities. In addition to functioning as an assessment, this document notes vulnerable areas of preparedness and makes specific recommendations for research priorities in the future.
http://www.nap.edu/books/0309061954/html/index.html

**Defense Against Toxic Weapons from the Veterinary Corps, United States Army** Authored by David R. Franz, Ph.D., of the Veterinary Corps of the U.S Army, this document is intended to provide basic information regarding biological toxins so that military leaders can better protect their troops from this threat. This document focuses specifically on toxins rather than on conventional chemical and biological weapons. The first half of this work discusses the threat of toxic weapons, providing comparisons between toxins and conventional chemical weapons, use of toxins in battle, classifications and examples, how toxins function, and populations at risk. The latter portion addresses practical countermeasures including physical protection, real-time detection of an attack, diagnosis, prevention, and treatment and decontamination concerns. In addition, the text devotes a section to providing detailed answers to frequently asked questions regarding protection of healthcare providers, sampling procedures, toxin analysis and identification, and water treatment. http://www.vnh.org/DATW/toc.html

**Health Aspects of Biological and Chemical Weapons from the World Health Organization** With the original draft of this report dating back to 1970, this second edition of the World Health Organization's (WHO) "Health Aspects of Chemical and Biological Weapons" is an updated analysis of the health aspects, threat, and concerns over possible release of hostile biological agents. Unlike other reports of its kind, this document focuses specifically on the civilian aspects of a bioterrorist threat rather than the military aspects. In nearly 100 pages of content, this report covers assessing the threat to public health, information on biological and chemical agents, public health preparedness, legal background on chemical and biological warfare (CBW) policy, and international sources of assistance in CBW-related matters. Readers will also find clinical and technical information on health effects and analytical information on public health preparedness.
http://www.who.int/emc/pdfs/BIOWEAPONS_FULL_TEXT2.pdf

**Initial Management of Irradiated or Radioactively Contaminated Personnel** This manual has been designed with the intention of providing military and civilian medical personnel with directions for initial assessment, management, and therapy for patients who have been irradiated or radioactively contaminated. A number of forms of radioactive contamination are covered in this document including external irradiation, external contamination, wound contamination, and internal contamination. Additionally, the authors have provided useful information on radioactive elements such as chromium, cobalt, depleted uranium, iodine, plutonium, radium, and tritium, including scientific background information, half-life, exposure evaluation, internal contamination, and treatment.
http://www.vnh.org/BUMEDINST6470.10A/TOC.html

**NATO Handbook on the Medical Aspects of Nuclear, Biological, and Chemical Defensive Operations from the Department of the Army** This NATO handbook contains 12 chapters of information on defense against chemical weapons. Nerve agents, vesicants, lung-damaging agents, cyanogen agents, incapacitants, riot control agents, incendiary materials, and herbicides are among the many categories of chemical agents covered by this text. Each chapter is further subdivided to address physical and chemical properties, signs and symptoms of exposure, health effects, diagnosis, pre- and postexposure treatment, emergency field therapy, and other aspects of specific chemical agents. The handbook is designed to provide detailed clinical and technical information in a concise format. The final chapters are dedicated to recognition of chemical exposure, medical support in chemical operations, and removal of contaminated food, water, and supplies.
http://www.fas.org/nuke/
guide/usa/doctrine/dod/fm8-9/3toc.htm

**Treatment of Chemical Agent Casualties and Conventional Military Chemical Injuries from the U.S. Armed Forces** A joint effort between the Departments of the Army, Navy, Air Force and Commandant, and Marine Corps, this two-part document is intended for use by Armed Forces and trained medical personnel in the recognition and treatment of exposure to conventional and chemical warfare agents. The first section of this manual addresses chemical agent casualties

including nerve agents, incapacitants, vesicants, lung-damaging agents, and cyanogen agents, with information on general properties, absorption and protection, health effects, diagnosis, prevention and treatment, and side effects of antidotes. The second section discusses the injuries resulting from conventional military chemicals such as riot control agents, smokes, incediary agents, and noxious chemicals. Additional information regarding first aid, self-aid, and combat lifesaver aid for chemical injuries is provided.
http://www.vnh.org/FM8285/cover.html

## 18.5 MAILING LISTS AND DISCUSSION FORUMS

**BIOWAR List** BIOWAR is a discussion server designed to provide a forum for researchers on biowarfare, bioterrorism, and biological toxins. Individuals may post articles, opinion papers, research proposals, and other information to be shared with the member community. Membership to this LISTSERV is by invitation only and requires the completion of a membership questionnaire for approval, but the general public may access read-only versions of the site and can review any postings. Recent information on the BIOWAR servers includes articles focusing on anthrax and the surrounding investigation, clinical information, and other anthrax warnings.
http://www.sonic.net/~west/biowar/index.htm

**Centers for Disease Control and Prevention Mailing Lists** The CDC offers subscriptions to mailing lists on a variety of topics. Visitors to this site may subscribe to any combination of over 20 different mailing lists by submitting a name and e-mail address. Updates are sent out periodically in electronic format. Lists cover recent contents from *Emerging Infectious Diseases,* HIV/AIDS information, surveillance report updates, surveys, health and nutrition, and *Morbidity and Mortality Weekly Report.*
http://www.cdc.gov/subscribe.html

**Environmental Protection Agency LISTSERVs** The Environmental Protection Agency sponsors nearly 50 LISTSERVs addressing a wide variety of topics on environmental health. These LISTSERVs provide a forum for discussion, information transfer, and research initiatives, covering subject areas that range from "Biological Criteria and Bioassessment" to "Environmental Technol-

ogy." The more popular and extensive LISTSERVs are accompanied by exclusive Web sites or brief descriptions providing more information. Visitors to this site will find step-by-step instructions on how to subscribe and unsubscribe to these information resources.
http://www.epa.gov/epahome/listserv.htm

**RealNews Daily Delivery from the Terrorism Research Center** The Terrorism Research Center RealNews Summary works to provide the convenience of up-to-the-minute terrorism-related news delivered directly to a user's e-mail account. Daily headlines are available on this site, as well as access to full-text versions of news articles drawn from a variety of media sources. RealNews also maintains an archive of all previous postings dating back to October of 1999. In order to receive updates via e-mail, a brief registration is required.
http://www.terrorism.org/mailman/listinfo/realnews

## 18.6 Education and Training Resources

**American Military University** In the 10 years since its founding, the American Military University (AMU) has grown to become a comprehensive academic and research institution, offering undergraduate and advanced studies in a broad spectrum of fields. Site contents include information on AMU history, academic programs and curricula, admission criteria, and an academic calendar. As part of its continuing education program, AMU offers a variety of distance education programs. Enrollment information for these programs is also available via this site. Advanced courses of study include criminal justice, intelligence, political science, and national security studies, along with over 25 undergraduate degrees. The university also offers special programs in homeland security and security management.
http://www.amunet.edu/home/default.asp

**Chemical Education Foundation** The Chemical Education Foundation provides educational programs for responsible use and management of chemical products. Chemical news and updates, training programs and materials, waste disposal information, and hazardous material regulations are among the many resources that can be found on this page. The foundation also produces educational materials for specific audiences including the chemical industry, community groups, teachers/students, and consumers; many publications can be downloaded as Adobe Acrobat files. http://www.chemed.org/html-index.html

**Community Disaster Education Materials from the American Red Cross** Resources provided by the American Red Cross are intended to inform and educate the community before and after a disaster strikes. This site provides access to an extensive listing of educational resources including terrorism information, chemical emergencies and natural disasters, general disaster preparedness, teacher and school training materials, and content especially designed for children. Many of these resources are available for download in their full-text version. Videotapes must be ordered through a local Red Cross chapter. These resources provide valuable information for all members of a community in preparing for and coping with crisis situations.
http://www.redcross.org/pubs/dspubs/cde.html

**Compendium of Weapons of Mass Destruction Courses Sponsored by the Federal Government** Sponsored by the federal government and released in July 2000, this 137-page document was compiled to inform state and local agencies of available federal training opportunities in the area of weapons of mass destruction. The training courses listed in this document are indexed according to sponsoring agency. Additional information includes course descriptions, objectives, target audiences, type of instruction, and prerequisites. Courses are sponsored by federal agencies such as the Departments of Defense, Health and Human Services, and Energy, as well as the Federal Emergency Management Agency, and they address topics ranging from chemical accidents and biological warfare to domestic preparedness and nuclear emergencies. http://www.ndpo.gov/compenium.pdf

**Directory of Civilian Emergency Response Training Programs by State** The Community Emergency Response Team (CERT) maintains this listing of response and emergency management organizations that provide training programs in disaster education and response. Information for each listing includes geographic area, the name of the program, sponsoring agency, contact information, Web site address (if available), and a brief summary of program goals. Dozens of programs sponsored by agencies in over 30 states are listed in alphabetical order by geographic location.
http://www.fema.gov/emi/cert/dir.htm

**Distance Learning Websites from the Centers for Disease Control and Prevention** This CDC-maintained Web site is an index of outside institutions that provide distance learning resources and initiatives. Visitors to this site will find links to over 40 distance learning Web sites. Organizations listed include the American Public Health Association, the Federal Government Distance Learning Association, and the Learning Resource Center.
http://www.phppo.cdc.gov/phtn/sites.asp

**Domestic Preparedness Campus, U.S. Department of Justice** The U.S. Department of Justice in cooperation with Texas A&M University has created the Domestic Preparedness Campus, an educational institution providing distance learning courses covering the material required for advanced training by local chapters of the National Emergency Response and Rescue Training Center as well as other subjects relating to domestic preparedness. Current available courses address "Emergency Medical Service Concepts for Weapons of Mass Destruction Incidents," "Public Works," and "Terrorism Awareness for Emergency First-Responders." Registration is free and is required in order to access course materials.
http://www.teex.com/campus/index.cfm

**Emergency Education Network, Federal Emergency Management Agency** The Emergency Education Network (EENET) is a satellite-based learning system designed to provide training and education to a diverse audience around the United States. EENET provides a wide variety of programs for all members of the public safety community including programs focusing on emergency services trainers, disaster operations, national alert, and disaster loss mitigation; all are broadcast once per month on Wednesday afternoons. As EENET Webcasts are part of the public domain, any user with a C-band or Ku-band satellite dish can receive these transmissions and participate in training. Videotapes of broadcasts are also available for order. In addition to the regular schedule of broadcasts, EENET frequently airs special programming. Times, dates, and topic information on these special broadcasts is available via this site.
http://www.fema.gov/emi/eenet.htm

**Emergency Management Institute** Designed to provide training geared to enhancing U.S. emergency management practices, the Emergency Management Institute presents an assortment of educational resources on this Web site. Online content includes information on training program enrollment policy and procedures, Integrated Emergency Management Courses, higher education projects, the Emergency Education Network, disaster-related job training, and community emergency support programs. The institute maintains an extensive listing of available courses and links to outside organizations whose focus is on emergency management and domestic preparedness. Course information, enrollment requirements, and some course materials are accessible online. http://www.fema.gov/emi/

**Learning Resources from the Centers for Disease Control and Prevention** CDC educational resources address a variety of topics relating to bioterrorism. Documents listed on this page cover bioterrorism preparedness, biological warfare and terrorism response, chemical warfare, threats, policy, legislation, contingency planning, and safety guidelines. Approximately 10 major resources, including official statements, reports, and analyses on bioterrorism are available on this site in PDF format. http://www.bt.cdc.gov/learningresources.asp

**National Emergency Response and Rescue Training Center** A part of the Texas Engineering Extension Service, the National Emergency Response and Rescue Training Center (NERRTC) is responsible for developing and implementing educational programs such as classroom work, field exercises, and computer simulations to enhance the preparedness and response capability of state and local emergency personnel. These training programs are specifically designed to address terrorist attacks involving weapons of mass destruction. Resources on this site include a search engine that provides information on training courses offered by 12 different institutions, as well as online course information. Other features include NERRTC training products such as software and curriculum overviews, programs sponsored by the Bush School of Government and Public Service, details on virtual reality training, publications, news, and other media and activity updates.
http://teexweb.tamu.edu/nerrtc/

**National Laboratory Training Network, Centers for Disease Control and Prevention** Jointly sponsored by the Association of Public Health Laboratories

and the CDC, the National Laboratory Training Network (NLTN) administers laboratory training courses in clinical, environmental, and public health areas. NLTN has a number of online and distance learning resources including conferences, workshops, seminars, computer-assisted instruction, self-study, facilitated study, and interactive tools. Under the "Special Interest" section of this site, users will find resources devoted specifically to bioterrorism. This page includes CDC updates, a bioterrorism overview, public health emergency preparedness documents, reports and recommendations, and a calendar of NLTN bioterrorism preparedness training events including date, workshop title, and location. Resources on this site cover a wide range of information from clinical resources on anthrax, plague, and related diseases to laboratory protocols to be enacted in the event of release of a hostile bioterrorism agent.

http://www.phppo.cdc.gov/nltn/default.asp

### National Terrorism Preparedness Institute

Maintained by St. Petersburg College, the National Terrorism Preparedness Institute (NTPI) aims at better preparing America's civil and military emergency first responders for coping with a weapon of mass destruction incident. To this end, NTPI has a number of online and onsite educational and information resources. Training materials include course offerings in critical incident stress management, terrorism response and planning, decontamination, medical strategies, and nuclear, biological, and chemical hazards. In addition, NTPI sponsors ComNET, Consequence Management News, Equipment, and Training, a live broadcast network that airs a variety of programs dedicated to training, response, and recovery. For a complete listing of ComNET programs and schedule, users should access the "Broadcasts" section. NTPI also maintains an archive of all broadcasts available free of charge on the Web.

http://terrorism.spjc.edu/index.htm

### Public Education from DrinkingH2O.com

Intended as a resource for the general public, this site provides information on concerns related to the safety of drinking water. Features of the site include fact sheets, presentations, conservation recommendations, and answers to frequently asked questions. Visitors to this site can find Environmental Protection Agency (EPA) news on counterterrorism measures designed to protect drink-

ing water sources, monitoring drinking water safety following disasters, statistical information on water use and conservation efforts, and an EPA-sponsored "Consumer's Guide to the Nation's Drinking Water." Other features of interest are sections devoted to water news, providing information on the latest water-related developments, and the events calendar, an extensive and detailed yearly guide of water-related activities.
http://www.drinkingh2o.com/html/public.html

### Public Health Training Network, Centers for Disease Control and Prevention

Utilizing a number of media formats from instructional video to multimedia interactive Web sites, the Public Health Training Network (PHTN) is a distance learning initiative working to provide training opportunities for government and community public health professionals. Major site resources include fact sheets and technical information and the opportunity to view live Web casts of CDC information broadcasts. These broadcasts cover a variety of topics including risk communication and bioterrorism, smallpox, anthrax, and bioterrorism response. Past broadcasts are available for viewing online in the site archives. Additional resources include the PHTN catalog of training materials, a newsletter, and an image library.
http://www.phppo.cdc.gov/phtn/default.asp

### Training and Technical Assistance from the Office for Domestic Preparedness

In order to enhance the capacity to respond to domestic incidents, the Office of Domestic Preparedness (ODP) provides direct technical assistance to local and state agencies. This site provides an overview of all ODP training programs and the institutions that deliver these education programs. Visitors will find information on the National Domestic Preparedness Consortium, the Center for Domestic Preparedness, the New Mexico Institute of Mining and Technology, and the U.S. Department of Energy. In addition, ODP provides detailed outlines of its technical assistance programs in the areas of state strategy, information management, and equipment technical assistance.
http://www.ojp.usdoj.gov/odp/ta/overview.htm

### Training Resources from the National Fire Academy

The National Fire Academy (NFA) offers a variety of training resources for firefighters, emergency response personnel, and fire administrators. In addition to educational resources, this Web site also offers refresher materials, distance learning programs through the Emergency Education Network, and information on fire and emergency management subjects in the Learning Resource Center. State and local fire training systems are also represented on the site, as well as the Training Resource and Data Exchange Program, which promotes the sharing of fire-related training information among federal, state, and local levels of government. The site also features a "Train-the-Trainer" section, which allows fire service professionals to participate in academy courses. Select NFA course materials are available for download. Other materials, including instructor guides, a student manual, and audiovisuals, are indexed by title and year of release and can be obtained from the National Technical Information Service.

http://www.usfa.fema.gov/nfa/tr_act.htm

**Training Resources from the Office of Emergency Preparedness Counterterrorism Program** As a service of the Office of Emergency Preparedness, this Web site provides links to federal training materials on weapons of mass destruction, points of contact, and information on obtaining grants or contracts related to domestic preparedness. Informational resources include a satellite broadcast of the U.S. Army Medical Research Institute of Chemical Defense conference on "Medical Response to Chemical Warfare," links to the National Domestic Preparedness Office, basic concepts for Emergency Response to Terrorism, and a compendium of federal courses. Each resource listed on this page is accompanied by a brief description of the information contained therein or information that can be found from an outside organization.

http://ndms.dhhs.gov/CT_Program/Training/training.html

## 18.7 REFERENCE RESOURCES

**Catalog of Federal Domestic Assistance** As a service of the Federal Register, the Catalog of Federal Domestic Assistance contains information on financial and nonfinancial assistance opportunities granted by a number of federal government agencies. Resources listed on this site include federal programs, projects, services, and activities designed to provide assistance for the benefit of the American public. Each listing contains information on the sponsoring agency, authorization, program

objectives, type of assistance available, uses and restrictions, eligibility requirements, application materials, and contact information. Grants are available to fund a variety of projects including domestic preparedness planning programs and the purchase of fire and emergency equipment for response to weapons of mass destruction incidents. A complete listing of all available grants and examples of funded programming are among the many features offered on this site.
http://www.cmi-services.org/grants.asp

**CDC Health Topics A to Z**  Health Topics A to Z is the continually expanding index for all health- and disease-related topics that can be found on the CDC Web site. For those interested in finding information regarding disease or health concerns, this extensive catalog provides an excellent starting point with links to fact sheets, articles, and research findings.
http://www.cdc.gov/health/diseases.htm

**ClinicalTrials.gov**  As a service of the National Institutes of Health, ClinicalTrials.gov has been developed to provide patients, family members, and the general public with information regarding ongoing clinical research. Over 5,600 clinical research studies are currently cataloged on this site. Searches can be performed by such criteria as disease, location, treatment, and sponsor. http://www.clinicaltrials.gov/

**Health.gov**  Providing links to the Department of Health and Human Services and other federal agencies, Health.gov serves as a portal to information on government health initiatives and activities. This site is a comprehensive listing of online resources available from a variety of organizations. Resources relate to disease, health, nutrition, guidelines, and bioterrorism. Each section contains updates, fact sheets, information on treatments, and related links.
http://www.health.gov/

**Links to Public Health Organizations and Resources Online from the Public Health Foundation**  The Public Health Foundation maintains an extensive listing of public health organizations with online resources. Organizations listed at this site include federal agencies, state departments of health, and national organizations. Other resources available cover academic and training programs, best practices for public health, databanks, environmental health, planning and policy, and safety. Many links are accompanied by brief descriptions. http://www.phf.org/links.htm#State%20Health

**NBC Product and Services Handbook**   A collaboration between the U.S. Joint Service Material Group and the Nuclear, Chemical, and Biological (NBC) Industry Group, this handbook catalogs all nuclear, biological, and chemical products manufactured by domestic companies as well as the NBC-related services provided by those companies. Handbook contents cover agent characteristics, minimization of contamination, individual protection, collective protection, decontamination, medical systems, communications, research and development and several related topics. The section on "Agent Characteristics" provides a table of NBC agents including bacterial, viral, blood, and chemical toxins. Information listed in this table includes the scientific name of the agent or its chemical formula, a description, transmission potential, incubation period, duration of illness, symptoms, treatment, and potential means of delivery. This document provides nearly 200 pages of clinical, technical, policy, and procedural information designed for use by a diverse audience.
http://www.nbcindustrygroup.com/handbook/index08.htm

**Pocket Guide to Chemical Hazards from the National Institute for Occupational Safety and Health**   Published as a resource for workers, employers, and occupational health professionals, the National Institute of Occupational Safety and Health *Pocket Guide to Chemical Hazards* is intended to provide general industrial hygiene information on hundreds of chemical substances. The guide covers a variety of topics including chemical names and designation numbers, permissible exposure limits, physical and chemical descriptions of agents, measurement methods, personal protection and sanitation recommendations, and symptoms of excess exposure. The chemicals index provides an alphabetical listing of names and synonyms for nearly 700 chemical agents. The entire pocket guide is available for download via this Web site. Print and CD-ROM versions are available on request from several vendors listed on the site.
http://www.cdc.gov/niosh/npg/npg.html

**Publications Available Online from the Armed Forces Radiobiology Research Institute**   The

Armed Forces Radiobiology Research Institute (AFRRI) provides online access to a number of clinical and technical information resources related to radiation and human health effects. Information provided is of a technical nature and is intended as an educational resource for radiology professionals and radiobiology researchers. Additional online publications include access to previous news headlines and event highlights. Other site features are devoted to collaborations, products, training material, and seminar information from the AFRRI.

http://www.afrri.usuhs.mil/www/news/news.htm

**Publications from the National Institute for Occupational Safety and Health**    For those interested in publications produced by the National Institute for Occupational Safety and Health, this Web site is the definitive resource. Hundreds of publications are indexed on this site, the majority of which can be viewed online free of charge. Documents provided address topics relating to occupational safety and health concerns. Publications date back as far as 1971 and include all documents up to the present. This resource is a chronological index according to year of publication.

http://www.cdc.gov/niosh/publistd.html

**Publications from the Occupational Safety and Health Administration**    The Occupational Safety and Health Administration (OSHA) produces a number of publications that address work safety concerns in a variety of working environments. This site is an index of all OSHA publications ranging from fact sheets to surveillance data and work safety statistics to procedural and policy recommendations. Over 100 publications are cataloged here, the vast majority of which are available for download and review. Resources are listed alphabetically by title and also contain the publication date and OSHA publication number. Users should note that this index is not linked to a search engine.

http://www.osha-slc.gov/OshDoc/Additional.html

**State Public Health Associations, American Public Health Association**    With over 50,000 members worldwide, the American Public Health Association (APHA) works to fight disease and promote human health. This section of the APHA Web site contains information related to state public health associations including rosters, calendars of annual meetings, links to online resources, action alerts, and advocacy tips. Information is designed to be of use to APHA affiliate organizations. http://www.apha.org/state_local/

**U.S. Army Medical Department Information Resources** The Virtual Reference Desk is an extensive listing of online resources relating to a variety of subjects categorized alphabetically. Categories include almanacs, biographies, distance learning, government resources, information management, legal sources, military sources, and surveillance and statistical sources. Each category contains a list of links to available resources, with each accompanied by a brief description. A section devoted exclusively to bioterrorism provides descriptions and links to news resources; journal articles; overviews of terrorism, preparedness, and planning; textbooks; government sites; and counterterrorism organizations.
http://www.armymedicine.army.mil/
medcom/medlinet/virtual2.htm

## 18.8 REGIONAL RESOURCES

**Emergency Services WWW Site** With over 2,000 listings, this Web site is an extensive index of known fire, rescue, and emergency services resources found on the Web. Sites listed here are divided into categories according to sponsoring organization. These include fire, disaster management, dispatch, hazardous materials, rescue, commercial, and personal sites. Due to the number of sites posted, listings are necessarily concise. Links are accompanied by the date added, location of sponsoring organization, and classification. The search function allows users to narrow down the number of sites by phrase, keyword, or site classification.
http://www.district.north-van.bc.ca/eswsl/www-911.htm

**Fairfax County Urban Search and Rescue Team** One of the premier urban search and rescue operations in the nation, Virginia Task Force One, sponsored by the Fairfax County Fire and Rescue Department, is composed of approximately 130 highly trained individuals including fire and rescue workers, paramedics, emergency medicine physicians, canine handlers, structural engineers, and equipment specialists. Task Force One is prepared to respond at a moment's notice to domestic and international situations, the most recent mission having been the Pentagon incident. As home to such a large-

scale and important national operation, this Web site offers an enormous number of features and resources, including sections devoted to urban search and rescue information, team information, a resource center, mission reports, family support, and disaster news. Each section contains an average of five or six additional resources. The resource center, for example, features a news center, live earthquake data, a weather center, live video cams and dispatch audio, an urban search and rescue library, and training materials.
http://www.vatf1.org/

### Local Emergency Planning Committee Database, Environmental Protection Agency
Maintained by the Chemical Emergency Preparedness and Prevention Office of the Environmental Protection Agency, the Local Emergency Planning Committee (LEPC) Database is an index of over 3,000 U.S. emergency management agencies categorized by state of origin. A search engine enables users to locate an agency by zip code, state, or organization name and address. Information provided in each listing includes the LEPC name, mailing address, point of contact, and e-mail address, if available.
http://www.epa.gov/ceppo/lepclist.htm

### New York State Incident Command System
The Incident Command System (ICS), is a standardized emergency management system designed to coordinate the various response and recovery efforts of federal, state, and local agencies following a disaster. Materials on this site are dedicated to the New York State ICS, containing historical information, organizational charts, and training materials for use of the ICS. This site provides a summary of various aspects and functions of the ICS. Concise training modules are provided as an introduction to proper use of the system.
http://www.nysemo.state.ny.us/ICS/explain.htm

### North Carolina Hazardous Materials Regional Response Team
The six North Carolina Hazardous Materials Regional Response Teams (RRTs) were designed to provide assistance to local authorities with technical support, manpower, special equipment, and supplies when an incident is beyond the local response capabilities. This site features news updates pertaining to hazardous materials and disaster management, information on the RRT program, recent event coverage, a train-

ing calendar and access to training materials, and contact information for members and team leaders.
http://www.duke.edu/~pirre001/rrt4.html

 **Northern New England Disaster Recovery Information X-change Group** With over 1,150 members, the Northern New England Disaster Recovery Information X-change Group (NEDRIX) is an extensive network of organizations from both the public and private sectors dedicated to the sharing of information relating to disaster recovery and business resumption. General information about NEDRIX, a staff directory, and recent news including past meetings and newsletter archives are among the resources that can be found on the NEDRIX home page. Membership is open to anyone interested in business continuity, disaster recovery, and emergency management; registration can be completed at the site.
http://www.nedrix.com/

 **State Offices of Emergency Management** Supported by Emergency Response Planning, this resource page provides a brief summary of the various responsibilities and functions of a state emergency and disaster response agency. In addition, this Web site is a growing index of links to state and local emergency response agency online resources. Links to the offices of all 50 states and the District of Columbia are provided as well as additional useful resources.
http://www.erplan.com/resources.htm

 **State Offices of Emergency Preparedness and Response** This CDC resource is intended to provide information on U.S. state and local efforts for preparedness and response to bioterrorism. This site allows the user to choose any state or area and receive a profile of that area's current preparedness and response activities and programs. In addition, emergency and key contact information are provided.
http://www.bt.cdc.gov/STAndLocal/

 **State Offices of Homeland Security** The National Conference of State Legislatures (NCLS) works to improve the quality and effectiveness of state legislatures and to promote interstate cooperation and communications. This section of the NCSL Web site catalogs information regarding state responses to the events of Sep-

tember 11, 2001. A number of states have begun to create state offices for domestic security or commissions designed to address in-state terrorism. This site provides a summary of the actions, considerations, and proposed legislation of each state and provides links to press releases and other important information from each state's officials regarding the matter.
http://www.ncsl.org/programs/
legman/nlssa/sthomelandoffcs.htm

## State/Territorial Links from the Association of State and Territorial Health Officials
The Association of State and Territorial Health Officials (ASTHO) brings together local health representatives from across the nation to forge bonds, make policy recommendations, and promote public health. Materials on this site include information on ASTHO committees and projects along with fact sheets on preventive health, immunization, chronic disease, and public health threats. Under the section titled "Government Relations," users will find policy statements, a calendar of events, public health resources, and media releases. Information from specific state and local governments is also available.
http://www.astho.org/state.html

**19**

# GLOSSARIES

## 19.1 GENERAL RESOURCES

**2T-0497**

**Glossary from the HazMat Guide for First Responders, U.S. Fire Administration** This extensive listing of common terms and abbreviations from the U.S. Fire Administration is designed as a resource for emergency personnel, especially first responders. Approximately 60 terms and explanations have been compiled in the *Hazardous Materials Guide* available at this Web site.
http://www.usfa.fema.gov/hazmat/glossary.htm

**2T-0498**

**Glossary of Biochemterrorism from yourDictionary.com** The Glossary of Biochemterrorism defines commonly used terms relating to biological weapons, diseases, national and international security, and weapons of mass destruction. Hotlinks within the definitions take the visitor to related terms elsewhere in the glossary.
http://www.yourdictionary.com/library/bioterrorism.html

**2T-0499**

**Glossary of Healthcare Terminology from the Department of Defense** This glossary from the Department of Defense includes abbreviations and acronyms and provides links to nearly 20 other subsections of terminology related to healthcare used throughout the department. The file requires Adobe Acrobat for viewing.
http://www.tricare.osd.mil/references/acroterms.html

**2T-0500**

**Glossary of Terms from the Agency for Toxic Substances and Disease Registry** The Agency for Toxic Substances and Disease Registry (ATSDR) has published this extensive listing of general and ATSDR-specific terms. Over 50 terms related to chemistry, biology, and terrorism are provided, with detailed explanations.
http://www.atsdr.cdc.gov/glossary.html

**Glossary of Terms from the Centers for Disease Control and Prevention** The Special Pathogens Branch of the Centers for Disease Control and Prevention has provided a listing of commonly used terms with accompanying definitions. More than 30 clinical terms and their definitions are available on this Web site, some with links to related articles.

http://www.cdc.gov/ncidod/dvrd/spb/mnpages/glossary.htm

# 20

# WEB SITE AND
# TOPICAL INDEX

**N**

## Q

**NOTES**

**NOTES**